BE REVERENT

D1236156

Be Reverent

WARREN W. WIERSBE

While this book is intended for
the reader's personal enjoyment
and profit, it is also designed for
group study. Study questions are
located at the end of the text.

David C Cook

transforming lives together

BE REVERENT
Published by David C. Cook
4050 Lee Vance View
Colorado Springs, CO 80918 U.S.A.

David C. Cook Distribution Canada
55 Woodslee Avenue, Paris, Ontario, Canada N3L 3E5

David C. Cook U.K., Kingsway Communications
Eastbourne, East Sussex BN23 6NT, England

David C. Cook and the graphic circle C logo
are registered trademarks of Cook Communications Ministries.

Unless otherwise noted, Scripture quotations are from the *King James Version*. Other quotations are taken from the *New International Version* (NIV), © 1973, 1978, 1984. International Bible Society. Used by permission of Zondervan Bible Publishers; *The New King James Version* (NKJV), © 1979, 1980, 1982 by Thomas Nelson, Inc. Publishers; *New American Standard Bible* (NASB), © the Lockman Foundation 1960, 1962, 1963, 1968, 1971, 1972, 1973, 1975, 1977; the Holy Bible, *New Living Translation* (NLT), copyright © 1996 by Tyndale Charitable Trust. All rights reserved; and *The Amplified Bible* (AMP), © 1962, 1964, by Zondervan Publishing House, and 1954, 1958 The Lockman Foundation.

Library of Congress Cataloging-in-Publication Data
Wiersbe, Warren W.
Be reverent / by Warren Wiersbe
p. cm.
Includes Bibliographical references.
ISBN 978-0-7814-3304-4
1. Bible O.T. Ezekiel--Commentaries. I. Title.

BS1545.3.W54 2000
224'.407--dc21
00-040829

Editor: Barbara Williams
Design: iDesignEtc.
Cover Photo: Dynamic Graphics
Study Questions: Carol Smith

Printed in the United States of America
First Edition 2007

6 7 8 9 10 11 12 13 14 15 16

081507

CONTENTS

PREFACE

One thing that is lacking in the church today is a sincere reverence for the name and glory of the Lord. At least a dozen times in the Book of Psalms, you find the psalmist praising God's holy name. In fact, God's people are identified in Scripture as those who reverence God's name (Rev. 11:18).

Associated with God's name is God's glory, for His name is a glorious name (1 Chron. 29:13). When God's people glorify Him, they bring honor to His name, just as obedient children bring honor to their family name. "Hallowed be thy name" is the first petition in the Lord's Prayer (Matt. 6:9), and one of the reasons God answers prayer is that His name might be glorified.

The messages of the Prophet Ezekiel focus on the glory of God, the throne of God, and the honor of the name of God. God is called "Lord God" ("Sovereign Lord," NIV) over 400 times in this book, and you find the solemn phrase "I am the Lord" 59 times. In all that God says and does, He has one purpose in mind: "You will know that I am the Lord" (Ezek. 6:7, NIV).

When Ezekiel lived, spoke, and wrote his book, the Jewish people were captives in Babylon, and Ezekiel was there with them. He was not only a servant sent to speak to his people, but he was also a sign to the people (24:24, 27). God asked him to do many unusual things in order to get the attention of the people so they would hear the Word of God. His spoken messages and his "sign messages" were both needed, because the people had blind eyes and hard hearts. Ezekiel was a master of metaphor and imagery.

Is the prophecy of Ezekiel a book that's needed today? The eminent Jewish writer Elie Wiesel says, "No generation could understand Ezekiel as well—as profoundly—as ours." One thing is sure: our generation *needs* the message of Ezekiel, for we are a people who lack the reverence we should have for the glory of God and the name of God.

We can write "Ichabod—the glory has departed" over the doors of many homes, churches, and Christian ministries.

Yet Ezekiel's message isn't only a negative exposure of the sins of God's people; it's also a positive encouragement because of the future God has planned. The prophet closes his book with the glorious vision of a restored people with a renewed worship and the glory of God dwelling with them. The prophet gives Jerusalem a new name: "Jehovah Shammah—the Lord is there" (48:35).

"Hallowed be Thy name!"

Warren W. Wiersbe

A Suggested Outline of Ezekiel

Key Theme: Showing reverence for the name and glory of God
Key Verse: "You will know that I am the Lord" (6:7, NIV)
(This statement is found seventy times in the book)

I. The prophet's call (1–3)
1. Seeing God's glory—1
2. Hearing God's Word—2
3. Becoming God's watchman—3

II. The fall of Jerusalem (4–24)
1. The judgment predicted—4–7
2. God's glory departs—8–11
3. Godless leaders exposed—12–17
4. God's justice defended—18–21
5. The end of the city—22–24

III. The nations judged (25–32)
1. Ammon—25:1-7
2. Moab— 25:8-11
3. Edom—25:12-14
4. Philistia—25:15-17
5. Tyre—26:1–28:19
6. Sidon—28:20-24
7. Egypt—29–32

IV. The glorious future of Israel (33–48)
1. The city of Jerusalem restored —33–34
2. The land of Israel renewed—35–36
3. The nation of Israel resurrected and reunited—37–39
4. The temple and the priesthood reestablished—40–48

A Time Line for Ezekiel's Ministry

605 B.C.   Nebuchadnezzar takes the temple treasures to Babylon; Daniel taken captive

597 B.C.   Ezekiel taken captive to Babylon at age twenty-five

593 B.C.   Ezekiel called to ministry at age 30 (Ezek. 1–3)

592 B.C.   Ezekiel's vision of the temple in Jerusalem (Ezek. 8:1ff)

591 B.C.   Ezekiel interprets Israel's history (Ezek. 20:1ff)

588 B.C.   Siege of Jerusalem begins (Ezek. 24:1ff)

587–585 B.C.   Ezekiel's messages against Egypt (Ezek. 29–32) and Tyre (Ezek. 26:1ff)

586 B.C.   Jerusalem destroyed by the Babylonian army

585 B.C.   News comes to Ezekiel of Jerusalem's destruction (Ezek. 33:21-22)

573 B.C.   Visions of Israel's glorious future (Ezek. 40–48)

571 B.C.   Ezekiel's message that Babylon will defeat Egypt (Ezek. 29:17-21)

ONE

From Priest to Prophet

Like Jeremiah (1:2), Zechariah (1:1), and John the Baptist (Luke 1:5ff), Ezekiel ("God strengthens") was called by God from being a priest to serving as a prophet. As Jehovah's spokesman to the Jewish exiles in the land of Babylon, he would rebuke their sins and expose their idolatry, but he would also reveal the glorious future the Lord had prepared for them. He was thirty years old at the time of his call (Ezek. 1:1), the normal age for a priest to begin his ministry (Num. 4:1-3, 23).[1]

It would have been much easier for Ezekiel to remain a priest, for priests were highly esteemed by the Jews, and a priest could read the Law and learn everything he needed to know to do his work. Prophets were usually despised and persecuted. They received their messages and orders from the Lord as the occasion demanded and could never be sure what would happen next. It was dangerous to be a prophet. Most people resent being told about their sins and prefer to hear messages of cheer, not declarations of judgment.

Jeremiah had been ministering in Jerusalem for four years when Ezekiel was born in 622, but surely as the young priest grew up, he paid close attention to what Jeremiah was saying.[2] It's likely that Daniel and Ezekiel were friends before the Captivity, though there's no evidence they saw each other in Babylon. Ezekiel's prophetic ministry was greatly needed in Babylon because false prophets abounded and were giving the Jewish people false hopes of a quick miraculous deliverance (usually by Egypt) and a triumphant return to their land (Jer. 5:30-31; 27:1-11; 28:1-17). It's possible that King Zedekiah's visit to Babylon (51:59-61) and the arrival of Jeremiah's letter to the exiles (Jer. 29) both occurred the same year Ezekiel received his call. This letter told the Jews that they would be in Babylon for seventy years and therefore should settle down, raise families, and pray for their captors. But Jeremiah also announced the ultimate fall of Babylon, a message the exiles were only too eager to hear.

The most difficult task of a prophet is to change people's minds. This means pulling up the weeds of false theology and planting the good seed of the Word of God. It also means tearing down the flimsy thought structures that false prophets build and constructing in their place lasting buildings on solid foundations of truth (Ezek. 1:10; 2 Cor. 10:3-6). To prepare him for his difficult ministry, the Lord caused Ezekiel to participate in three dramatic experiences.

1. Beholding the glory of the Lord (Ezek. 1)
The kingdom of Judah had suffered greatly at the hands of victorious Babylon, and many Jewish people wondered if Jehovah was still the God of Abraham, Isaac, and Jacob (see Ps. 74). Were the Jews not God's chosen people? Had not Jehovah defeated their enemies and given them the Promised Land? Was not Jerusalem His holy city and did He not dwell in their holy temple? Yet now His chosen people were exiles in a pagan land, their Promised Land was devastated, Jerusalem was in enemy hands, and the temple had been robbed of its precious treasures. It was a dark day for Israel, and the first thing Ezekiel needed to understand was that, no matter how discouraging the circumstances, God was still on the throne accomplishing His divine purposes in the world. There are many unexplained mysteries in the vision

Ezekiel had, but one message comes through with clarity and power: Jehovah is the sovereign Lord of Israel and of all the nations of the earth.

The storm (Ezek. 1:3-4). The Chebar River (Kebar, NIV) or canal flowed from the Euphrates River, south of the city of Babylon, where the Jewish exiles gathered for prayer (see Acts 16:13). Ezekiel mentions it in Ezekiel 1:1; 3:23; 10:15, 20, 22; and 43:3. Apparently Ezekiel was there interceding with the other captives when the Lord called him to his new ministry. Isaiah was worshiping in the temple when God called him (Isa. 6) and Paul and Barnabas were engaged in worship at Antioch when they received their call (Acts 13:1-3). When Ezekiel went to the prayer meeting, it was just like any other day; but the Lord made it a turning point in his life. We never know what a difference a day will make when we're in the path of duty.

The word of the Lord came to Ezekiel in the form of a vision, and the hand of the Lord laid hold of him and claimed him for special service. The phrase "the word of the Lord came" is used fifty times in his prophecy and speaks of the authority of his message; and "the hand of the Lord" is found also in Ezekiel 3:14, 22; 8:1; 33:22; 37:1; and 40:1. The word of the Lord brings enlightenment and the hand of the Lord enablement (see Eph. 1:15-23). In Scripture, a storm is often an image of divine judgment (Prov. 1:27; Isa. 66:15; Jer. 4:13; 23:19; Nahum 1:3). Since the immense whirlwind cloud Ezekiel beheld was coming from the north, it indicated the invasion of Judah by the Babylonian army and the destruction of the land, the city of Jerusalem, and the temple (Jer. 4:6; 6:1). For forty years, God had graciously led Israel by a fiery cloud; but now a fiery cloud was bringing chastening to His disobedient people. The Prophet Jeremiah saw a similar vision at the beginning of his ministry (Jer. 1:13-16).

Ezekiel saw bright light around the cloud and an enfolding fire, like molten metal, within the cloud. Both are reminders of the holiness of God, for "our God is a consuming fire" (Ex. 19:16, 18; Deut. 4:24; Heb. 12:29). As he describes this vision, Ezekiel uses the words "like" and "likeness" at least twenty-five times, indicating that what he saw was symbolic of realities God wanted to reveal to him. Throughout the Bible, the Lord uses familiar things to illustrate spiritual truths that are beyond human vocabulary and description. *The cherubim (Ezek. 1:5-14)*. In 10:15 and 20, Ezekiel identified the living creatures as the cherubim, heavenly creatures first mentioned in Genesis 3:24. The tabernacle curtains were embroidered with images of the cherubim (Ex. 26:1), and two cherubim were on the golden covering of the ark, the mercy seat (Ex. 25:18-22). Cherubim were very much in evidence in Solomon's temple (1 Kings 6:23-29; 2 Chron. 3:10-13) and in John's visions in the Book of Revelation (Rev. 4:6-9; 5:6-14; 6:1-11; 14:3; 15:7; 19:4). The creatures had the body of a human, straight feet like that of a calf, four faces and four wings, with human hands under the wings. Their wings were so arranged that the creatures did not have to turn; they could fly straight forward and change directions quickly. Their wings touched so that each creature was at the corner of a square that would outlined by their wings.

Of special interest are their four faces: a man, a lion, an ox and an eagle (Ezek. 1:10). Man is the highest of God's creatures, being made in the image of God. The lion is the greatest of the untamed beasts of the forest, while the ox is the strongest of the domesticated beasts of the field. The eagle is the greatest of the birds and is even a picture of God (Deut. 32:11-12). But there is also a connection here with the covenant God made with Noah after the Flood (Gen. 9:8-17). God promised not to destroy the world again with a flood, and He gave this promise to Noah (a man) and his descendants, the birds (the eagle), the livestock (the ox), and the wild animals (the lion). The presence of the cherubim before the throne of God is assurance that God remembers His promise and cares for His creatures. But it also reminds us that all of creation is used by the Lord to bless or to chasten His people. In this vision, they are a part of God's judgment on His sinful people.

The life of these creatures came from the "spirit" (or Spirit)[3] within the cloud (Ezek. 1:12, 20), and this life enabled them to move like lightning; in fact, in their movements, they even looked like flashes of lightning. When Ezekiel first saw these creatures, he compared them to fiery amber or molten metal (v. 4); but as he watched them closely, he compared them to sparkling bronze (v. 7), burning coals of fire, lamps, and lightning (vv. 13-14). Like the Apostle John describing the beauty of the holy city (Rev. 21–22), the prophet ran out of words and had to draw pictures!

The wheels (Ezek. 1:15-21). There were four wheels (v. 16), each with an intersecting wheel and each associated with one of the cherubim. The intersecting wheels enabled the creatures and the cloud to move in any direction instantly without having to turn, moving like a flash of lightning. These wheels looked like chrysolite, a yellow or greenish-yellow precious stone; they were very high, as though reaching from earth to heaven, and their rims were awesome and full of eyes. The spirit (Spirit) of the living creatures was in the wheels, so that the living creatures moved in whatever direction the wheels moved. It was indeed an awesome sight, the huge wheels, the living creatures, the enfolding fire, and the eyes in the rims of the wheels. What an arresting picture of the providence of God, always at work, intricately designed, never wrong, and never late!

The firmament (Ezek. 1:22-25). This awesome expanse looked like sparkling ice (crystal) and stood over the heads of the cherubim. Now we get the total picture: a heavenly chariot with four wheels, moving quickly from place to place at the direction of the Lord. As it moved, the noise of the wings of the cherubim sounded like the noise of great waters coming together, "like the voice of the Almighty," and like the sound of a mighty army (3:13; 10:5; Ps. 46:3; Rev. 1:15; 14:2; 19:6). The wheels symbolize the omnipresence of God, while the eyes on their rims suggest the omniscience of God, seeing and knowing everything. Ezekiel was beholding a representation of the providence of God as He worked in His world. But one more item remained.

The throne (Ezek. 1:26-28). The wheels depicted God's

omnipresence and omniscience, and the throne speaks of God's omnipotent authority. The throne was azure blue, with flashes of fire within it (holiness; see Rev. 15:2) and a rainbow around it (covenant grace). Noah saw the rainbow *after the storm* (Gen. 9:13-16), the Apostle John saw it *before the storm* (Rev. 4:3), but Ezekiel saw it *over the storm and in control of the storm.* In His wrath, God remembers mercy (Hab. 3:2). Ezekiel realized that he was beholding the glory of the Lord (Ezek. 1:28), and he fell on his face in awesome fear (3:23; Dan. 8:17; 10:9, 15, 17; Rev. 1:17). The "man" he saw upon the throne was probably a preincarnate appearance of our Lord Jesus Christ. (See Ezek. 8:2 and 40:3.)

The glory of the Lord is one of the key themes in the prophecy of Ezekiel (3:12, 23; 8:4; 9:3; 10:4, 18-19; 11:22-23; 39:21; 43:2, 4-5; 44:4). The prophet will watch God's glory leave the temple and go over the Mount of Olives, and he will also see it return to the kingdom temple. Because of Israel's sins, the glory left the temple; but God's promise is that one day the city of Jerusalem and the temple will be blessed by the glorious presence of the Lord. The city will be called "Jehovah Shammah—the Lord is there" (48:35).

Now we can begin to grasp the message that God was giving His prophet. Though His people were in exile and their nation was about to be destroyed, God was still on the throne and able to handle every situation. In His marvelous providence, He moves in the affairs of nations and works out His hidden plan. Israel wasn't the victim of Babylonian aggression. It was God who enabled the Babylonians to conquer His people and chasten them for their rebellion, but God would also bring the Medes and the Persians to conquer Babylon, and Cyrus, king of Persia, would permit the Jews to return to their land. "Oh, the depth of the riches both of the wisdom and knowledge of God! How unsearchable are His judgments and His ways past finding out!" (Rom. 11:33, NKJV)

No matter what message God gave him to preach, or what opposition arose from the people, Ezekiel would be encouraged and strengthened because he had seen the mighty throne of God in the midst of the fiery trial. He had seen the glory of God.

2. Accepting the burden of the Lord (Ezek. 2:1–3:3)

Ezekiel was now to receive his official commission as a prophet of the Lord God, and the Lord told him he was facing a very difficult task. Whether it's raising a family, teaching a Sunday School class, shepherding a church, or evangelizing in a distant nation, we have to accept people as they are before we can lead them to what God wants them to be. God gave Ezekiel four important commandments to obey.

Stand and listen (Ezek. 2:1-2). As a result of beholding the vision, Ezekiel fell to the ground, completely overwhelmed by the glory of the Lord and the wonder of His providential working in the world. Who but the sovereign Lord could have a throne like a chariot and move as quickly as He pleased? Who but the Lord could travel in the midst of a fiery whirlwind to accomplish His great purposes?

Ezekiel is called "son of man" ninety-three times in his book, a title that the Lord also gave to Daniel (Dan. 8:17). "Son of man" is also a messianic title (Ezek. 7:13) which the Lord Jesus applied to Himself at least eighty-two times when He was ministering on earth. But in the case of Daniel and Ezekiel, the title "son of man" emphasized their humanity and mortality. Ezekiel was facedown in the dust when God spoke to him, reminding him and us of mankind's humble beginning in the dust (Gen. 1:26; 3:19). "For He knows our frame; He remembers that we are dust" (Ps. 103:14, NKJV). God remembers, but sometimes we forget.

There is a time to fall down in humble adoration, and there is a time to stand up and take orders (Josh. 7:6ff). The command of the Word and the power of the Spirit enabled Ezekiel to stand to his feet, and the Spirit entered him and strengthened him. On many occasions, the Spirit would lift him up (Ezek. 2:2, 3:14; 8:3; 11:1, 24; 37:1; 43:5) and give him special power for his tasks (3:24; 11:5). The important thing was that Ezekiel stand obediently before the Lord and listen to His Word.

Go and speak (Ezek. 2:3-5). Prophets weren't people who majored only in foretelling the future, although that was part of their ministry. They were primarily *forth-tellers* who declared God's Word to the people. Sometimes they gave a message of judgment, but it was usually followed by a message of hope and forgiveness. The Jews needed to hear Ezekiel's messages because they were rebellious, stiff-necked, and hard-hearted.[4] At least sixteen times in this book you find the Jews described as "rebellious." They had revolted against the Lord and were obstinate in their refusal to submit to His will. Their refusal to obey the terms of the covenant had led to their defeat and capture by the Babylonian army. Even in their captivity, they were nursing false hopes that Egypt would come to their rescue or the Lord would do a great miracle.

So rebellious were the Jewish people that God called them "a rebellious nation" and used the Hebrew word *goy*, which was usually reserved for the Gentiles! Israel was God's chosen people, a special nation, and yet they were acting like the Gentiles who didn't have all the blessings and privileges God had given the Jews. This wasn't a very encouraging word for the young prophet, but he needed to know in advance that his work would be difficult. God gave the same kind of message to Isaiah when He called him (Isa. 6:8-13). But whether the people listened and obeyed or turned a deaf ear, Ezekiel had to be faithful to his task (1 Cor. 4:2).

Don't be afraid (Ezek. 2:6-7). Three times in verse 6 the Lord admonished the prophet not to be afraid of the people, and He repeated it again (3:9). He had given a similar caution to Jeremiah (Jer. 1:8), and Jesus gave the same warning to His disciples (Matt. 10:26, 28, 31). "Who are you that you should be afraid of a man who will die, and of the son a of man who will be made like grass?" (Isa. 51:12, NKJV) Ezekiel was to declare God's Word boldly no matter how his listeners responded. His own people might act like briars and thorns,[5] and even like painful scorpions, but that must not deter His servant.

Receive the Word within (Ezek. 2:8–3:3). Being a priest, Ezekiel knew that the Hebrew Scriptures pictured God's Word as food to be received within the heart and digested inwardly. Job valued God's Word more than his "necessary food" (Job 23:12), and Moses admonished the Jews to live on God's Word as well as on the bread (manna) that the Lord supplied daily (Deut. 8:3; see Matt. 4:4). The Prophet Jeremiah "ate" the Word of God (Jer. 15:16) and so did the Apostle John (Rev. 10:8-10). God's prophets must speak from within their hearts or their messages will not be authentic.

A hand stretched out and handed Ezekiel a scroll that didn't have any good news written on it, because it was filled on both sides with "words of lament and mourning and woe" (Ezek.2:10, NIV). Perhaps it contained the messages that are recorded in chapters 4 through 32, God's judgments on Jerusalem and the Gentile nations. (See the suggested outline of the book.) God commanded him to eat the scroll and it tasted sweet like honey (Pss. 19:10; 119:103), although later he tasted bitterness (Ezek. 3:14), not unlike the Apostle John (Rev. 10:8-11). It's a great honor to be a spokesperson for the Lord, but we must be able to handle both the bitter and the sweet.

Had Ezekiel heard the description of the hardness of his people before he saw the vision of God's glory, he might have had a difficult time accepting his call. But having seen the glorious throne of the sovereign Lord, Ezekiel knew that he had all the help he needed to obey the will of God. In his difficult ministry to the Israelites, Moses was encouraged by meeting God on the mountaintop and seeing the display of His glory, and the Prophet Isaiah saw the glory of Christ in the temple before he launched into his ministry (Isa. 6; John 12:37-41). The Prophet Habakkuk was lifted from the valley of despair to the mountain peak of victory by contemplating the glory of God in the history of Israel (Hab. 3). Before Stephen laid down his life for the sake of Jesus Christ, he saw the glory of the Son of God in heaven (Acts 7:55-60). The only motivation that never fails is doing all for the glory of God.

3. Declaring the Word of the Lord (Ezek. 3:4-27)

What the people needed more than anything else was to hear the Word of the Lord. Even before the nation fell, Jeremiah had warned them not to listen to the false prophets, but neither the leaders nor the common people would obey (Jer. 5:30-31; 6:14; 7:8; 8:10). God had spoken loudly in Israel's shameful defeat and captivity, but now the Jews were still clinging to empty hopes and listening to the lying words of false prophets in Babylon (Jer. 29:15-32). The human heart would rather hear lies that bring comfort than truths that bring conviction and cleansing. Ezekiel declared God's Word as a messenger (Ezek. 3:4-10), a sufferer (vv. 10-15), a watchman (vv. 16-21), and a sign (vv. 22-27).

The messenger (Ezek. 3:4-9). Three elements are involved here: speaking, receiving (understanding) the message, and obeying. "Go and speak my word!" (v. 4) was God's commission. Ezekiel was the messenger, the people of Israel were the audience, and the Word of God was the message to be delivered. The prophet wasn't allowed to send a substitute messenger, nor was he permitted to alter the message or go to a different audience. One of the New Testament words for preaching is *kerusso*, which means "to proclaim as a herald." In ancient days, rulers would send out royal heralds to convey their messages to the people, and the herald was obligated to deliver the message just as he received it. If Ezekiel wanted to be a faithful herald, every part of God's commission had to be obeyed to the last detail.

The second element is *receiving (vv. 5-7)*. To receive the Word of God means to understand it and take it into the heart and mind (Matt. 13:19). Since Ezekiel was a chosen prophet of the Lord, what he said was important and the people were obligated to receive it. He was speaking their own language, so they couldn't make excuses and say, "We don't understand what you're saying." He understood their speech and they understood his. If God had sent Ezekiel to a nation where he had to use an interpreter, they would have understood his message and received it; but his own people turned a deaf ear to him. Jesus used a similar approach in 11:21-24 when He condemned the Jewish cities for rejecting

Him. Had He done those same miracles in heathen cities, they would have repented and turned to the Lord.

The third element is *obeying (Ezek. 3:7-9)*. God doesn't send us His messengers to His people to entertain them or give them good advice. He expects us to obey what He commands. Unfortunately, the nation of Israel had a tragic history of disobedience to the law of God and rebellion against the will of God. That was their record during 40 years in the wilderness (Deut. 9:7) as well as during over 800 years in their own land (2 Chron. 36:11-21). No other nation has been blessed by God as Israel has been blessed, for the Jews had God's holy law, the covenants, a wealthy land, the temple, and the prophets to give them warnings and promises as they needed them (Rom. 9:1-5). Like the people of Israel, many people today hear God's Word but won't try to understand, or if they do understand, they refuse to obey.

God assured His prophet that He would give him all he needed to withstand their opposition and disobedience. In Ezekiel 3:8, there is a play on words involving Ezekiel's name which means "God is strong" or "God strengthens." It also means "God hardens." If the people harden their hearts and faces, God will harden His servant and keep him faithful to his mission. He gave a similar promise to Jeremiah (Jer. 1:17).

The sufferer (Ezek. 3:10-15). Ezekiel was by the river Chebar when he saw the vision and heard God's Word (1:3), but now he was commanded to join the other exiles at a place called Tel-Abib. This site hasn't been identified, but it was not at the same location as the modern Tel-Aviv. There were a number of villages along the river (Ezra 2:59; 8:17), and some of the Jewish captives had been settled there by the Babylonians. The Spirit of God lifted the prophet up (Ezek. 3:12, 14)[6] and took him to the place where the captives were gathered together and probably praying. This remarkable experience would be repeated (8:3; 43:5), and Ezekiel would no doubt recall that the Prophet Elijah had been caught away by God (2 Kings 2:11, 16; see 1 Kings 18:12 and Acts 8:39). The prophet had received God's Word, and now he must take it to God's people.

As the Spirit began to work, Ezekiel heard behind him several sounds: the rustling of the cherubims' wings, the whirring of the wheels, and "a loud rumbling sound" (NIV), like an earthquake. He knew that God's glorious throne was moving and that the Lord was working out His purposes. What was the origin of the praise statement, "Blessed be the glory of the Lord from His place"? (Ezek. 3:12) Both the KJV and the NASB translate it as coming from the cherubim, but the NIV suggests that it was Ezekiel himself who spoke it. However, it could also be translated "as the glory of the Lord arose from its place," a description rather than a declaration. As we shall see in chapters 8 to 11, the movement of God's glory is a key theme in this book.

The Lord brought His servant to Tel-Abib so he could sit with the captives and feel their burden of disappointment and grief. Psalm 137 reveals both their misery and their hatred for the Babylonians. When they should have been repenting and seeking God's face, the Jews were regretting what had happened and praying that one day they might be able to retaliate and defeat their Babylonian captors who taunted them. As Ezekiel sat there with the people, overwhelmed by what the Lord had said to him and done for him, he realized the seriousness of his calling and how great was the responsibility God had placed on his shoulders. It's a good thing for the servant of God to be among his people, to weep with those who weep and rejoice with those who rejoice, for he can better minister to them when he knows their hearts and feels their pain.[7] It isn't enough simply to proclaim the message of God; we must also seek to have the caring heart of God.

The watchman (Ezek. 3:16-21). The watchmen on the walls were important to the safety of the city and the image shows up frequently in the Scriptures (Isa. 21:11-12; 56:10; 62:6; Jer. 6:17; Pss. 127:1; 130:6; Heb. 13:17). The emphasis here is on judgment, while in Ezekiel 33 it is on hope, but the message is the same: the prophet must be faithful to warn the people of judgment, and the people must heed the warning and turn from their sin. Spiritually speaking, the "wall" that protected Israel was their covenant relationship with the Lord. If they obeyed the terms of the covenant declared by Moses, God would care for His people, protect them, and bless them; but if they disobeyed, God would chasten them. But whether He was chastening or blessing, God would always be faithful to His covenant. (See Lev. 26 and Deut. 28.)

Ezekiel is the prophet of human responsibility. Some of the captives were blaming God for their sad plight, while others blamed their ancestors. Ezekiel made it clear that each individual is held responsible and accountable before God (see Ezek. 18). He presented four scenarios. The first is that of *the people dying because the watchman was unfaithful and didn't warn them (3:18).* Their blood would be on the watchman's hands and he would be held accountable (see v. 20; 18:13; 33:4-8). The image of blood on the hands (or the head) goes back to Genesis 9:5 and appears in the law of Moses (Lev. 20). See also Joshua 2:19; 2 Samuel 1:16 and 3:29; and Isaiah 1:15 and 59:3. Jesus used this image in Matthew 23:35 and Luke 11:50-51; and see Acts 5:28; 18:6; and 20:26. The second scenario is obvious.

A second scenario pictures *the watchman being faithful to warn the wicked but they refuse to listen (Ezek. 3:19).* That was the problem Ezekiel faced as he preached to the hardhearted Jewish captives in Babylon. Jesus wept over Jerusalem because the people would not come to Him (Matt. 23:37-39). The third scenario describes *the righteous dying because they turned from their covenant obedience and the watchman did not warn them (Ezek. 3:20).* The watchman-prophet should not only warn sinners to turn from their sin, but he must also warn those who are obeying the covenant ("the righteous") not to turn from it and disobey God. No matter how much obedience they had practiced, it would mean nothing if they deliberately rebelled against God. However, their blood would be on the watchman's hands if he didn't warn them. By putting a barrier in the way, God seeks to prevent the righteous person from sinning; but that doesn't excuse the watchman from being alert and giving warning.

The final scenario is that of *the righteous heeding the watchman's warning and not being judged (v. 21).* It was a serious thing for the

Jewish people to treat lightly the covenant that had been accepted and sealed at Sinai (Ex. 19–20). If the watchman-prophet saw faithful people about to break the covenant, he had to warn them that they would be judged. Sometimes godly people get the idea that their obedience has "earned" them the right to do as they please, but that idea is a great lie. God gives His people many privileges, but He never gives the privilege to sin.

These four examples were given to Jewish people under the Old Covenant and have to do with obedience to the law and the danger of physical death. The righteousness of the law was external, but the righteousness we have through faith in Jesus Christ is internal, and the two must not be confused (Rom. 9:30–10:13). Faith righteousness is God's gift to those who believe in Jesus Christ, and their righteous standing before God doesn't depend on their good works (Rom. 3–4). However, our fellowship with the Father depends on a heart of obedience (2 Cor. 6:14–7:1), and He will discipline those of His children who deliberately oppose His will (Heb. 12:1-11). If they persist in resisting His will, He may take their lives (Heb. 12:9). "There is a sin unto death " (1 John 5:16-17). Personal responsibility is the key here, both of the watchman and of the people. If the Jews under the Old Covenant were held responsible for their actions, how much more responsible are believers today who have the complete Bible, the indwelling Holy Spirit and the revelation of God through Jesus Christ? See Hebrews 12:12-28.

The sign (Ezek. 3:22-27). Ezekiel not only spoke God's Word to the people, but he also lived before them in such a way that they *saw* God's message portrayed before their very eyes. God said to him, "I have made you a sign to the house of Israel" (12:6, NIV; see 4:4; 14:8; 24:24, 27). You will find the prophet performing twelve "action sermons" to convey God's truth to people who were becoming more and more deaf to the voice of God.[8] Pharaoh wouldn't listen to God's Word, so the Lord spoke to him through a series of miracles and plagues. The Prophet Jeremiah also tried to reach the people through "action sermons," such as burying a new belt (Jer. 13), refusing to take a wife (Jer. 16), and breaking clay jars (Jer. 19).

It's likely that there is a break between Ezekiel 3:21 and 22. Ezekiel did go to the people and give them God's warning, but they would not listen. God told him to leave the gathering by the river and go out into the plain for a new set of instructions. What do you do when the people close their ears to the Word of God? God certainly could have judged them for their wickedness, but in His grace He gave them further opportunities to hear His saving Word. Jesus took the same approach when He began to teach in parables. He clothed the truth in interesting images and in that way sought to reach the people (Matt. 13:10-17). The careless would hear and brush it aside, but the concerned would ponder the parable and learn God's truth.

The Word of God may not have penetrated the hearts of the people, but the glory of God and the Spirit of God were still with God's servant. If the people wouldn't respond to Ezekiel's public ministry, perhaps he could reach them in his own house. The elders of the people could come to hear his messages (Ezek. 8:1; 14:1; 20:1) and then share them with the people. The prophet shut himself up in his house, although at times he did leave for special reasons (5:2; 12:3), and he never spoke unless he had a message from the Lord. When the news came of the destruction of Jerusalem, this command of silence was removed and he was able to speak as other people (24:25-27; 33:21-22). From the time this command was given to the time it was removed, seven years elapsed (from 593 B.C. to 586 B.C.).

Ezekiel's silence was a sign to the Jews that God's Word is not to be taken for granted or treated lightly like trivial daily conversation. When God speaks, we had better listen and obey! "He that hears, let him hear" (3:27, NIV) is a familiar and important phrase in Scripture because it indicates that we have the responsibility to pay attention to God's Word, cherish what He says, meditate on it, and obey it. At least five times in Deuteronomy Moses said, "Hear, O Israel!" as he repeated the law and reminded them of the great privilege Israel had to hear the very voice of God at Sinai (Deut. 4:1-13). At least eight times in the Gospels Jesus said, "He who has ears to hear, let him hear," (NASB) or similar words (Matt. 11:15, 13:9, 43; Mark 4:9, 23; 7:16; Luke 8:8; 14:35). What about the "binding" of the prophet? (Ezek. 3:25) This is probably a figurative statement, because there's no evidence that Ezekiel was literally bound and forced to remain in his house. As we have seen, he did leave the house (5:2; 12:3) and nobody prevented him. The Jewish people "bound" Ezekiel in the sense that their sins made it necessary for him to remain home in silence until God gave him a message. The attitude of the people wasn't that of militant opposition but rather passive indifference; hence, the necessity for Ezekiel to use "action sermons" to get their attention.

"I am the Lord!" is repeated fifty-nine times in this book, because it was Ezekiel's task to remind his people who was in charge. The name of God used almost exclusively in the book is "Jehovah Adonai—the Sovereign Lord." A.W. Tozer was right when he wrote, "God being who and what he is, and we being who and what we are, the only thinkable relation between us is one of full lordship on His part and complete submission on ours."[9]

Are we a rebellious people, or, like Ezekiel, are we obedient servants?

TWO

EZEKIEL 4–7

The Death of a Great City

When the sons of Asaph wanted to describe the city of Jerusalem, they wrote, "Beautiful in elevation, the joy of the whole earth, is Mount Zion on the sides of the north, the city of the great King" (Ps. 48:2, NKJV). The Babylonian Talmud says, "Of the ten measures of beauty that came down to the world, Jerusalem took nine" (*Kidushin 49b*), and, "Whoever has not seen Jerusalem in its splendor has never seen a lovely city" (*Succah 51b*). Of modern Jerusalem, Samuel Heilman wrote, "It is a place in which people actually live; it is a place that lives in them."[1] One of the Jewish exiles in Babylonian wrote: "If I forget you, O Jerusalem, let my right hand forget her skill! If I do not remember you, let my tongue cling to the roof of my mouth—if I do not exalt Jerusalem above my chief joy" (Ps. 137:5-6, NKJV). When Jewish families around the world celebrate Passover, they conclude the meal with, "Next year in Jerusalem!"

The Jewish exiles wouldn't be happy with the three messages Ezekiel would bring them from the Lord, for he was going to announce the destruction of Jerusalem and the ravaging of the Promised Land. It was bad enough that the Jews were exiles in a pagan land, but to be told that they would have no city to return to was more than they could bear. No wonder they preferred the encouraging messages of the false prophets.

1. The sign messages: the siege of Jerusalem (Ezek. 4–5)
Most of the Jewish people had become so calloused they could no longer hear God's Word, so the Lord commanded Ezekiel to take a different approach. The prophet stayed home for the most part and didn't take part in the everyday conversation of the people. He remained silent at all times except when he had a message to deliver from the Lord. That made people want to listen. Furthermore, the prophet often "preached" his messages silently through "action sermons" that aroused the interest of the people. In this way, he was a visible sign to the "spiritually deaf" people (4:3; 12:6, 11; 24:24). Word got around that Ezekiel occasionally did strange things, and he soon became a curiosity and a celebrity among the exiles. People stood before his house and waited to see what he would do next (4:12). These two chapters record four "action sermons" that conveyed startling news to the Jewish people in Babylon.

The siege of Jerusalem (Ezek. 4:1-3). This "tile" was probably an unbaked brick or a soft clay tablet, both of which were commonplace in Babylon. On it, Ezekiel drew a sketch of the city of Jerusalem, which the people would easily recognize, and then he set it on the ground and began to "play soldier" as he acted out the siege of Jerusalem. Using earth and various objects, he set up fortifications around the city so nobody could get in or get out. He built a ramp to facilitate scaling the walls, and he provided battering rams for breaking down the gates and the walls. This, of course, was what would happen at Jerusalem in 588 B.C. when the Babylonian army began the siege of the city.

Imagine how shocked the spectators were when Ezekiel's face became hard and resolute and he placed a flat iron griddle between his face and the besieged city. It was the kind of utensil that the priests used in the temple for preparing some of the offerings (Lev. 2:5; 6:21; 7:9). The iron griddle symbolized the wall that stood between God and the sinful Jewish nation so that

He could no longer look on them with approval and blessing. Ezekiel the priest could not pronounce on them the priestly blessing of Numbers 6:24-26, for God's face was not shining on them with blessing. God was *against* them (Ezek. 5:8; Isa. 59:1-3) and would permit the pagan Babylonians to destroy the city and the temple. Years later, Jeremiah would write, "You have covered yourself with a cloud, so that no prayer can get through" (Lam. 3:44, NIV, and see Ezek. 3:8-9).

During all this activity, Ezekiel didn't say a word, but the spectators surely got the message. It's possible for people to rebel against God such a long time that all God can do is allow them to reap the consequences of their own sins. The Jews were sinning against a flood of light. They knew the terms of the covenant, and they knew that God had sent prophet after prophet to rebuke their idolatry (2 Chron. 36:11-21), yet they had persisted in disobeying His will. Now it was too late. "Ephraim is joined to idols, let him alone" (Hosea 4:17, NKJV).

The judgment of Judah (Ezek. 4:4-8). At specified times each day (v. 10, NIV), Ezekiel was commanded to lie on the ground, facing the model he constructed of the siege of Jerusalem. He was to be bound (v. 8), his arm was to be bared, and he had to eat the meager food described in verses 9-17. He was to lie on his left side for 390 days and then on his right side for 40 days. This symbolic act told the Jewish exiles why the Lord was allowing their holy city to be ravaged and ruined: the nation had sinned and their sins had caught up with them. Of course, Ezekiel didn't "bear their sins" in the sense of atoning for them, for only the Son of God can do that (1 Peter 2:24). But "bearing the iniquity"[2] of the nation before God was one of the ministries of the priesthood, and Ezekiel was a priest (Ex. 28:36-38; Num. 18:1). The binding of the prophet and the baring of his arm spoke of the future binding of the prisoners and the baring of God's arm in judgment.

The Lord explained to Ezekiel that each day represented a year in the sinful history of the Jewish nation, and somehow he conveyed this fact to the people who watched him each day. But why did the Lord choose the numbers 390 and 40? Since one day was the equivalent of one year of Israel's rebellion, the Lord was undoubtedly looking back at the nation's past sins and not ahead at future disobedience. The forty years probably represented Israel's rebellion during their forty-year journey from Egypt to the Promised Land, but what is the starting point for the 390 years? The ministry of Ezekiel focused primarily on Jerusalem, the des-ecration of the temple by idolatry, and the departing of God's glory. It's likely that the 390-year period begins with Solomon's son Rehoboam who became king in 930 (1 Kings 14:21ff). When you add the years of the reigns of the kings of Judah from Rehoboam to Zedekiah, as recorded in 1 and 2 Kings, you have a total of 394 years. Since during three of the years of his reign Rehoboam walked with God (2 Chron. 11:16-17), we end up with a number very close to Ezekiel's 390 years.[3]

However we calculate the mathematics of this sign, the mes-sage is clear: God had been long-suffering toward the sinful peo-ple of Judah, warning them and chastening them, but they would not remain true to Him. Some of their kings were very godly men and sought to bring the people back to God, but no sooner did these kings die than the people returned to idolatry. Eventually, there came a time when their sins caught up with them and God's patience had come to an end. God would rather see His land devastated, the city of Jerusalem ruined, His temple destroyed, and His people killed and exiled, than to have them give such a false witness to the Gentile nations. Judgment begins with the people of God, not with the godless pagans (1 Peter 4:17-19), and it behooves believers and congregations today to walk in the fear of the Lord.

The famine in the city (Ezek. 4:9-17). In the first two "action ser-mons," Ezekiel showed the Jewish people the reality of the siege of Jerusalem and reason for it, and in the next two, he will display the horror of it, beginning with famine. The Lord commanded him to combine three grains (wheat, barley, and spelt) and two vegetables (beans and lentils) and grind them into flour and bake bread. This combination would produce the very poorest kind of bread and therefore represented the scarcity of food during the siege of Jerusalem. The people would eat almost anything, including one another (Deut. 28:49-57). God had warned them of this judgment in His covenant, so they shouldn't have been shocked.

The Jews sometimes cooked over fires made from cow dung mixed with straw, and this was not against the Law of Moses; but the use of human excrement was a sign of abject poverty and want. Of course, no priest would defile himself and his food by using human excrement for cooking his food (Deut. 14:3; 23:12-14), so the Lord allowed Ezekiel to use cow dung. His protest reminds us of that of Peter in Acts 10:14. Each day, the prophet would eat about eight ounces of bread and drink about two-thirds of a quart of water, reminding the spectators that the people within Jerusalem's walls would be starving and thirsting for water, but there would be no relief (see Lam. 1:11, 19; 2:11-12, 19). In His covenant, God had warned them about this judgment, but the people didn't listen (Lev. 26:26). Ezekiel was careful to obey the dietary laws, but the Jews scattered among the Gentile nations would be forced to eat defiled bread or else die of starvation.

God gave His chosen people a land of milk and honey and promised to bless their crops, their flocks and herds, and their families, if they obeyed His covenant. But they took their blessings for granted and turned away from the Lord and worshiped idols, so God cursed their blessings (Mal. 2:2). The land of milk and honey and the rich city of Jerusalem became places of scarcity and hunger, to the extent of parents eating their own children to stay alive during the siege (Ezek. 5:10; Deut. 29:22-28).

The destiny of the people (Ezek. 5:1-17). The Prophet Isaiah compared the invasion of an enemy to the shaving of a man's head and beard (Isa. 7:20), so Ezekiel used that image for his fourth "action sermon." Shaving could be a part of a purification ritual (Num. 6:5; 8:7), but the Jews had to be careful how they dressed their hair and their beards (Lev. 19:27; Deut. 14:1), and the priests had to be especially careful (Lev. 21:5-6). When Ezekiel, a priest, publicly shaved his head and his beard, the people must have been stunned; but it took extreme measures to get their attention so they would get the message. The shaving of the head and the beard would be a sign of humiliation and great sorrow and mourning, and that's the way the Lord felt about the impending destruction of Jerusalem and the holy temple. By using a sword and not a razor, Ezekiel made the message even more dramatic: an army was coming whose swords would "cut down" the people of the land.

The prophet was commanded to weigh the hair carefully and divide it into three parts. One part he burned on the "siege brick" to symbolize the people who died of famine or pestilence in Jerusalem. A second part was hacked to bits with the sword, symbolizing those slain by the Babylonian soldiers. The third part was thrown to the winds, picturing the Jews scattered among the Gentiles and the exiles taken to Babylon. However, before Ezekiel threw the hair to the winds, he took a small portion of it and hid it in the hem of his garment, a symbol of God's special care for a remnant of the people who would be spared to return to the land. The Lord in His covenant promised the sparing of a remnant (Lev. 26:36-39), for Israel still had a work to do in the world. But Ezekiel 5:4 indicates that anyone who was spared must not take their safety for granted, for more fire could come out from God's judgment of Jerusalem. This prophecy was fulfilled in the days after the siege of the city when innocent Jewish people were killed by scheming criminals (Jer. 40–44).

In Ezekiel 5:5-6, the Lord explained why He would permit His chosen people to suffer and die so shamefully at the hands of the Babylonians. As far as His eternal purposes were concerned, Jerusalem was His city and the center of the nations (38:12).[4] "Salvation is of the Jews" (John 4:22). Israel was a privileged people, but privilege involves responsibility and accountability. The day of reckoning had come and there was no escape. Israel was called to be a light to the Gentiles, to lead them to the true and living God (Isa. 42:6; 49:6); but instead, they adopted the wicked ways of the Gentiles and became greater sinners than their neighbors.

The Lord in His message drew some telling conclusions or

applications from this fact (Ezek. 5:7-11). God would punish Israel openly, in the sight of the nations whose evil practices they followed.[5] This would not only chasten Israel, but it would be a warning to the Gentiles that the God of Israel is a God of justice. Whereas before, God had been with and for His people, now He would be against them,[6] which reminds us of the iron skillet Ezekiel held between his face and the city of Jerusalem (4:3). The leaders had defiled the temple with their idols, a theme we'll hear more about later in Ezekiel's prophecy, and the Lord responded by withdrawing His favor and refusing to pity His people in their great distress. "I will also diminish thee" in 5:11 can be translated "I myself will shave you," taking us back to Ezekiel's fourth "action sermon."

In verses 12-17, the Lord explains again the awfulness of the judgment coming to the people left in the city and the land. Pestilence and famine will take one-third of them; another one-third will be killed by the Babylonian army; the remainder will be scattered. Why? Because God was "spending His wrath"[7]and "accomplishing His fury" upon His sinful people. God's anger against sin is a holy anger, not a temper tantrum, for He is a holy God. "Our God is a consuming fire" (Deut. 4:24; Heb. 12:29). There could be no doubt that these great judgments would come, because it was the Lord Himself who had spoken (Ezek. 5:13).[8] The whole land would be devastated and people would perish from famine and the pestilence that often accompanies famine, as well as bloodshed from enemy soldiers and hungry wild beasts. But as terrible as these judgments were, perhaps the greatest tragedy was that Israel would cease to bring glory to Jehovah God (v. 14) and would become a shameful reproach among the nations (Deut. 28:37; Jer. 18:15-17; 48:27; 2 Chron. 7:19-22).

Jesus Christ warned the church of Ephesus that they would lose their light if they refused to repent and obey His instructions (Rev. 2:6). What a tragedy it is when a local assembly openly dis-obeys God's Word and begins to act like the unsaved people of the world! Once a church has lost its witness for the Lord, is there anything left?

Throughout Old Testament history, the presence of a "faithful remnant" in Israel was important to the fulfillment of God's plan. The entire nation of Israel accepted God's covenant at Mount Sinai (Ex. 20:18-21) but most of them failed to obey the Lord and died in the wilderness. In the years that followed the nation's entrance into the Promised Land, the people gradually declined spiritually, and it was the remnant that prayed, obeyed God's Word, and remained faithful to the Lord. It is this remnant that will play an important role in the future of Israel (Isa. 1:9; 10:20-23; 11:11, 16; 37:31; Joel 2:32; Micah 2:12; 5:7; Zeph. 2:4-7; Zech. 8:1-8; Mal. 3:16; Rom. 9:27; 11:5). According to the letters to the seven churches of Asia Minor, there is a faithful remnant in the professing church today (Rev. 2:24; 3:4-6; and note our Lord's words to the "overcomers").

2. The first spoken message: the judgment of the land (Ezek. 6:1-14)
God had commanded His prophet to remain silent except for those times when He opened his mouth and commanded him to preach a special message. In these two chapters, there are two messages of judgment from the Lord. The first explains that the idolatry of the people had defiled the land and the temple, and the second describes the terrible disaster that would come with the arrival of the Babylonian army. Ezekiel the watchman was warning the people that an invasion was coming because God had seen their sins and was about to punish them.

God's judgment of the high places (Ezek. 6:1-7).[9] The land belonged to the Lord, and He allowed the Jewish people to use it as long as they didn't defile it with their sins (Lev. 25:23; 18:25, 27-28). If the Jews obeyed His law, God would bless them in their land (26:1-13). But if they failed to keep the terms of His covenant, the Lord would punish them by withholding blessing from the land He had given them or by "vomiting" them out of the land (Lev. 18:24-30; 26:14ff; Deut. 28:38-42, 49-52). This explains why Ezekiel "set his face"[10] against the mountains, hills, rivers (ravines), and valleys of the land, for they had been defiled by the idolatry of Israel. Of course, it wasn't the physical terrain that had sinned but the Jewish people who had polluted the Holy Land by erecting their "high places [idolatrous shrines] under every green tree" (Ezek. 6:13; see Deut. 12:2; 1 Kings 14:23; Jer. 2:20; 3:6, 13).

The Jewish prophets despised idolatry and spoke scornfully about the idols that the people valued so much. The prophets called the idols "nothings" or "vanity" (Isa. 66:3; 1 Chron. 16:26; Jer. 14:14), "abominations" (2 Chron. 15:8) and "terrors" (1 Kings 15:13); but the word Ezekiel used is even more derisive because it can mean "pellets of dung."[11] The people treated their false gods as the highest things in the land, but God saw them as the lowest and most defiling thing—dung.

The Babylonian army would come into the land and break down the shrines and altars and destroy the idols. But even more, the soldiers would kill the worshipers and leave their rotting corpses as "sacrifices" to the fallen idols. "I will bring a sword upon you" (v. 3)[12] and "you shall know that I am the Lord" (Ezek. 6:7).The enemy would stack the corpses around the shrines like so many logs and pieces of defiled flesh. In His covenant with Israel, God warned Israel that this would happen if they turned from Him and worshiped false gods. During Israel's history, godly kings would destroy these abominable places and evil kings would rebuild them (2 Kings 18:3-4; 21:1-6; 23:8-9).

God's grace to the Jewish remnant (Ezek. 6:8-10). Against the somber background of this nationwide slaughter, Ezekiel reminds the people of the grace of God in sparing a remnant, a topic that he had illustrated when he put some of the shaved hair in the hem of his garment (5:1-3). He will mention the remnant again in 7:16; 11:16-21; 12:15-16; 14:22-23; and 16:60-63. That a remnant of faithful people would be spared was part of the covenant promise (Lev. 26:40-46). It was this feeble remnant that returned to the land, rebuilt the temple, restored the worship of the Lord, and eventually made possible the coming of the Messiah (Luke 1–2).

Not only was the worship of idols an abomination and a participation in filth, but it was adultery (Ezek. 6:9).[13] The nation had been married to Jehovah at Sinai, and the worship of any other god was an act of adultery (Isa. 54:5; Jer. 2:1-8; 3:14; 31:32; Hosea 2:16). Here we see God's heart broken over the unfaithfulness of His people: "How I have been grieved by their adulterous hearts" (Ezek. 6:9, NIV). The jealousy of God over Israel, His adulterous wife, is often mentioned in Ezekiel's prophecy (8:3, 5; 16:38, 42; 23:25; 36:5; 38:19).

God's chaste love for Israel, His wife, is the major theme of the Prophet Hosea, whose wife became a prostitute and had to be bought back by her loving husband. This was an "action sermon" (and a costly one) that rebuked Israel for their unfaithfulness to God, but the prophet assured them that the Lord would forgive if they would repent and return. Ezekiel announced that the Jews scattered throughout the Gentile nations would realize their sins, remember their God, loathe themselves, and return to the Lord; and this remnant would become the future of the nation. In the midst of judgment, God would remember mercy (Hab. 3:2).

God's weapons of destruction (Ezek. 6:11-14). As he lamented the abominations that his people had committed, the prophet combined both speech and action (clapping, stamping his foot). In 21:14 and 17, these actions represented God's response to the invasion and assault of the Babylonians. From the context, when Ezekiel struck his hands together, it symbolized the marching of soldiers and the clashing of the swords as God's wrath was "spent" or "accomplished" against His disobedient people.[14] This wasn't something the Lord enjoyed doing, because He has no pleasure in the death of the wicked (18:23; 33:11). The Lord unleashed His three weapons against His people: the swords of the Babylonians, famine in the city, and the pestilence that usually accompanies famine (see 5:1-2).

Once again, Ezekiel described the unfaithful Jews being slaughtered at their idolatrous shrines and their corpses stacked up around the altars like so much dead wood (6:13; see vv. 3-5). When God "stretches out his hand" (v. 14), it means that judgment is coming (14:9, 13; 16:27; 25:7, 13, 16). The word "Diblah" might be a shortened form of Beth Diblathaim in Moab (Jer. 48:22), but if it is, the significance of the reference has been lost to us. Some Hebrew manuscripts read "Riblah," a city in Syria, and this seems to fit. God promised to devastate the land "from the desert to Riblah [Diblah]" (NIV), that is, from the south to the north. It's like saying "from Dan to Beersheba," from the north to the south.

At least sixty times, Ezekiel writes, "And they shall know that I am the Lord" (Ezek. 6:14). Whether in blessing or chastening, the Lord's purpose is to reveal Himself to us in His love and grace. If the people of Israel had truly known the character and ways of their God, they could never have rebelled against Him as they did. "Oh, that they had such a heart in them that they would fear Me and always keep all My commandments, that it might be well with them and with their children forever!" (Deut. 5:29, NKJV)

3. The second spoken message: the devastation of the land (Ezek. 7:1-27)
The nation of Israel was blessed with a gracious Lord to worship and love, a fruitful land to enjoy, and a holy law to obey. Their love for the Lord and their obedience to His law would determine how much blessing He could entrust to them in the land. These were the terms of the covenant and the Jewish people knew them well. The generation that first entered the land obeyed God's covenant, as did the succeeding generation, but the third generation provoked the Lord, broke their "marriage vows," and prostituted themselves to idols (Jud. 2:10-13). They disobeyed the law, defied their Lord, and defiled the land, and the Lord would not accept that kind of conduct. First, He punished them *in their land* by permitting seven enemy nations to occupy the land and oppress the people, as recorded in the Book of Judges. But each time God delivered Israel from their oppressors, the Jews eventually returned to the worship of idols; so He finally took them *away from the land*, some through death and others through exile in Babylon. It's a tragic story, but it reminds us that the Lord is serious about His covenant and our obedience.

Disaster announced (Ezek. 7:1-9). In this second spoken message, the key phrases are "the land," "an end," and "it is come." The land is personified in this message and Ezekiel speaks to it and announces that disaster is about to fall. The judgment was certain because the prophet announced "It is come!" at least nine times in verses 1-12. He was a faithful watchman, warning the people that the Babylonian army was coming from the north to invade the land, rob it, and ruin it. Babylon was God's weapon through which He would unleash His anger, judge Israel's abominable behavior, and repay them for their disobedience. In previous chastisements, the Lord had shown pity and spared His people, but this judgment would be different. They had defiled His land with their sins, and the only way the land could be cleansed was by punishing the people for their sins.

In verses 7 and 10, the KJV has the phrase "the morning is come," but both the NKJV and the NIV translate it "doom has come." The Hebrew word means "to plait, to braid," such as braiding a garland of flowers for the head, and it's translated "diadem" in Isaiah 28:5. How do the translators get either "morning" or "doom" out of this word? Probably from the image of "that which comes around," for a braided garland is the result of the weaving of flowers into a circle. "Morning" is that which comes around, day after day, and the doom of the Israelites had "come around." They had "woven" their own shameful crown of sin when they could have worn a diadem of glory to the Lord.

The disaster pictured (Ezek. 7:10-21). Always the master of vivid language to help the people "see" the truth, Ezekiel painted four word pictures to arouse their interest and perhaps reach their hearts. The first is *the budding rod (vv. 10-11),* an image from nature. God had been long-suffering as His people disobeyed His law and defied His prophets, but now their sins had "ripened" and the nation would have to reap what they sowed. In their pride, they had cultivated a false confidence that the Lord would never allow His people to be exiled or His temple destroyed, but their sin had now "matured" and both were now about to happen. Isaiah had used a similar image when describing the Assyrian invasion of the land (Isa. 10:5), only he saw the invaders as the "rod" in His hand. If that's the image Ezekiel had in mind, then the rod is Nebuchadnezzar and the "blossoming" means that the time was ripe for God to punish the people. Violence in the land had grown into a rod of wickedness, and the people's sins would find them out.

The second picture is taken from *the business world* (*Ezek. 7:12-13*), with the Jewish "Year of Jubilee" as the background (Lev. 25). Every seventh year was set apart as a Sabbatic Year, during which the land lay fallow and debts were cancelled (vv. 1-7; Deut. 15:1-6). After seven of these Sabbatic Years, the fiftieth year was set apart as a Year of Jubilee, when the land lay fallow, debts were cancelled, servants were set free, and the land was returned to the original owners. The price of a parcel of land was determined by the number of years until the Year of Jubilee and the amount of crops that could be harvested during that time. If a poor man sold his land or himself to be a servant, he knew the land would be returned to his family in the Year of Jubilee and he would be set free.

With the Babylonian invasion imminent, the price of land would certainly drop and wealthy people could quickly increase their holdings, but there was no guarantee that they would hold what they purchased. Furthermore, the seller couldn't be sure that he would get his land back when the Year of Jubilee arrived. Jeremiah had told the captives that they would be in Babylon for seventy years (Jer. 29:10), so they would spend their Sabbatic years and the next Year of Jubilee in captivity—if they were alive. The vision of coming judgment would "not be reversed" (Ezek. 7:13, NIV); instead, the whole economic pattern would be reversed. Had the Jews obeyed God's law, the slaves would have been freed and the ownership of the land would have been protected, but now the surviving Jews would be enslaved and their land taken from them. The people had not obeyed the laws concerning the Sabbaths for the land, so the Lord took the land from them until those Sabbaths were fulfilled (2 Chron. 36:14-21). What we selfishly keep for ourselves, we eventually lose; but what we give to the Lord, we keep forever.

The third picture is that of *the watchman (Ezek. 7:14-15)*. God had made Ezekiel a watchman (3:17-21), and it was his responsibility to warn the people when danger was at hand. If an enemy army approached, the watchmen on the walls would blow their trumpets and summon the soldiers to man their posts and protect the city. But it was futile for the watchmen in Jerusalem to blow their trumpets because there was no Jewish army available and any resistance was futile. If the soldiers went outside the city into the country, they would be slain by the swords of the Babylonian army; and if the warriors stayed inside the city, they would die from famine and pestilence. Why risk your life in such a hopeless cause?

In his fourth picture, Ezekiel compares the fugitives who escape to *mourning doves (7:16-18)*, frightened and alone in the mountains. It is from this group that the Lord would form His remnant, so they were important to Him. Instead of rejoicing at their escape, these people were mourning over their sins (Isa. 59:11), wearing sackcloth and shaving their heads in sorrow and repentance, a fulfillment of Ezekiel's prophecy in Ezekiel 6:9-10. They will be too weak and frightened to fight the enemy; all they can do is throw themselves on the mercy of the Lord.

People throwing away their valuables (Ezek. 7:19-21) is the fifth and final picture. During the final years of the kingdom of Judah, the rich were getting richer and the poor were getting poorer, with the rich robbing the poor without any interference from the courts. The prophets thundered against this evil, but the leaders would not listen. The refugees couldn't carry their wealth as they fled from Jerusalem, so they treated it like garbage and threw it into the streets. You can't eat money, and what good is money when there's no food to buy in the city? Furthermore, there wouldn't be any places to purchase supplies as the people fled to the mountains. Their gold and silver were only excess baggage that would slow them down, and their idols were even more worthless. In a time of crisis, we quickly learn what's valuable and important to life. The lust for wealth lured them into sin, and their sins brought about judgment. The Babylonian soldiers took the wealth of the Jews as loot, along with their expensive idols; this was God's payment to Babylon for their services in chastening Israel.

The disruption from the disaster (Ezek. 7:22-27). First, there would be no help from the religious leaders, neither the prophets nor the priests (v. 26); and the holy temple would be defiled and destroyed. The Jews had depended on the temple to save them, for surely God wouldn't permit His beautiful house to be ruined by pagan soldiers (Jer. 7:1-5). But the temple had become a den of thieves (v. 11), and the Lord was no longer pleased with the sacrifices the people offered there (Isa. 1:11-20). God would allow pagans to pollute His treasured place. The priests could give no encouragement from the Word of God because the people had broken the covenant and were outside the place of blessing. The false prophets could see no vision because they had rejected the truth.

Not only would there be religious chaos, but the political system would fall apart (Ezek. 7:27). In the eyes of Ezekiel, the king was Jehoiachin (1:2) and the prince was Zedekiah. Though Zedekiah was the last king of Judah, the prophet didn't recognize his reign but considered him only a prince (12:10, 12). The leadership in Judah began to collapse when the kings refused to listen to Jeremiah's messages from the Lord, admonishing them to surrender to Babylon and thus save the city and the temple. Whenever leaders of the Jewish nation depended on politics rather than the prophetic Word, they gradually moved into compromise and confusion (Isa. 8:20). Judah sought alliances with Egypt and tried to negotiate a way to peace (Ezek. 7:25), but the Lord had determined that His people should be chastened, and no political power can overrule the sovereign will of God.

"The Lord brings the counsel of the nations to nothing; He makes the plans of the peoples of no effect. The counsel of the Lord stands forever; the plans of His heart to all generations" (Ps. 33:10-11, NKJV).

THREE

The Glory Has Departed

The Gentile nations had their temples, priests, religious laws, and sacrifices, but only the nation of Israel had the glory of the true and living God dwelling in their midst (Rom. 9:4). When Moses dedicated the tabernacle, God's glory moved in (Ex. 40:34-35), but the sins of the people caused the glory to depart (1 Sam. 4:19-22). When Solomon dedicated the temple, once again God's glory filled the sanctuary (1 Kings 8:11); but centuries later, the Prophet Ezekiel watched that glory leave the temple—and then come back again! Without the presence of the glory of the Lord, God's people are just another religious crowd, going through the motions. "If Your presence does not go with us," said Moses to the Lord, "do not bring us up from here" (Ex. 33:15, NKJV). The people of God are identified by the presence of God.

Recorded in these chapters is a remarkable vision that God gave Ezekiel, which he shared with the elders of the people of Israel (Ezek. 11:25). It wasn't an easy message to preach because it dealt with three great tragedies in the life of the Jewish nation: the temple was defiled (8:1-18), the people were doomed (9:1–10:22), and the leaders were deceived (11:1-25). The truths he shared in this message were opposite to what the false

43

prophets were declaring both in Jerusalem and in Babylon. In their blind overconfidence, the false prophets and the officials who followed them all claimed that God would never permit His holy temple to fall into the hands of pagan Gentiles, but they proved to be wrong.

1. The temple is defiled (Ezek. 8:1-18)

Seeing dramatic visions and hearing God's voice were not everyday experiences for God's servants the prophets. As far as the record is concerned, fourteen months passed since Ezekiel was called and given his first visions. During that time he and his wife lived normal lives as Jeremiah had instructed (Jer. 29:4-9). Since the exiles in Babylon didn't have Jewish kings or princes to direct the affairs of the people, they chose elders to be their leaders; and some of these elders occasionally visited Ezekiel (see Ezek. 14:1; 20:1; 33:30-33). In this chapter, Ezekiel had two vivid experiences that led to a sad declaration: God would unleash His fury and judge His people without pity.

The glory of God was revealed (Ezek. 8:1-2). Above everything else, God's servants need to focus on the glory of God. It was seeing God's glory that kept Moses going when he was heavily burdened for the people (Ex. 33:18-23), and Ezekiel needed that same kind of encouragement. He saw the same glorious being and the same "chariot throne" that he had seen in the first vision (Ezek. 1). It's likely that this awesome being was Jesus Christ in a preincarnate appearance, and "the glory of God" in 8:4 was undoubtedly the spectacular vision of the wheels, cherubim, firmament, and throne which accompanied his prophetic call. God's servants may think that their greatest need is to see new visions and hear new voices, but the Lord doesn't always work that way. Instead, He often meets the need by giving us *a fresh experience of the original call.* The Lord reminded His servant that He was still on the throne and that His providential care for him and his people had never ceased. What more did Ezekiel need to know?

The idolatry of the people was exposed (Ezek. 8:3-16). Ezekiel

44

was lifted from his house in Babylon and taken to the temple in Jerusalem! He wasn't transported bodily; he remained in his house and saw what was going on in the temple. (See 11:1, 24; 37:1; 43:5.) The first thing he saw in the temple was an idol! It's called "the image of jealousy" because idolatry provokes the Lord who is jealous over His people (Deut. 32:21). As the nation decayed spiritually, the religious leaders incorporated into the temple rituals the worship of other gods along with the worship of Jehovah. The stages in their idolatry were clear. First the Jewish people became curious about their neighbors' religion and then they investigated it. Its baser elements appealed to their fleshly appetites, and before long they were secretly participating in pagan worship. It was just a short step to start worshiping idols openly and then moving this false worship into the temple, as though Jehovah was just one of many gods (Deut. 7:1-11). Since the Lord and Israel were "married" in a covenant relationship, Israel's "religious prostitution" aroused the Lord's holy jealousy, just as a husband or wife would be jealous if a "lover" invaded their marriage (Ex. 20:5; Deut. 32:16).

King Hezekiah had removed idolatry from the land (2 Kings 18:1-5), but King Manasseh not only restored it but made it worse. It was he who put an idol into the Lord's temple (21:1-7), and Amon, his son and successor, continued his father's evil practices. But godly King Josiah purged the land of idolatry and burned that idol and crushed it to powder (23:4-20). But the idol had been replaced! The remarkable thing is that the glory of God was present in the same temple, but God was about to remove His glory and Ezekiel would watch it occur. Without the presence of God, the temple was just another building. It was the blasphemous sins of the religious leaders that drove God away from His holy house, and Ezekiel was about to see how wicked these leaders really were.

The Lord then led him to a place in the temple where there was a hole in the wall leading to a secret chamber. When Ezekiel entered the room, he saw seventy elders of the people (Ex. 24:9-10; Num. 11:16ff) burning incense before various idols whose images were painted on the wall, each man worshiping his own idol (see Ezek. 12, NASB). So gross was their appetite for false gods that they were even worshiping creeping things! (See Deut. 4:14-19; Rom. 1:18-25.) Ezekiel recognized Jaazaniah, one of the leading men in Jerusalem. (This is not the Jaazaniah of Ezek. 11:1.) It's possible that his father Shaphan was the same man who found the Book of the Law in the days of King Josiah and served the Lord so faithfully (2 Chron. 34). If so, he had at least three other sons: Ahikam, who protected Jeremiah from being killed (Jer. 26:24); Gemariah, who begged King Jehoiakim not to destroy Jeremiah's scroll (36:12ff); and Elasah, who delivered Jeremiah's scroll to the Jews in Babylon (29:1-3). Nebuchadnezzar appointed Shaphan's grandson Gedaliah to serve as governor of Judah after Jerusalem was destroyed (39:14). With this kind of godly heritage, it's difficult to believe that Jaazaniah became an idolater.

God knew what was in the hearts of these men and how they justified their sin: "The Lord does not see us, the Lord has forsaken the land" (Ezek. 8:12, NKJV). But the Lord isn't like the dead idols they worshiped which "have eyes but see not" (Ps. 115:5), and the people had forsaken the Lord long before He forsook them (2 Chron. 24:20; Jer. 1:16; 2:13, 17; 7:29, 15:6). Sad to say, the false thinking of these elders reached to the people, and they adopted it as their excuse for sin (Ezek. 9:9).

But there was more sin for Ezekiel to see in the temple. This time, it was the women at the gate of the temple, who were openly taking part in a heathen ritual dedicated to Tammuz (8:13-14). While not all scholars agree, Tammuz is usually identified as a fertility god whom the Egyptians called Osiris and the Greeks called Adonis. According to their myths, Tammuz was killed by a wild boar and went to the underworld, and this tragedy brought winter each year. But his wife Ishtar (Astarte) would rescue him and this would bring the return of springtime and the rebirth of nature. It was nothing but superstition; the Jewish women had forsaken the truth of God for lies and were depending on gods that didn't exist. The rituals associated with the worship of Tammuz were unspeakably vile, as most fertility rituals were.

The fourth sight that would grieve Ezekiel's heart was that of twenty-five men at the door of the temple, between the porch (entry) and the brazen altar, openly bowing down to the sun (vv. 15-16). Since they were standing in an area by the altar of sacrifice available only to the priests, it's likely these men were priests, although in 9:6, these men are called elders. In worshiping the sun, they had to face the east, and this meant they turned their backs on the temple of God and the God of the temple. The idolatry of the seventy elders was hidden in the temple, but these men practiced their idolatry openly! It was contrary to God's law for the Jews to worship the heavenly bodies (Ex. 20:1-6; Deut. 17:3), but these men were worshiping the creation instead of the Creator (Rom. 1:25) and doing it openly in the temple precincts.

Idolatry was a besetting sin among the Jewish people. Abraham belonged to an idol-worshiping family before God called him (Josh. 24:2), and the Jews learned a great deal about idolatry when they sojourned in Egypt (Ezek. 20:7; Josh. 24:14). When they captured the Promised Land, they failed to destroy the idols and shrines of the residents of the land, and this idolatry became a snare to them (Jud. 2:10-15). While believers today may not bow before grotesque idols like those named in the Bible, we must still beware of idols, for an idol is anything that has our devotion and commands our will and takes the place of the true and living God. "Little children, keep yourselves from idols" (1 John 5:21) is an admonition that needs to be heeded by the church today.

The divine judgment is announced (Ezek. 8:17-18). Ezekiel had seen only a part of the evidence that the people in Jerusalem had abandoned themselves to idolatry. He had seen an idol in the temple, defiling its very precincts and yet being worshiped by people who also claimed to worship the Lord, as though Jehovah were one God among many, not the Lord of Lords. Then he saw the leaders secretly worshiping false gods in the temple. After that, everything was out in the open: the women weeping for Tammuz, and the priests/elders bowing down to the sun. In God's sight, these things were abominable and detestable and they provoked Him to anger. Except for the faithful remnant, the Jewish people no longer feared God or cared about pleasing Him.

The strange phrase "put the branch to the nose" has no parallel in Scripture and may describe a part of an idolatrous ritual. Some see it as an insulting gesture, similar to our "sticking up the nose" at someone or something, while others suggest it should be translated "a stench in my nose." Whatever it means, the gesture was repulsive to God. He announced that the nation's idolatry was the cause of the violence in the land. Because the leaders despised God's law, they didn't care whether the courts were just toward everyone or partial toward the rich. When people lose their fear of God, they do as they please and don't worry about the consequences.

The Lord had presented the evidence and announced the verdict, and now He declared the sentence: He would obey His covenant and severely punish His people for their multiplied sins. "Unsparing fury" was the sentence, and no pity added. The guilty nation could cry out for mercy, but He would not listen to them,[1] and they couldn't appeal to a higher court. He had given them opportunity after opportunity to turn from their sins, but they refused to listen; and now He wouldn't listen to them.

2. The people are doomed (Ezek. 9:1–10:22)
This is the heart of Ezekiel's message, and it must have broken his heart to deliver it. Read the Book of Lamentations and see how thoroughly the Lord "dealt in fury" with His people. The Prophet Jeremiah was an eyewitness of the destruction of Jerusalem, and what Ezekiel predicted, Jeremiah saw fulfilled.

The remnant spared (Ezek. 9:1-4). In his vision, Ezekiel was still in the temple in Jerusalem when he heard the Lord summon six "men" to prepare the way for the slaughter. These were probably angels who appeared as men, the angels assigned to the city of Jerusalem. Daniel learned that there were angels in charge of nations (Dan. 10:12-21), so it isn't unusual that Jerusalem should have six guardian angels. These angels were appointed to execute God's judgment in the city. But with the six angels was a seventh person bearing the equipment of a scribe, clothed in linen as though he were a priest. On the basis of his garment (Dan. 10:5; Rev. 1:13), some students have identified this man as the Lord Jesus Christ who came to preserve His faithful remnant, but this is only conjecture. On his belt or sash, the scribe wore a leather or metal container, about ten inches long and an inch and a half square, in which were reed pens and a container of ink. In ancient cities, the scribe would register the citizens and identify the aliens. These seven angels congregated at the altar of burnt offering, the place where the fire of God's holy judgment consumed the sacrifices.[2] The fire declared the holiness of God, but the blood sacrifice on the altar declared the grace of God.

At this point, the shekinah[3] glory that had been on the "chariot throne" (Ezek. 8:2, 4) moved from the throne to the threshold of the temple, in preparation for leaving the temple. It's interesting that the glory of God should be associated with the judgment of a polluted city, but it is for His glory that God judges sin.[4] It is also for His glory that that God graciously saves those who put their trust in Him (Eph. 1:6, 12, 14). The Jewish people who had God's glory dwelling among them didn't seek to glorify Him by obeying His will, so He received glory by punishing their sins.

The scribe-angel was commanded to go through the city and mark the people who lamented and grieved because of the sins of the city. No matter how dark the day, God has always had His faithful remnant who obeyed His will and trusted Him for deliverance, and Ezekiel was among them (Ezek. 6:11; 21:6). See Psalms 12:5; 119:53; 136; Isaiah 66:2; Jeremiah 13:17; Amos 6:6 and Malachi 3:16. The marking of people will also be a feature of the end times (Rev. 7:3; 9:4; 13:16-17; 20:4). Believers today are "marked" by the Spirit of God (Eph. 1:13-14) and should be "marked" by holy lives that glorify Christ.

The rebels judged (Ezek. 9:5–10:7). The other six angels were to follow the scribe-angel and kill everybody on whom he didn't put the mark, and nobody was to be spared because of sex or age. The word for "mark" in the Hebrew text is the last letter of the Hebrew alphabet (*taw* or *tau*), which in that day was written like a cross (X). The angels see to it that God's plans are fulfilled for individuals and nations, but they perform their duties invisibly, unseen by the people whose lives they affect. It was now the year 592 B.C. (8:1), and the city of Jerusalem wouldn't be taken until 586 B.C. Some of the inhabitants had already died of famine and pestilence, but when the Babylonian army broke through the walls, many more were to be slaughtered with the sword (5:8-13).

"Begin at my sanctuary" seems like a strange order, but it was the idolatry in the temple that had aroused the anger of the Lord. Often in Scripture you find God sending judgment, not because unbelievers have sinned, but because His own people have disobeyed His law! Twice Abraham brought judgment on innocent Gentiles because he lied about his wife (Gen. 12:10-20; 20:1-18). Aaron the high priest led Israel into idolatry and 3,000 people were slain (Ex. 32:1-6, 26-29). David committed adultery with Bathsheba and then murdered her husband, Uriah, and his sins brought years of trouble to his family and the nation. A crew of Gentile sailors almost drowned because of the disobedience of God's prophet Jonah. God's people are to be the salt of the earth and the light of the world (Matt. 5:13-16). If there were more salt in this world, there would be less decay, and more light would mean less darkness. Our good works glorify the Lord, but our sins invite His discipline. Peter warned believers in the first century that "judgment must begin at the house [household] of God" (1 Peter 4:17), a warning we need to heed today as our Lord's coming draws near.

A corpse was an unclean thing to a Jew, so corpses in the temple would defile the house of God. These people had defiled God's house by their wicked lives, and now they would defile it further in their terrible deaths. The idolaters would be as dead as the idols they worshiped (Ps. 115:8). When the Prophet Ezekiel saw this scene, he fell on his face to intercede for the remnant God had promised to protect. This attitude is the mark of a true shepherd (see Ezek. 4:14; 11:13). Abraham interceded for Lot in Sodom (Gen. 18:16ff), and Moses interceded for his brother Aaron and the idolatrous Jews (Ex. 32:11ff). The prophets asked

God to spare the people of Israel, and Jesus prayed for the ignorant people who crucified Him (Luke 23:34). God informed Ezekiel that the land was defiled by innocent blood and the city was full of injustice, and the time had come for the people to reap what they had sown.

In response to Ezekiel's concern and prayer, the Lord revealed His glory once again, just as it had been revealed when Moses dedicated the tabernacle and Solomon dedicated the temple. The glory cloud left the chariot-throne and hovered over the threshold. The Lord commanded the scribe-angel to enter between the wheels and take coals from the fire that was there and to scatter the coals over the city of Jerusalem. Not only would the city be visited by famine, pestilence, and sword, but it would be burned by the Babylonian army. This was not a fire of purification, such as Isaiah experienced (Isa. 6:5-7), but a fire of condemnation (2 Kings 25:8-9).

The glory revealed (Ezek. 10:8-22). Ezekiel describes the vision of God's glory that he had seen on the day of his ordination (vv. 15, 20-22). One new feature is the fact that the living creatures were "full of eyes" even as the wheels were, which suggests God's omniscience (see 1:18). God's providential working in this world is not aimless or haphazard. Everything is done "according to the purpose of Him who works all things according to the counsel of His will" (Eph. 1:11, NKJV). Another new feature is the identifying of the wheels as "the whirling wheels" (Ezek. 10:13, NIV).

One problem that this new description presents relates to the description of the faces of the cherubim in verse 14. In 1:10, each cherub had the face of a man, a lion, an ox, and an eagle; while in 10:14, the face of the ox is apparently replaced by the face of "the cherub." The so-called contradiction is only apparent. From where Ezekiel was standing, he saw a different face of each of the cherubs. "The cherub" must have been the one that gave the coals of fire to the scribe-angel. We might paraphrase it, "The first face I saw was of the cherub and it was an ox, since the faces I saw of the other three cherubim were of a man, a lion, and an eagle." Each face was indeed the face of the cherub since each of the living creatures was a cherub.

God's glory departed from the threshold and stood over the throne-chariot which was on the right side of the house (v. 3), as though the Lord were calling His glory back to His throne. At the same time, the chariot-throne arose and stood at the door of the east gate of the temple. There Ezekiel would see some of the leaders of the nation engaged in worshiping the sun, and the Lord would judge one of them.

Ezekiel was learning that the most important part of the nation's life was to magnify the glory of God. The presence of God in the sanctuary was a great privilege for the people of Israel, but it was also a great responsibility. The glory of God cannot dwell with the sins of God's people, so it was necessary for the glory to leave, and the sanctuary and the people to be judged.

3. The leaders are deceived (Ezek. 11:1-25)
When you read the prophecy of Jeremiah, you discover that the civil and religious leaders of the kingdom of Judah, as well as the rulers of Jerusalem, were not interested in knowing and doing the will of God. When one of the kings inquired of Jeremiah, he did it secretly because he was afraid of what his advisers might do (Jer. 37:17). During Judah's last years, the people were ruled by weak men who promoted idolatry and would not call the people to repentance and prayer (2 Chron. 7:14). By publicly wearing a yoke, Jeremiah had made it clear that the only way to spare the city and the temple from destruction was for the Jewish leaders to surrender to the Babylonians (Jer. 27). Instead, the Jewish leaders secretly made an agreement with the Egyptians, asking them to rescue them from Babylon, but the Egyptians were help-less to do anything. God had decreed the fall of the nation, and He was using Nebuchadnezzar as His servant to accomplish His will (Jer. 25:9; 27:6; 43:10).

The city is like a cauldron (Ezek. 11:1-13). Ezekiel is still hav-ing his vision of Jerusalem and the temple, and the Lord showed him twenty-five men at the eastern door of the temple, worship-ing the sun. (See 8:15-18). Among them were the leaders of the people, Jaazaniah and Pelantiah. (This is not the Jaazaniah of v. 11.) These men were giving wicked advice to the king and other leaders in Jerusalem, but their counsel was not from the Lord. How could it be wise counsel when they were idolaters who worshiped the sun? At the same time, they were plotting evil so that they could benefit personally from the Babylonian attack on the city. In every crisis, you will find "opportunists" who seek to help themselves instead of helping their country, and they usually hide behind the mask of patriotism.

Not only were these leaders idolaters and wicked counselors, but they cultivated a philosophy that gave them and the other leaders a false confidence in their dangerous situation. "Is not the time near to build houses?" they asked. "This city is the pot and we are the flesh" (11:3, NASB). Jeremiah had told the exiles to build houses in Babylon and settle down and raise families, because they would live there for seventy years (Jer. 29:4ff). But it was foolish for the people in Jerusalem to build houses, for the Lord had ordained that the Babylonian army would destroy the city and slaughter most of the inhabitants. These evil leaders were sure that Jerusalem was as safe for them as a piece of meat in a cooking pot. The innuendo in this metaphor was that the people in Jerusalem were choice cuts of meat while the exiles in Babylon were just the scraps and rejected pieces. Of course, just the opposite was true! Had the leaders in Jerusalem listened to Jeremiah's message about the baskets of figs, they would have seen their philosophy completely reversed. The good figs were the exiles and the bad figs were the people left in Jerusalem (Jer. 24:1-7). God would preserve a remnant from among the exiles, but the idolaters in Jerusalem would be slain.

The Lord told Ezekiel to prophesy against those evil leaders and point out that they weren't the meat—they were the butchers! They had killed innocent people in Jerusalem and stolen their possessions, and even if the leaders weren't slain in Jerusalem, they would not escape judgment. They might flee the city, but the Babylonians would catch them at the border, pass sentence on them, and kill them; and that is exactly what happened (2 Kings 25:18-21; Jer. 39:1-7; 52:1-11, 24-27). Then the Jewish officials would learn too late that Jehovah alone is Lord of heaven and earth.

In his vision, Ezekiel preached this message and Petaliah fell down dead! The Lord gave the sun-worshipers a vivid proof that their evil thoughts and plans could only lead to disaster. Once again, Ezekiel revealed his shepherd's heart as he fell on his face before the Lord and prayed for the people. As in Ezekiel 9:8, he prayed that the Lord would spare a remnant of the people so Israel would have a future.

Jehovah the sanctuary of His people (Ezek. 11:14-21). This is God's word of encouragement to His servant that He would fulfill His promise and spare a remnant of the people. The people in Jerusalem were sure that God would deliver them and give back their land, because the exiles had left the land and were far from Jerusalem and the temple. In ancient days, people believed that each nation had its own gods, and when you left your home country, you left your gods behind.[5] Of course, Jehovah had revealed Himself to Abraham as "possessor of heaven and earth" (Gen. 14:22), so the Jewish leaders shouldn't have had such a narrow view of God. What they said was probably just an excuse for confiscating land that belonged to some of the exiles.

But the Lord made it clear that He had not forsaken the Jews in Babylon, for the "I will" statements in Ezekiel 11:16-20 declare His promises to the exiles. First, God Himself would be to them "a sanctuary for a little while" during their captivity. "Lord, You have been our dwelling place in all generations" (Ps. 90:1, NKJV). The self-confident Jews in Jerusalem thought they were secure as long as they had the temple, but the true temple was with the exiles in Babylon! Long before there ever was a tabernacle or a temple, the patriarchs had God as their refuge and strength, their sanctuary, and their abiding place. Wherever Abraham pitched his tent, he also built an altar to the Lord, because he knew that God was with him (Gen. 12:8; 13:1-4, 18). The New Testament equivalent of this experience is to abide in Christ (John 15:1-10).

His second promise is "I will even gather you" (Ezek. 11:17).

A remnant of Jews would one day return to the land and rebuild the temple. No matter where the Jews had been scattered, the Lord would find them and bring them home. This promise goes far beyond the restoration after the Captivity, for the Lord has promised that in the end times He will gather His people back to their land (28:25-26; 34:11-16; 36:24-38; 37:11-28; Isa. 11:11-16; Jer. 24:4-7). His third promise is, "I will give you the land of Israel" (Ezek. 11:17). Since God had already given this land to Abraham and his descendants (Gen. 12:7; 13:14-17; 15:7), nobody else could successfully lay claim to it. When the exiles returned to their land, they would be cured of idolatry and would remove all the pagan worship.

The promises in Ezekiel 11:19-21 go beyond the return of the Jewish exiles after the Babylonian Captivity, for Scripture records no evidence of this kind of spiritual renewal in the post-exilic period. In fact, the account given in Ezra, Nehemiah, Haggai, and Malachi is just the opposite. The promises apply to the end times when God's people Israel will be regathered to their land, will repent of their sins and trust their Messiah (Zech. 12–14), and welcome Him as their King. They will experience a spiritual regeneration, a new birth. However, those who will not believe will be judged (Ezek. 11:21). Later in this book, Ezekiel will describe in greater detail the glorious blessings God has prepared for the Jewish nation (chaps. 33–48). Jeremiah had also announced a "New Covenant" for the people of Israel (Jer. 31:33; 32:38-39), a covenant not written on stones but engraved on the human mind and heart; and Christian believers today share in that covenant (2 Cor. 3; Heb. 9–10).

The glory departs (Ezek. 11:22-25). The chariot-throne had been lingering at the threshold of the east gate of the temple, with the glory of God above it (10:18-19). Now the glory of God departed and rested over the Mount of Olives, east of Jerusalem. Ezekiel could have written "Ichabod" over the east gate, for indeed, "the glory has departed" (1 Sam. 4:19-22). However, Ezekiel saw the glory return, this time to the new temple that will stand during the reign of Christ in His kingdom (Ezek. 43:1-5).

After the temple was destroyed in 586 B.C., the glory of God disappeared from the earth and didn't return until the birth of Christ in Bethlehem (Luke 2:9, 32; John 1:14). Wicked men crucified the Lord of glory (1 Cor. 2:8), but He arose again and ascended back to heaven from Bethany (Luke 24:50-51; Acts 1:9-12) which is on the eastern slope of Mount Olivet. One day Jesus will return to the Mount of Olives (Zech. 14:4) to deliver His people and establish His kingdom. The glory will have returned!

When the vision ended, Ezekiel found himself back in his own house in Babylon, and he told the Jewish elders and the other exiles what the Lord had shown him. Some no doubt believed and prayed for the peace of Jerusalem, while others preferred to listen to the deadly soothing words of the false prophets. But four years later (Ezek. 24:1), Ezekiel would get the message that the siege of Jerusalem had begun. The date was January 15, 588 B.C. Three years later (January 8, 585 B.C.), a fugitive would arrive in Babylon with the news that the city had fallen (32:21).

God's Word never fails.

FOUR

The Truth About the False

In his *Notes on the State of Virginia*, Thomas Jefferson wrote, "It is error alone which needs the support of government. Truth can stand by itself."[1] During the siege of Jerusalem (606–586 B.C.), error had the support of government, religion, and the masses of citizens, and most of the Jewish exiles in Babylon agreed with them. "We will never give in to the Babylonian army!" was the cry of the Jewish people in Jerusalem. "The Lord will never allow the Gentiles to destroy His holy city or defile His holy temple!" One public dissenting voice in Jerusalem was the Prophet Jeremiah, and in Babylon it was the Prophet Ezekiel. Both in his "action sermons" and his oral messages, Ezekiel warned the people that they were trusting in illusions. No matter what the officials, the false prophets, and the people said, the city and the nation were doomed. In these chapters, Ezekiel exposes the errors that brought the nation to ruin.

1. False confidence (Ezek. 12:1-28)
When the Lord called Ezekiel, He warned him that he would be ministering to a rebellious people (2:3-8) who were spiritually blind and deaf (12:2). In order to understand God's truth, we must

57

be obedient to God's will (John 7:17; Ps. 25:8-10), but Israel was far from being obedient. Years before, Isaiah spoke to people who were spiritually blind and deaf (Isa. 6:9-10), and that was the kind of people Jeremiah was preaching to in Jerusalem (Jer. 5:21). When our Lord was here on earth, many of the people were spiritually blind and deaf (Matt. 13:13-14) and so were the people who heard Paul (Acts 28:26-28). In order to get the attention of the exiles and excite their interest, Ezekiel performed two "action sermons" and after each one gave a message from the Lord.

The leaders cannot escape (Ezek. 12:1-16). The Lord instructed Ezekiel to play the part of a fugitive escaping from a besieged city. Part of his activity occurred in the daytime and part at twilight, and the curious but perplexed Jewish exiles watched his strange actions. First, Ezekiel prepared a knapsack with essentials for a journey and took it outside in the daylight and hid it somewhere away from his house. Then he returned to the house and that evening dug through one of its walls, probably from the outside since the people could see him work. Houses were constructed of sun-dried bricks, so digging through the wall wasn't a problem. After that, he retrieved his knapsack, went into the house, and climbed out through the hole, while his face was covered and his eyes were fixed on the ground. As the people watched, they asked, "What is he doing?"

Packing the knapsack and leaving it at a distance from his house conveyed the message that the leaders in Jerusalem were planning to flee for their lives. Digging through the wall from outside the house pictured the Babylonian army's assault on the walls of Jerusalem. That evening, when Ezekiel climbed out of the house through the hole, the knapsack on his back, he depicted the Jewish leaders secretly trying to flee from the city to save their lives. History tells us that King Zedekiah, his officers, and his army escaped from Jerusalem exactly that way, but they were pursued by the Babylonians and captured (2 Kings 25:1-7; Jer. 52:4-11). The Babylonians killed the king's sons and officers before his very eyes,[2] put out Zedekiah's eyes, and took him prisoner to Babylon, where he died.

The next morning, in the message that followed the "action sermon,"[3] Ezekiel predicted that these events would occur. He also announced that though Zedekiah would be taken to Babylon, he would not see it (Ezek. 12:13; Jer. 52:11). How could such a thing happen? It was very simple: the Babylonians gouged out his eyes and *Zedekiah couldn't see anything!* But it wasn't the Babylonian army that captured the king of Judah and his officers; it was God's "net" that caught them. Nebuchadnezzar and the Babylonian army didn't win because of their own skill; they were God's instruments to defeat the people of Judah and Jerusalem (Jer. 27:1-22). Jeremiah had admonished Zedekiah to surrender to the Babylonians (38:14ff), but the king didn't have the faith to trust God's Word and obey it. Had he humbled himself and surrendered, the people, the city, the temple, and the lives of the people would have been spared.

Not only would the Jewish officials be slain and their king humiliated, but the people in Jerusalem who survived the siege would be scattered abroad, and some of them would be taken to Babylon (Ezek. 12:14-16). Again, this would be the work of God—"I shall scatter them"—and not because these surviving Jews had been especially holy. Quite the opposite was true: the Lord allowed the survivors to go to Babylon as witnesses that their evil deeds deserved the punishment that God had sent to the nation. This will come up again in 14:22-23.

The people will live in terror (Ezek. 12:17-28). The prophet's second "action sermon" probably took place the next day when it was time for his meal. Perhaps some of the Jews were in the house with him, or what's more likely, he ate the meal outside and continued the fugitive image. He ate his bread and drank his water—a frugal meal—while shaking and trembling as if in fear. He was illustrating the tragic condition of the people in Jerusalem during the Babylonian siege. They would have very little food and would eat it with fear and trembling because it might well be their last meal. Their plight would be the fulfillment of the Lord's promise in 4:16-17. Anxiety, worry, fear, and consternation would grip the people as the fall of the city became more imminent.

The theme of Ezekiel's message (12:21-28) was the certainty and the nearness of God's judgment on Jerusalem and the land of Judah. The people were quoting a proverb that may have been devised by the false prophets to humiliate Ezekiel: "The days drag on and every vision comes to nothing and is not fulfilled" (v. 22, AMP). In other words, "Ezekiel tells us about all his visions, but nothing ever happens. Why worry? His prophecies will come to nothing!" The Jews had said a similar thing to Isaiah (Isa. 5:19), and people today say this about the return of Jesus Christ (2 Peter 3). People can predict the weather, but they don't discern "the signs of the times" (Matt. 16:3).

The Lord gave His servant a new proverb to share with the exiles: "The days are near when every vision will be fulfilled" (Ezek. 12:23, NIV). Because Ezekiel's prophecies had not been fulfilled immediately, the people were paying more attention to the false prophets than to the true Word of God. The visions of the false prophets were false and misleading, and they delivered only the soothing and encouraging words that the people wanted to hear (Jer. 28–29). The Lord made it clear that there would be no more "delays" and that His Word would be fulfilled. He had said to Jeremiah, "I am watching over My word to perform it" (1:12, NASB), and He told Isaiah that His Word always fulfilled the purposes for which it was sent (Isa. 55:8-11). God's Word has its appointed time and will never fail (Hab. 2:3).

Among the exiles, one part said that Ezekiel's words would never be fulfilled, but another group said, "Yes, they will be fulfilled, but not in our time. We don't have to worry about what will happen because it will take place a long time from now" (paraphrase of Ezek. 12:27). Their interpretation was wrong and so was their selfish attitude. Even if the Lord did delay His judgments, how could the Jewish people be content with the present knowing that a future generation would be wiped out and the holy city and temple destroyed? They were like King Hezekiah when Isaiah rebuked him for his pride and warned him that Babylon would conquer Judah: "At least there will peace and truth in my days" (Isa. 39:8, NKJV).

The Lord made it clear that Ezekiel's words would be fulfilled very soon. "The word which I have spoken shall be done" (Ezek. 12:28). Six years later, the Babylonian army breached the walls of Jerusalem and Ezekiel's predictions came true. How tragic it is when people deliberately ignore or reject the dependable Word of God and put their faith in the empty but soothing words of false religious leaders! It reminds me of a story that came out of World War II. A group of soldiers asked their new chaplain if he believed in hell, and he laughed and said that he didn't. The men said, "Well, sir, if there isn't a hell, then we don't need you. But if there is a hell, then you're leading us astray—and that's worse!" There is no substitute for God's Word.

2. False prophecy (Ezek. 13:1-23)

Ezekiel had answered the shallow selfish thinking of the exiles and the people in Jerusalem, but now he attacked the source of their blind optimism: the messages of the false prophets. Jeremiah in Jerusalem had to confront a similar group of men who claimed to have a word from the Lord. The false prophets claimed to speak in the name of the Lord, just as Jeremiah and Ezekiel did, but they didn't get their messages from the Lord. Ezekiel spoke against both false prophets (vv. 1-16) and false prophetesses (vv. 17-23) who were actually using the occult practices forbidden to the people of Israel (Deut. 18:9-14).

The lying prophets (Ezek. 13:1-16). Four times in this paragraph God declares that the false prophets saw vanity (nothingness) and spoke lies. God hadn't called them (Jer. 23:21-22) and God didn't give them their messages, yet they claimed to be His prophets. They spoke out of their own imaginations and their "inspiration" was self-induced. Ezekiel compared them to the foxes (jackals) that lived as scavengers in the deserted ruins of the land. They cared only for themselves, they did nothing to improve the situation, and they lived off the fears of the people. In times of crisis, there are always religious opportunists who prey on weak and ignorant people who are seeking cheap assurance and comfort.

Ezekiel also compared the false prophets to workmen who failed to build something that would last. The spiritual "wall" that had protected the Jewish people for centuries had fallen into ruin, and prophets like Ezekiel and Jeremiah were trying to rebuild and strengthen it by proclaiming the Word and calling the people back to God. But the false prophets ignored the Word of God and substituted their own lies ("untempered mortar," KJV = whitewash).[4] They were like workmen who whitewashed a weak wall to make it look sturdy, because they promised peace when God had promised destruction (Ezek. 13:10, 16; Jer. 6:14; 7:8; 8:11). Just as the storm would come, and the rain, hail, and wind knock down the wall, so God's wrath would come and destroy Jerusalem, the prophets, and their deceptive messages. A true prophet tells people what they _need_ to hear, but a false prophet tells them what they _want_ to hear (2 Tim. 4:1-5). A true servant of God builds carefully on a strong foundation and keeps the wall in good repair, but a hireling builds carelessly and whitewashes things to make them look better.

God explained how He would judge the false prophets (Ezek. 13:9). First, they would be exposed as counterfeits and no longer have an exalted reputation among the people. They would lose their prominent places in the councils of the nation. God would treat them like Jews who had also lost their citizenship (Ezra 2:59, 62) and therefore be deprived of the privilege of returning to their land. It appears that the false prophets in Jerusalem would be slain by the enemy and those in Babylon would be left there to die. The counterfeit prophets gave the people a false hope, so God gave them no hope at all.

It's a serious thing to be called of God and to speak His Word to His people. To assume a place of ministry without being called and gifted is arrogance, and to manufacture messages without receiving them from the Lord is impertinence. The false prophets in Ezekiel's day were guilty of both. Popularity is not a test of truth. History shows that those who spoke the truth were usually rejected by the majority, persecuted, and even killed. Jesus used the same image of a storm to warn us about false prophets

(Matt. 7:15-27). It's easy for people to say "Lord, Lord," but it's not easy to walk the narrow road and confront the crowd that's going in the opposite direction.

The lying sorceresses (Ezek. 13:17-23). The gift of prophecy wasn't given exclusively to men, for several prophetesses are named in Scripture: Miriam (Ex. 15:20), Deborah (Jud. 4:4-5), the wife of Isaiah (Isa. 8:3), Hulda (2 Kings 22:14), and the daughters of Philip the evangelist (Acts 21:8-9). Noadiah (Neh. 6:14) was apparently a self-styled prophetess and not a true servant of God.

The Jewish women Ezekiel was exposing were more like sorceresses who claimed to be prophetesses. They practiced the magical arts they had probably learned in Babylon, all of which were forbidden to the Jews (Deut. 18:9-14). They manufactured magic charms that people could wear on various parts of the body and thus ward off evil. They also told fortunes and enticed people to buy their services. Like the false prophets, they were using the crisis situation for personal gain and preying on the fears of the people. A Christian executive in Chicago told me that during the Depression, worried businessmen frequently visited a fortuneteller who sold her services from a fine restaurant.

But these women weren't helping people; they were hunting them and catching them like birds in a trap to take their money. They told the people lies, they didn't expose their sins, and they kept them from trusting the true and living God and depending on His Word alone. Instead of condemning the evil and rewarding the good, they were slaying the good and rewarding the evil! Through their divinations, they gave false hope to the wicked and condemned the just, and they were willing to do it for just a handful of barley and a scrap of bread![5] But their end would come. God would strip them of their charms and amulets and then take His people back to their land, leaving these evil women behind to die.

3. False piety (Ezek. 14:1-11)
Except when God told him to leave, Ezekiel was confined to his

house (3:24) and was not allowed to speak unless he was declaring a message from the Lord. The elders of the exiled people came to visit him to see what he was doing and to hear what he had to say about their situation (8:1; 20:1). The prophet gave them two messages from the Lord.

He exposed their hidden sin (Ezek. 14:1-5). God told His servant that these elders were like some of the spiritual leaders Ezekiel had seen in his vision of the temple (chap. 8): outwardly they were serving the Lord, but secretly they were worshiping idols. Instead of having a love for God and His Word in their hearts, the elders had idols in their hearts. Yet they piously sat before God's prophet and acted spiritual, but to them, listening to Ezekiel speak was more like religious entertainment than receiving spiritual enlightenment (33:31). They were like the people in Isaiah's day who drew near to God with words but not with their hearts (Isa. 29:13). Jesus said that the Pharisees in His day were guilty of the same sin (Matt. 15:8-9), and so are some professed Christians today. Idolatry in the heart puts a stumbling block before the eyes (Ezek. 13:7; 7:19; 18:10; 44:12) and this leads to a tragic fall.

It's not likely that believers today would have a love in their hearts for actual images, but anything that replaces God in our affections and our obedience is certainly an idol. It might be wealth, as in the case of Achan (Josh. 7), Ananias and Sapphira (Acts 5), and the man we call "the rich young ruler" (Matt. 19:16-26). Jonah's idol was a selfish patriotism that made him turn his back on the Gentiles who needed to hear his message. Pilate's idol was holding the approval of the people and his status in the Roman Empire (Mark 15:15; John 19:12-16). What we have in our hearts affects what we see and how we live. If Christ is Lord in our hearts (1 Peter 3:15), then there will be no place for idols.

Loving and accepting the false prevents us from knowing and loving the true (2 Thes. 2:10) and results in our becoming estranged from the Lord (Ezek. 13:5). By worshiping false gods, Israel abandoned the Lord whom they had "married" at Sinai

(Jer. 2:1-14), and they needed to turn back to the Lord. Like the believers in the church of Ephesus, they had "left their first love" (Rev. 2:4). God told Ezekiel that the Jewish people had deserted Him to follow after idols and that He would discipline them in order to "recapture" their hearts.

He called them to repent (Ezek. 14:6-11). Repentance is a change of mind; it means turning from sin and turning to the Lord. The Jewish exiles needed to change their minds about idols and the sin of worshiping idols, and then turn to the Lord who alone is worthy of worship. God would judge each sinner personally and deal with each one personally (v. 7), and some of them He would use as examples to warn the other exiles (v. 8).

A casual reading of verse 9 would give the impression that it was the Lord's fault that people were worshiping idols, but that isn't the case. Everybody in Israel knew the Ten Commandments and understood that it was a sin to make and worship idols (Ex. 20:1-6). Even if someone very close to them enticed them to practice idolatry, they were not to yield (Deut. 13). God permitted these enticements to test the people to make sure they were loyal to Him. Of course, God knows what's in the human heart, but we don't know our own hearts, and these tests help us to stay humble before the Lord and walk in the fear of the Lord. An illustration of this truth is seen in 1 Kings 22. God permitted a lying spirit to work in the minds of the false prophets to convince Ahab to go into battle. Micaiah, the true prophet, told the assembly what would happen, but they rejected the truth and put their trust in lies. God spared the life of the king of Judah but took the life of wicked King Ahab.

When people will not receive "the love of the truth, that they might be saved," God may "send them strong delusion, that they should believe the lie, so that they all may be condemned" (2 Thes. 2:10-11, NKJV). It's the condition of the person's heart that determines the response to the Lord's test, for God deals with people according to their hearts (Ps. 18:26-27). The attitude of the lost world today is that there are no absolutes, and therefore there can be no "truth." Satan is the liar and the deceiver and he has blinded the minds of people so that they believe lies and reject the truth of God. We must do all we can to share the truth of the Word with a blind and deaf world, trusting the Holy Spirit to open their eyes and ears and save them by His grace.

4. False hope (Ezek. 14:12-23)
In this particular message, the Lord described once again the four judgments He would send on the people of Judah and Jerusalem, and He emphasized one compelling fact: there would be no escape. Perhaps some of the Jews remembered how their father Abraham interceded for Sodom and Gomorrah, and how the Lord promised to spare the city if He could locate in it ten righteous men (Gen. 18:16-33). God had told Jeremiah to stop praying for the people because they were beyond hope (Jer. 7:16; 11:14; 14:11), and now He would tell Ezekiel that the presence of three righteous men whom the Jews revered would not save the city of Jerusalem.

The judgments described (Ezek. 14:12-21). The first judgment is *famine (vv. 12-14).* God would break the staff of bread and cut off the lives of humans and animals. Both Jeremiah and Ezekiel mention this judgment (Jer. 14; Ezek. 5:12, 16-17; 6:11-12; 7:15; 12:16), and it came as promised. But God in His covenant with Israel had warned that famine would come if the people disobeyed His Word (Deut. 28:15-20, 38-40, 50-57). "But surely there are enough righteous men in Jerusalem to turn away God's anger," the leaders argued; but God silenced their lips. If Noah, Daniel, and Job were in the city, their righteousness would deliver only themselves and could not save the city.

Why did the Lord choose these three men? For one thing, all three of them are identified in the Old Testament Scripture as righteous men (Gen. 6:9; Job 1:1, 8; 2:3; Dan. 6:4-5, 22). All of them were tested and proved faithful, Noah by the Flood, Daniel in the lions' den, and Job by painful trials from Satan. They were all men of faith. Noah's faith helped to save his family and animal creation; Daniel's faith saved his own life and the lives of his friends (Dan. 2:24); and Job's faith saved his three friends from God's judgment (Job 42:7-8). However, the faith and righteousness of these three men could not be accredited to others. Noah's family had to trust God and enter the ark; Daniel's friends had to pray and trust God; and Job's friends had to repent and bring the proper sacrifices. There is no such thing as "borrowed faith."

The responsibility of each person before God is a key subject in the Book of Ezekiel, and he will deal with it in chapter 18. God doesn't punish people because of the sins of others, nor will God accept the righteousness of others to compensate for the wicked deeds of sinners. This principle is made clear in both the Law of Moses and the covenant God made with Israel. The only time God abandoned this principle was when Jesus Christ His Son died on the cross, for He suffered for the sins of the whole world. When we trust Jesus as Savior and Lord, we receive the gift of His righteousness and God accepts us because of His Son (Rom. 3:21-4:25; 2 Cor. 5:19-21).

The second judgment was *wild beasts in the land (Ezek. 14:15-16)*. This judgment was also mentioned in the covenant: "I will also send wild beasts among you, which shall rob you of your children, and destroy your cattle, and make you few in number; and your highways shall be desolate" (Lev. 26:22). The Lord gave Israel victory in the Promised Land in about seven years, but the "mopping up" operation took a little longer. God gave the Jews victory over the residents "little by little" so that the land wouldn't revert to its natural state and the wild animals take over (Deut. 7:22). But now in a developed land, with many people, towns, and cities, the animals would still take over at the command of God! Unfortunately, it would be innocent children who would suffer most. But even if these three righteous men were living in the land, they couldn't deliver anybody other than themselves.

The third judgment was *the sword (Ezek. 14:17-18)*, which means war. The word "sword" is used at least eighty-six times in Ezekiel. The Babylonian army would sweep through the land and show no mercy (Hab. 1:5-11). They would surround Jerusalem and besiege it until its food ran out and its fortifications failed. The presence of Noah, Daniel, and Job could not have saved the city.

The final judgment was *pestilence* (*Ezek. 14:19-20*), which usually accompanies famine and war (Rev. 6:3-8). Dying people and decaying corpses certainly don't make a besieged city a healthier place in which to live. Again, God gave the warning about the inability of the three righteous men to rescue the people. The fourfold repetition of this truth surely got the message across to the elders, but the Jewish people had a tendency to rest all their hopes on the righteousness of their "great men." Both John the Baptist and Jesus warned the Pharisees and Sadducees that they couldn't please God just because Abraham was their father (Matt. 3:7-9; John 8:33-47) or Moses was their leader (9:28).

God's judgments vindicated (Ezek. 14:21-23). The absence of even three righteous people in Jerusalem would make God's judgments of the city even worse, and when all four of His judgments converge, how terrible it will be! No doubt the false prophets and some of the other captives would debate with the Lord and argue that He was being too hard on Judah and Jerusalem. But in His grace, He would allow some of the people to escape the four judgments and be taken captive to Babylon (12:16). When the exiles who preceded them to Babylon see the wickedness of these people, they will have to agree that the Lord was righteous in His judgments (Jer. 22:8-9). The hearts of these survivors must have been incurably sinful if they could watch the siege, see thousands die, be spared themselves, and still not repent and turn to the Lord. Indeed, their eyes were blind, their ears were deaf, and they were a stubborn and rebellious people.

FIVE

Pictures of Failure

The Prophet Ezekiel remained silent except when the word of the Lord came to him and God permitted him to speak (3:25-27). The three messages recorded in these chapters were given to the elders who were seated before him in his own house, men who outwardly appeared interested in hearing God's Word but inwardly were idolatrous (14:1-3). The Lord knew that neither the elders nor the people took Ezekiel's messages seriously because they saw him as a "religious entertainer" whose words were only "beautiful music" (33:30-33). Whenever God's people turn from His Word and become satisfied with substitutes, they are indeed headed for failure.

Because the people who heard him were spiritually blind and deaf, Ezekiel had to hold their attention, arouse their interest, and motivate them to think about God's truth. One way he did this was through his "action sermons," and another way was by means of sermons filled with vivid and arresting vocabulary and intriguing imagery. In these three messages, Ezekiel spoke about a vine, an unfaithful wife, and three shoots from a tree, and each of these images conveyed God's truth to those who really wanted to understand. These pictures and parables not only described the sins of the nation of Israel, but they also declared her terrible judgment. Ezekiel spoke to his people in the most vivid language found anywhere in Scripture, but the messages fell on deaf ears.

One more fact should be noted: these three "parables" answered the complaints of the people that God had rejected His people and was breaking His own covenant. False prophets in both Jerusalem and Babylon were building up the confidence of the people by telling them that the Lord would never allow Jerusalem and the temple to fall into the defiled hands of the Gentiles (Jer. 29:20-32). After all, Israel was Jehovah's special vine, planted by Him in the Promised Land. The nation was married to Jehovah in a divine covenant, and He would never divorce her. But even more, didn't the Lord promise David an endless dynasty? (2 Sam. 7) The Davidic dynasty was like a tall sturdy cedar tree that could never be felled by the Gentiles. Ezekiel used these same three images to teach the nation that the Lord was judging His people *because He did have these special relationships to them!* Privilege brings responsibility, and responsibility brings accountability.

1. The worthless vine (Ezek. 15:1-8)
The vine is an image found frequently in Scripture. Jesus compared Himself to a vine and His disciples to branches in the vine, because we depend wholly on Him for life and fruitfulness (John 15). Without Him, we can do nothing. Revelation 14:17-20 speaks of "the vine of the earth," and this is a symbol of corrupt Gentile society at the end of the age, ripening for judgment in the winepress of God's wrath. But the image of the vine is often applied to the nation of Israel (Ps. 80; Isa. 5:1-7; Jer. 2:21; Matt. 21:28-46; Luke 20:9-19). In fact, Ezekiel will bring the image of the vine into his parable about the "shoots" (Ezek. 17:6-8).

When you study the references listed above, you learn that Israel was a lowly vine when God planted her in the Promised Land, but by His blessing she increased and prospered. During the reign of David and the early years of Solomon, the vine was fragrant and fruitful, a witness to the Gentile nations of the blessing of the God of Israel. However, Solomon introduced idolatry into the nation, the kingdom divided, and the Jewish people began to bear "wild grapes" (Isa. 5:2) instead of fruit for God's glory. Subsequent kings, both of Israel and Judah, worshiped idols and engaged in the evil practices of the neighboring nations. God allowed the Gentiles to invade the land and eventually destroy Jerusalem and the temple (Ps. 80:12-13). The holy vineyard was defiled and devastated.

Ezekiel's contribution to the "vineyard story" is to point out the worthlessness of the vine if it doesn't bear fruit. If a tree becomes useless, you can at least cut it down and make something useful out of the wood; but what can you make out of the wood of a vine? You can't even carve a tent peg or a wall peg out of it! It's good for only one thing, and that's fuel for the fire. If the wood was useless *before* it was thrown into the fire, it's even more worthless *after* it's been singed and marred by the flames.

Ezekiel saw the nation's first taste of the fire in 605 B.C. when Nebuchadnezzar took the temple treasures to Babylon along with some of the best of the young men, including Daniel. In 597 B.C., there was a second deportation of exiles, Ezekiel among them, so the fire was growing hotter. The siege of Jerusalem began in 588 B.C. and the fire began to blaze; and in 586 B.C., the Babylonians destroyed Jerusalem and the temple and took thousands of Jewish captives to Babylon. The vine was burned at both ends and in the middle! The inhabitants of the holy city certainly went from the "fire" of invasion and assault to the literal fire of destruction. "Then they [the Babylonians] burned the house of God, and broke down the wall of Jerusalem, burned all its palaces with fire, and destroyed all its precious possessions" (2 Chron. 36:19, NKJV).

Those of us who are branches in Jesus Christ, the true vine, need to take this lesson to heart. If we fail to abide in Christ, we lose our spiritual power, wither, and fail to bear fruit for His glory. The fruitless branch is tossed aside and eventually burned (John 15:6). I don't think this burning means condemnation in the lake of fire, for no true believer can be condemned for sins for which Jesus died (John 6:37; 10:27-29; Rom. 8:1).[1] The image of the burning branch is that of a worthless life, a life useless to God. John Wesley, the founder of the Methodist church, prayed, "Lord, let me not live to be useless!"

2. The unfaithful wife (Ezek. 16:1-63)

This long chapter contains some of the most vivid language found anywhere in Scripture. It is addressed to the city of Jerusalem but refers to the entire nation. The chapter traces the spiritual history of the Jews from "birth" (God's call of Abraham) through "marriage" (God's covenant with the people), and up to their "spiritual prostitution" (idolatry)[2] and the sad consequences that followed (ruin and exile). The Lord takes His "wife" to court and bears witness of her unfaithfulness to Him. At the same time, the Lord is replying to the complaints of the people that He had not kept His promises when He allowed the Babylonians to invade the land. God did keep His covenant; it was Israel who broke her marriage vow and also broke the heart of her Lord and invited His chastening (Ezek. 6:9). But as we read the chapter, we must see not only the dark background of Israel's wickedness but also the bright light of God's love and grace. "But where sin abounded, grace abounded much more" (Rom. 5:20, NKJV).

Israel experienced a great love (Ezek. 16:1-14). Israel is pictured here as an unwanted child that was exposed, abandoned, and left to die, but she was rescued by the Lord and became His wife. Many of the Jews were excessively proud of their heritage and called the Gentiles "dogs," but the Lord reminded them that they had descended from the Amorites and the Hittites (see Gen. 10:15-16; Deut. 20:17), and that their great city of Jerusalem was once inhabited by the Jebusites (Josh. 15:63). It wasn't until the time of David that Jerusalem belonged to the Jews and became the capital of the nation (Josh. 10:5; 2 Sam. 5:6-10). For that matter, their esteemed ancestor Abraham was an idol-worshiping pagan when God graciously called him! (Josh. 24:2-3) So much for national pride.

The parents of the newborn child didn't even given her the

humane treatment that every baby deserves. They didn't cut the umbilical cord, wash the child, rub her skin with salt[3], or even wrap her in cloths ("swaddled," KJV) for her protection and to keep her limbs straight. Without pity or compassion, they threw her out into the open field and exposed her to the elements. The Lord passed by, saw the helpless baby, took pity on her, and saved her. By the power of His Word He gave her life, and this was wholly an act of divine grace. "The God of glory appeared to our father Abraham" (Acts 7:2, NKJV), not because Abraham earned it or deserved it, but because of God's great love and grace.

The baby grew and became a young woman ready for marriage. The KJV phrase "come to excellent ornaments" in Ezekiel 16:7 means "come to full maturity." But would any suitor want a young woman who was forsaken by her own parents? By now, Israel was enslaved in the land of Egypt, so the Lord would have to redeem her. He wanted her for Himself so He "passed by" again (vv. 6, 8) and claimed her for His own bride. When a suitor spread his garment over a marriageable girl, that meant they were engaged (Ruth 3:9). He did deliver them from bondage, and at Sinai He entered into a "marriage covenant" with the people of Israel. (See Deut. 32:1-14.)

Once again, the Lord cleansed her and clothed her with beautiful expensive garments, fit for a queen. During the reign of King David and during Solomon's early years, Jerusalem was indeed a queenly city and Israel a prosperous kingdom. As long as Israel, Jehovah's wife, obeyed His Word and kept His covenant, He blessed her abundantly just as He promised. He gave her healthy children, fruitful flocks and herds, abundant harvests, and protection from disease, disaster, and invasion. There wasn't one word of the covenant that the Lord failed to keep, and the reputation of Israel spread far and wide. During Solomon's day, foreign rulers came to listen to him (1 Kings 10:1-10, 24-25).

Israel committed a great sin (Ezek. 16:15-34). When Israel became prosperous and famous, she forgot the Lord who gave her such great wealth and began to use God's generous gifts for worshiping idols (Hosea 2:8, 13-14; Deut. 6:10-12; 8:10-20). Like the ignorant heathen nations around her, she worshiped the creation rather than the Creator (Rom. 1:21-25) and abandoned her "husband" for false gods. She didn't simply occasionally commit adultery, as wicked as that is. She became a professional prostitute, but unlike other prostitutes, she sought out her lovers *and paid them to sin with her!* She took the very treasures and blessings that God generously gave to her and devoted them to the making and worshiping of idols—her jewels and garments, her food, and even her children (Ezek. 16:20-21)![4] Idolatry was Israel's besetting sin, and it wasn't cured until the nation was exiled for seventy years in Babylon.

But the nation of Israel practiced another kind of idolatry when she trusted other nations to protect and defend her rather than trusting the Lord Jehovah, her "husband" (vv. 23-34).[5] She not only borrowed the gods of other nations and abandoned the true God, but she hired the armies of other nations instead of believing that the Lord could care for her. King Solomon made treaties with other countries by marrying the daughters of their rulers, and this is what led him into idolatry (1 Kings 11). The Jews were especially tempted to turn to Egypt for help instead of confessing their sins and turning to the Lord (2 Chron. 7:14). The Jewish leaders used every means possible to secure the help of Egypt, all the while acting like a common prostitute (Ezek. 16:23-26). They also went after the Philistines, the Assyrians, and even the Babylonians! However, none of these alliances succeeded, and the Northern Kingdom (Israel) was taken captive by the Assyrians in 722 B.C., and the Southern Kingdom (Judah) was conquered by the Babylonians.

Israel's pride and ingratitude prepared the way for her idolatry. She forgot how good the Lord had been to her and became more concerned with the gifts than the Giver. Moses had warned about these sins (Deut. 6:10-15) but they didn't heed the warning. Believers today who live for the world and depend on the world are committing "adultery" in a similar way (James 4:4-6). The Lord desires and deserves our full and complete devotion (2 Cor. 11:1-4; Rev. 2:4).

Israel suffered a great discipline (Ezek. 16:35-42). The Lord was very patient with His people and warned them that their sins would bring them ruin, but they persisted in rejecting His Word, persecuting His prophets, and practicing the abominable sins of their neighbors. Many of the Jewish people were now exiled in Babylon and those left behind in Judah had either been slain by the Babylonians or were hopelessly imprisoned in Jerusalem and waiting for the siege to end. But the Jews shouldn't have complained to the Lord that He wasn't treating them fairly. They knew the terms of His covenant (Deut. 28–29) and He had already warned them many times that judgment was coming (32:22-43; 2 Chron. 36:14-21).

Their punishments are described as those of a prostitute, an adulteress, and an idolater, because the nation had committed those very sins. According to the law, prostitutes were to be burned (Lev. 21:9; see Gen. 38:24), adulterers and adulteresses stoned (Lev. 20:10), idolaters killed by the sword, and their possessions burned (Deut. 13:12-18). God used the Babylonian army to inflict these same judgments on the people of Israel (Ezek. 16:40-41). Many Jews were slain by the sword, and the city of Jerusalem and the temple were looted and burned.

Ezekiel gives a graphic description of the judgment of Israel, the prostitute. First the Lord would announce the crimes (vv. 35-36). She "poured out her lust" on the heathen idols[6] and exposed her nakedness in worshiping them. She disobeyed God's law, made idols of her own, and even sacrificed her children to them. Then the Lord announced the sentence (vv. 37-42). He would call her lovers (the heathen nations) to be her executioners, and they would gather around her and see her nakedness! She would be publicly exposed as an adulteress and a harlot. The enemy army would strip the city of Jerusalem, even as a convicted harlot is stripped, and then destroy the city (Deut. 22:23-24). Like adulterers and adulteresses, the people would be killed by stones; like idolaters, they would be slain by the sword; and like prostitutes, they would be burned in the fire. The Jews knew all these laws and their penalties, yet they flagrantly defied the Lord and persisted in their abominations.

Having described their sins, the Lord then *defended His sentence* (*Ezek. 16:43-52*). He not only knew what they had done, but He saw in their hearts why they had done it. In answer to the complaints of the people, the Lord proved that they deserved exactly what had happened to them. His judgment was not impulsive; He had waited a long time and they had refused to repent.

First, the nation had forgotten what the Lord had done for them (v. 43), and this was the very sin that Moses especially warned them to avoid (Deut. 6:10ff). God remembered the devotion they manifested in the early days of their commitment, like a young bride loving her husband (Jer. 2:2), but they didn't remember all that the Lord had done for them. When we forget to be thankful, we're in danger of taking credit for our blessings and failing to give God the glory He deserves.

Second, they failed to understand the enormity of their sins (Ezek. 16:44-52). The Jewish people excelled in quoting proverbs and ancient sayings, although such pithy statements usually don't go deep enough to answer the need. "As is the mother, so is her daughter" is the feminine version of "Like father, like son." Another version might be, "The apple doesn't fall too far from the tree." In other words, the children inherit their parents' nature, so don't be surprised if they repeat their parents' sins. The Jewish nation came from the Amorites and the Hittites, and they were worshipers of idols. Immorality and idolatry ran in the family, for Israel's "sisters," Samaria (the Northern Kingdom) and Sodom,[7] were famous for their godlessness.

However, since the Jews possessed the revelation of God's law and had enjoyed the blessing of God's goodness, their sins were far more heinous than those of their "sisters." If God judged Sodom and Gomorrah by sending burning sulfur on them, and if He permitted the Northern Kingdom to be captured by the Assyrians, then surely He would have to judge the people of Judah and Jerusalem if they didn't repent. But Judah and her leaders didn't take these other judgments to heart. To paraphrase verse 47, "You not only walked after their ways and imitated their abominations, but you went beyond them and sinned ever more than they did!"[8]

God names the sins of Sodom (Ezek. 16:48-50). The people were proud and haughty, overfed, idle, unconcerned about the poor and needy, and guilty of detestable acts, which probably refers to their homosexual lifestyle (Gen. 19). These were abominable sins of attitude and action, commission and omission; *and yet the people of Jerusalem and Judah were far guiltier than were the people of Sodom!* When you read the other prophets, especially Isaiah, Jeremiah, and Amos, you hear them naming the sins of the people of Judah and warning them that judgment was coming. The people of Judah were twice the sinners as the people in Samaria, and by comparison, the people of Judah made the citizens of Samaria and Sodom look righteous! What a terrible indictment against God's chosen people!

But is the church today any less guilty? Members of local churches commit the same sins we read about in the newspapers, but the news doesn't always get to the headlines. Congregations are being torn apart because of professed Christians who are involved in lawsuits, divorces, immorality, family feuds, crooked business deals, financial scandals, and a host of other activities that belong to the world. Is it any wonder that lost sinners pay little attention to our public ministry or our personal witness?

Israel will experience a great restoration (Ezek. 16:53-63). The phrase "bring again their captivity" means "restore their fortunes." The captives in Babylon would be restored, return to the land, and rebuild the temple. God's goodness in allowing this to happen would bring them to shame and repentance (Rom. 2:4). When you read the prayers of Ezra (Ezra 9), Daniel (Dan. 9), and the Levites who labored with Nehemiah (Neh. 9), you see that there was still a godly remnant that humbly sought the face of the Lord and confessed their sins.

However, it's likely that this restoration is reserved for the end times when Israel will see their Messiah, weep over their sins, and enter into His kingdom (Zech. 12:9–13:1). History records no restoration for Sodom and the cities of the plain that God destroyed, nor for the kingdom of Samaria that was conquered by Assyria in 722 B.C. Ezekiel writes about an "everlasting covenant" (Ezek. 16:60), which indicates that this prophecy will be fulfilled in the end times. (See Jer. 31:31-34; Isa. 59:21; 61:8.) Later in his book (Ezek. 37:15-28), Ezekiel will predict a reunion of Samaria (the Northern Kingdom) and Judah (the Southern Kingdom) under the kingship of the Messiah. The Lord makes it clear that this restoration and reunion will not be on the basis of the covenant made at Sinai but wholly because of His grace. The Jewish people broke that covenant and suffered for their disobedience, but nobody can be saved by keeping the law (Gal. 2:16, 21; Rom. 4:5). It is only through the redemption provided in Christ Jesus that sinners can be forgiven and received into the family of God (Eph. 2:8-10; Rom. 3:24).

There will come a time when God's people Israel will remember their sins and recognize God's goodness and grace on their behalf. Their mouths will be shut because of conviction (Ezek. 16:63; Rom. 3:19) and they will be saved. How can a holy God forgive the sins of rebels, Jews or Gentiles? Because of the atonement that He made on the cross when He gave His Son as a sacrifice for the sins of the world. "The Father sent the Son to be the Savior of the world" (1 John 4:14), and that included Israel. Christ not only died for the church (Eph. 5:25) and for the sins of the world (John 3:16), but He died for His people Israel (Isa. 53:8). One day, that New Covenant will bring to them the cleansing and forgiveness that only the blood of Christ can give.

3. The two eagles and three shoots (Ezek. 17:1-24)
From the images of a vine and a marriage, Ezekiel turned to the image of a great tree, two eagles, and three shoots. This message is called a "parable" or "riddle," which means a story with a deeper meaning, an allegory in which various objects refer to people and what they do. The Jewish people were fond of discussing the wise sayings of the ancients and were always seeking to discover deeper meanings (Ps. 78:1-3). Ezekiel hoped that his allegory would awaken his dull hearers and give them something to think

about. Perhaps the truth would grip their hearts and change their outlook on what God was doing.

This allegory is about three kings ("shoots"), because the cedar tree represents the royal dynasty of David.[9] David's dynasty was very important, because through it God had promised to bring a Savior to His people and to the world (2 Sam. 7:16; Luke 1:32-33, 69). It was essential that a descendant of David sit on the throne so that the blessing of God's covenant with David might rest on the land. At that time, the kingdom of Judah was a vassal state of Babylon and King Nebuchadnezzar was in charge. He is the first "great eagle" (Ezek. 17:3). The second eagle (v. 7) is the ruler of Egypt, probably Pharaoh Hophra who promised to help Judah in her fight against the Babylonians (v. 17). The eagle is used as a symbol of a strong ruler who invades a land (Jer. 48:40; 49:22). Now, let's consider the three kings, who are represented by three shoots.

King Jehoiachin (Ezek. 17:3-4, 11-12). When Nebuchadnezzar swooped down on Judah in 597 B.C., he deposed King Jehoiachin and took him and his family and staff to Babylon. He also took the temple treasures and 10,000 officers, artisans, and soldiers (2 Kings 24:8-17). This fulfilled the prophecy Isaiah had spoken to King Hezekiah after the king had shown all his wealth to the Babylonian visitors (Isa. 39; 2 Kings 20:17). Jehoiachin was the highest shoot or branch in David's family tree and he was "planted" in Babylon. Jehoiachin had reigned only three months and ten days (2 Chron. 36:9). He's the king that Jeremiah called "Coniah" (Jer. 22:24, 28; 37:1) and Jeconiah in Matthew's genealogy of Jesus (Matt. 1:11-12). In Ezekiel 19:5-9, Jehoiachin is compared to a lion who would be caught and taken to Babylon. During his three months on the throne, instead of leading the people back to faith in the Lord, Jehoiachin did evil in the sight of the Lord. He died in Babylon.

King Zedekiah (Ezek. 17:5-10, 13-21). After deposing Jehoiachin, Nebuchadnezzar made Jehoiachin's uncle Mattaniah the new king and changed his name to Zedekiah. He was the youngest son of good King Josiah and Nebuchadnezzar "planted" him in Judah where he "grew" for eleven years. But instead of producing a tree, King Zedekiah produced a humble vine. It was Zedekiah who asked Jeremiah to pray for him and the people and who hid him and cared for him (Jer. 37–38).

Nebuchadnezzar was kind to Zedekiah and the king took an oath to obey and serve him. Had he faithfully kept this treaty, Zedekiah would have saved the city and the temple; but instead he chose to break the covenant and turn to Egypt for help. The second eagle represents Pharaoh who tried to rescue the kingdom of Judah but failed. This foolish decision on the part of Zedekiah resulted in the uprooting and withering of the vine, and this was the end of the kingdom of Judah. Nebuchadnezzar would not tolerate his treachery in seeking Egypt as an ally, so he captured Zedekiah, killed his sons before his eyes, blinded him, and took him captive to Babylon where he died (Ezek. 17:16; 2 Kings 24:17–25:7).

But Ezekiel made it clear that it wasn't only Nebuchadnezzar's covenant that King Zedekiah broke, it was God's covenant; and it was God who punished him through Nebuchadnezzar. Zedekiah had sworn his oath in the name of the Lord (2 Chron. 36:11-14), and therefore he was obligated to keep it. In looking to Egypt for help, Zedekiah turned a deaf ear to the warnings of Jeremiah (Jer. 38), and Isaiah had preached the same message over a century before (Isa. 31:1; 36:9). It was the Lord who caught the king and his officers in His net and turned them over to the Babylonians (2 Kings 25:1-10; Jer. 52:1-11).

Messiah the King (Ezek. 17:22-24). Zedekiah had reigned for eleven years and was the twentieth and last king of Judah. His dethronement and death in Babylon seemed to mark the end of the Davidic line and therefore the failure of God's covenant with King David, but this was not the case. The Prophet Hosea predicted that the children of Israel would be "without a king, and without a prince" (Hosea 3:4), but the messianic line did not die out. After Babylon was conquered by the Medes and Persians, Cyrus allowed the Jews to return to their land, and one of their leaders was Zerubbabel, a great-great grandson of godly King

Josiah (1 Chron. 3:17-19) and an ancestor of the Lord Jesus Christ (Matt. 1:11-16; Luke 3:27). Once again, a godly remnant stayed true to the Lord and the promised Messiah was born. The name "Zerubbabel" means "shoot of Babylon," but he helped to make possible the birth of the "shoot of David," Jesus Christ, the Savior of the world.

King Jehoiachin had been a shoot plucked from the top of the cedar and taken to Babylon, but his descendants were rejected (Jer. 22:28-30), while King Zedekiah was a shoot planted in Judah; but both of these men failed to please the Lord or do His will. Was there any hope left for the people of God? Yes, for the Lord had promised to take a tender sprig "of the highest branch of the high cedar" (Ezek. 17:22) and plant it in the land of Israel where it would grow and become a great kingdom. This "shoot" is the Messiah, Jesus Christ, who came out of the stem of Jesse and one day will establish His glorious kingdom on earth (Isa. 11:1-10; Jer. 23:5-6; 33:15-17; Zech. 6:12-13). The "high mountain" Ezekiel wrote about is probably Mount Zion, where Messiah will reign over His people. The small "shoot" will grow into a mighty tree and provide shelter (see Dan. 4:17, 32-37).

But in order for the "shoot" to be planted, take root, and grow, the other "trees" (kingdoms) will have to be removed. Some of them will be cut down and others will just wither. The kingdoms of men seem large and powerful today, and the kingdom of the Lord seems small and withering, but when Jesus returns to earth to reign, the tables will be turned. This is why we must never be afraid or discouraged when we survey the world scene. Jesus came as "a root out of a dry ground" (Isa. 53:1-2), an insignificant shoot from David's family tree, but one day His kingdom will fill the earth. Never stop praying, "Thy kingdom come" for that prayer will be answered. The fulfillment of God's kingdom promises to David (2 Sam. 7) is in Jesus Christ (Luke 1:26-55, 67-80), and He shall not fail.

It was a dark day for the people of Israel, but when the day is the darkest, the Lord's promises shine the brightest. God's people today need to take heed to this prophetic Word, which is a light that shines in our dark world (2 Peter 1:19). Just as Jesus fulfilled prophecy and came the first time to die for the sins of the world, so He will the second time and reign over His righteous kingdom. The tender "shoot" of David will be the mighty monarch, the King of Kings and Lord of Lords!

S I X

God Is Just!

Responsibility is one of the major themes of these four chapters. The Jewish exiles in Babylon wére blaming their ancestors for the terrible judgment that had befallen them, so Ezekiel explained that God judges people individually for their own sins and not for somebody else's sins (chap. 18). He then pointed out that the Jewish leaders were responsible for the foolish decisions they had made (chap. 19), and that the nation itself had a long history of irresponsibility (chap. 20). Finally, the prophet reminded his listeners that the Lord Jehovah also had a responsibility to be faithful to Himself and His covenant with the Jews, and this was why He had chastened them (chap. 21). By dealing with the subject of personal and national responsibility, Ezekiel was able to answer the frequent complaints of the people that the Lord was treating them unfairly.

Responsibility and accountability are needed themes in our own day. Irresponsibility is rampant and very few people are willing to take the blame for wrongs committed or mistakes made. In his *Devil's Dictionary*, the cynical Ambrose Bierce defined responsibility as "a detachable burden easily shifted to the shoulders of God, Fate, Fortune, luck, or one's neighbor." After our first parents sinned, Adam blamed Eve and Eve blamed the serpent, but God still held Adam and Eve responsible for their disobedience and punished them accordingly. The Jews in Ezekiel's day were sure that God would deliver them and spare Jerusalem because Israel was God's chosen people, but they forgot that privilege always brings responsibility. They had the greatest law ever given to a nation, but they disobeyed it. The Lord gave them a wonderful land for their home, and they defiled it with idolatry. They violated the terms of the divine covenant and then were shocked when the Lord obeyed the covenant and chastened them.

1. Individual responsibility (Ezek. 18:1-32)

As you read this chapter, you find the prophet answering the erroneous statements the Jewish exiles were making about God and their difficult situation (vv. 2, 19, 25, 29). God knew what His people were saying and so did His prophet. Ignoring the inspired Word of God, the people were building their case on a popular proverb: "The fathers have eaten sour grapes, and the children's teeth are set on edge." In other words, "Our fathers have sinned and we, their children, are being punished for it." Their philosophy was a kind of irresponsible fatalism. "No matter what we do," they argued, "we still have to suffer because of what the older generation did." The Prophet Jeremiah quoted the same familiar proverb and preached the same truth that Ezekiel preached: God deals with us as individuals and punishes each of us justly for what we do (Jer. 31:29-30). He is a just and righteous God who shows no partiality (Deut. 10:17; 32:4). If He withholds punishment, it's only because of His grace and merciful long-suffering.

Where did Ezekiel's listeners get the idea that God punished the children for the sins of their fathers? This philosophy came from two sources: (1) a misinterpretation of what the Lord had said in His law, that He visited the sins of the fathers upon the children (Ex. 20:5; 34:6-7; Num. 14:18; Deut. 7:9-10), and (2) the Jewish idea of the oneness of the nation. According to the Law of Moses, innocent animals could suffer and die for guilty sinners, but nowhere was it taught that innocent people should be punished for sins committed by guilty people. In fact, Moses taught just the opposite: "The fathers shall not be put to death for their children, nor shall the children be put to death for their fathers; a person shall be put to death for his own sin" (Deut. 24:16, NKJV).[1] The warning in Exodus 20:5 and 34:6-7 implies that the Lord punishes the children *if they commit the sins their fathers committed*. Furthermore, God also promised to bless those children who followed godly examples and obeyed the Lord (20:6; Deut. 7:9-10), so He gave promises of blessing as well as warnings of chastening.

As for the solidarity of the nation, the Jewish people did consider themselves one people who descended from Abraham. Since each tribe descended from one of the sons of Jacob, Israel claimed both national and tribal solidarity. If only one Israelite disobeyed the Lord, it was as though all Israel had sinned, as in the case of Achan (Josh. 7:1, 11; and see Josh. 22, especially vv. 18-20). Knowing this fact, the Jewish people concluded that the Babylonian invasion and the nation's exile were the consequences of the sins of the previous generation.

Ezekiel answered the people's objections and explained the truth about God's judgment and justice by sharing some hypothetical situations and drawing some conclusions.

You cannot blame your ancestors (Ezek. 18:5-18). The prophet refutes the proverb by imagining a situation involving three men in a family, people with whom his listeners certainly could identify. He began with *a righteous father (vv. 5-9)*, a hypothetical Jew who kept God's law and therefore was just and would not die because of sin (vv. 4, 9). Death is frequently mentioned in this chapter (vv. 4, 13, 17-18, 20-21, 23-24, 26, 28, 32) and refers to physical death and not necessarily eternal punishment, although any Jew who didn't exercise saving faith in the Lord would not be accepted by Him. Whether people lived under the Old Covenant or the New Covenant, before or since the cross, the way of salvation is the same: faith in the Lord that is evidenced by a new life of obedience (Heb. 11:6; Hab. 2:4; see Rom. 4).

In describing this man, Ezekiel named eight negative offenses along with eight positive virtues. The negative sins this man avoids are: attending idol feasts in the "high places" and worshiping idols in his own land, committing adultery, incurring ritual uncleanness (Ezek. 18:6), exploiting people and using violence to rob people (v. 7), lending money with interest and demanding a profit (v. 8). The eight positive virtues are: returning a debtor's pledge, feeding the hungry and clothing the naked (v. 7), living justly and promoting justice (v. 8), living by God's statutes and obeying His ordinances, and living with integrity (v. 9). These offenses and virtues are mentioned in the Law of Moses,[2] but the man acted as he did because he loved God and had "a new heart and a new spirit" within him (v. 31). He put God first in his life, treated people with kindness and mercy, and used his material wealth to honor God and serve others. As evidence of his faith in Jehovah, he obeyed the two great commandments of the law, to love the Lord and to love his neighbor (Matt. 22:34-40)

This righteous father had an *unrighteous son (Ezek. 18:10-13)*, about whom Ezekiel had nothing good to say. He listed ten offenses against God's law, three of them capital crimes: murder (vv. 12, 14), idolatry (vv. 11-12), and adultery (v. 11). This godless son exploited the poor and took interest from his debtors. He never returned the debtor's pledge (Ex. 22:26; Deut. 24:12-13) and did all he could to make a profit, even if it meant hurting people and defying God's laws. The verdict is clear: "he shall surely die."

The third character in this drama was *a righteous grandson (Ezek. 18:14-18)*. How strange that the godly man of verses 5-9 should raise an ungodly son who himself had a godly son! The grandson followed the righteous example of his grandfather and not the evil example of his father. King Hezekiah was a godly father whose son Manasseh was evil, although late in life he did repent. Manasseh's son Amon was evil, but he fathered godly King Josiah! (See Matt. 1:10-11.) The ways of the Lord are sometimes strange, and "where sin abounded, grace abounded much more" (Rom. 5:20, NIV).

Twelve godly character traits are mentioned about this third man. The four that are lacking are ritual cleanness (Ezek. 18:6), living justly and promoting justice (vv. 12-13), and acting with integrity (v. 9). This doesn't mean that the man was actually guilty of these sins, because the first list doesn't mention every possible law in the Mosaic code. The point is that the third man the grandson, resisted the bad influence in the home and obeyed the Lord in spite of his father's bad example. The Lord didn't kill the grandson because of his father's sins or even spare him because of his grandfather's righteousness, but dealt with the man on the basis his own faith and righteousness.

You can blame yourselves (Ezek. 18:19-24). In this part of his message, Ezekiel responded to the questions of his hearers given in verse 19, just as he had responded to their question in verse 2. He described a wicked man who repented, turned from his sins, and lived (vv. 19-23), and then described a righteous man who returned to his sins and died (v. 24). The lesson from these two examples is obvious and answered their questions: people determine their own character and destiny by the decisions that they make. Neither the exiles in Babylon nor the citizens in Jerusalem were the prisoners and victims of some cosmic determinism that forced them to act as they did. It was their own unbelief (they rejected Jeremiah's message) and disobedience (they worshiped heathen idols and defiled the temple) that brought the Babylonian army to their gates; and it was King Zedekiah's breaking of the covenant with Nebuchadnezzar that brought the army back to destroy Jerusalem.

Ezekiel was giving the Jewish nation a message of hope! If they would truly repent and turn to the Lord, He would work on their behalf as He promised (1 Kings 8:46-53; Jer. 29:10-14). However, if they persisted in sinning, the Lord would continue to deal with them as rebellious children. God has no delight in the death of the wicked (Ezek. 18:23, 32; see 1 Tim. 2:4; 2 Peter 3:9), but He isn't obligated to invade their minds and hearts and force them to obey Him.

In Ezekiel 18:24, Ezekiel isn't dealing with what theologians call "the security of the believer," because the issue is physical life or death, as stated in God's covenant (Deut. 30:15-20; Jer. 21:8). The righteous man who adopted a sinful lifestyle[3] in defiance of God's law would suffer for that decision. It wasn't possible for the Jews to "accumulate points" with God and then lose a few of them when they sinned. People have the idea that God measures our good works against our bad works, and deals with us according to whichever is the greater. But from Adam to the end of time, people are saved only by faith in what God revealed to them, and their faith is demonstrated in a consistently godly life.

You cannot blame the Lord (Ezek. 18:25-32). For the third time, Ezekiel quoted the words of the complaining exiles, "The way of the Lord is not equal" (v. 25, see vv. 2, 19). The word "equal" means "fair." They were daring to say that God wasn't "playing fair" with His chosen people. But Ezekiel pointed out that it was the people who weren't being fair with God! When they obeyed the Lord, they wanted Him to keep the terms of the covenant that promised blessing, but when they disobeyed Him, they didn't want Him to keep the terms of the covenant that brought chastening. They wanted God to disobey His own Word and act contrary to His own holy nature.

"God is light" (1 John 1:5), which means He is holy and just, and "God is love" (4:8, 16), and His love is a holy love. Nowhere does Scripture say that we're saved from our sins by God's love, because salvation is by the grace of God (Eph. 2:8-10); and grace is love that pays a price. In His great love, God gave a gracious covenant to Israel, requiring only that they worship and serve Him alone with all their hearts. When sinners repented and sought the Lord, in His grace the Lord would forgive them; but when people deliberately rebelled against Him, in His holiness, God would punish them after bearing with them in His long-suffering. What could be fairer than that! For that matter, if God did what was fair, He would consign the whole world into hell!

The conclusion of this message was an invitation from the Lord for the people to repent (change their minds), turn from their sins, cast away their transgressions like filthy garments, and seek a new heart and a new spirit. God promised them a new heart if only they would seek Him by faith (Ezek. 11:19; see 36:26). This was one of the key themes in the letter Jeremiah had sent to the captives in Babylon (Jer. 29:10-14), but the people hadn't taken it to heart. God made it clear that He found no delight in the death of the wicked (Ezek. 18:23, 32), but if the wicked found delight in their sinful ways and would not repent, there was nothing the Lord could do but obey His own covenant and punish them. Ezekiel will develop this theme further in chapter 21.

2. Leadership responsibility (Ezek. 19:1-14)

Ezekiel had made it clear that individual Jews were responsible for their own sins, but it was also true that their leaders had led them astray because they had rebelled against God's will. Jeremiah had told the kings of Judah to surrender to Nebuchadnezzar because he was God's chosen servant to chasten Israel, but they had refused to obey. Zedekiah, Judah's last king, had agreed to a treaty with Nebuchadnezzar but then had broken it and sought help from Egypt. It was this foolish act that moved Nebuchadnezzar to send his army to Jerusalem and destroy the city and the temple.

Whether you read secular or sacred history, you soon discover that people become like their leaders. The same people who applauded Solomon when he built the temple also applauded Jeroboam when he set up the golden calves and instituted a new religion. One of the hardest tasks of Christian leaders today is to keep our churches true to the Word of God so that people don't follow every religious celebrity whose ideas run contrary to Scripture. It appears that being popular and being "successful" are more important today than being faithful.

In discussing the sins of the leaders, Ezekiel used two familiar images—the lion (vv. 1-9) and the vine (vv. 10-14)—and he couched his message in the form of a funeral dirge for "the princes of Israel." David's exalted dynasty had come to an end, but the men holding the scepter were nothing like David. Ezekiel wouldn't even call them "kings" but instead referred to them as "princes" (v. 1; see 7:27; 12:10, 12). Instead of lamenting their demise, the "funeral dirge" actually ridiculed the rulers of Israel; but later (21:27) Ezekiel would announce the coming of Messiah, the Son of David, who would be a worthy king.

Israel is like a lioness (Ezek. 19:1-9). The lioness represents the nation of Israel, or at least the royal tribe of Judah (Gen. 49:9; Num. 23:23; 24:9; 1 Kings 10:18-20; Micah 5:8). The first royal "whelp" was Jehoahaz, who reigned over Judah for only three months (Ezek. 19:2-4; 2 Kings 23:31-35). He was also known as "Shallum" (Jer. 22:10-12). Pharaoh Neco took him captive to Egypt where he died. The second royal "whelp" was Jehoiachin, who reigned three months and ten days (Ezek. 19:5-9; 2 Kings 24:8-16; 2 Chron. 36:9-10). Ezekiel describes him "strutting" and "roaring" (Ezek. 19:6-7) among the princes and the nations. Nebuchadnezzar took him to Babylon along with 10,000 captives and the temple treasures, and there he died. Jehoiachin turned a deaf ear to the preaching of Jeremiah, and the prophet didn't have anything good to say about him (Jer. 22:18-19). In this brief parable, the Lord made it clear that these two kings of Judah thought themselves to be great leaders, but they ignored the Word of God and He cut them down after their brief reigns.

Israel is like a vine (Ezek. 19:10-14). This is a familiar image in Scripture (Gen. 49:9-12;[4] Isa. 5; Ps. 80:8-13; Jer. 2:21) and in Ezekiel's prophecy (chap. 15; 17:1-10). The fruitful vine produced many kings who rebelled against God and was punished by being transplanted to Babylon, from "many waters" to a "desert" (Jer. 31:27-28). The last king of Judah, Zedekiah, broke his treaty with Babylon, rebelled against Nebuchadnezzar, and lost the scepter and the throne (2 Kings 24:17–25:7). With Zedekiah the Davidic dynasty ended, and he too died in captivity in Babylon (Jer. 52:11).

Had the nation of Israel obeyed the Lord, it would have become and remained a mighty lion and a fruitful vine that would have brought glory to the name of the Lord. Israel would have been a "light unto the Gentiles" (Isa. 42:6; 49:6) and many would have trusted in the true and living God. Israel didn't keep the terms of the covenant, but the Lord did; and that's why He chastened them and scattered them. God's chosen people have no temple, priesthood, sacrifice, or king (Hosea 3:4-5). Jesus Christ, Israel's Messiah, came as the lion of the tribe of Judah (Rev. 5:5) and the true vine (John 15:1), "a light to bring revelation to the Gentiles" (Luke 2:32), and the rightful heir to the throne of David (Luke 1:68-69), and His own people rejected Him. One day they shall see Him and receive Him, and God's gracious covenant with David will be completely fulfilled (2 Sam. 7) when Jesus reigns in His kingdom (Ezek. 34:23-24; 37:24-25; Matt. 1:1).

3. National responsibility (Ezek. 20:1-44)

Ezekiel delivered this message on August 14, 591 B.C., to some of the Jewish elders who came to his house to "inquire of the Lord." But the prophet knew that their hearts were not right with God and that they had no right to ask the Lord for instruction (vv. 30-32; see 14:1-3; 33:30-33).[5] A willingness to submit and obey is the mark of the person who can seek God's guidance and expect to receive it. Ezekiel's response to their request was to review the history of the nation of Israel and point out the repeated rebellion of the people and the gracious long-suffering of the Lord.

The American editor and writer Norman Cousins wrote in a *Saturday Review* editorial (April 15, 1978), "History is a vast early warning system." But some anonymous thinker has said, "The one thing we learn from history is that we don't learn from history"; or in the words of Dr. Laurence J. Peter, "History teaches us the mistakes we are going to make."[6] The Jewish historians, prophets, and psalmists were honest enough to declare the sins of the nation *and write them down for future generations to read!* Why? So that future generations wouldn't make the same mistakes that they made. But, alas, God's people haven't begun to learn the lessons, let alone obey them.

Scripture teaches that God is working out His plan for the nations (Acts 14:14-18; 17:22-31; Dan. 5:21; 7:27) and that His people Israel are at the heart of that plan. Other nations are mentioned in Scripture primarily as they relate to Israel, for Israel is the only nation with whom God has entered into covenant relationship. At Sinai, after Israel left Egypt, God gave them His law (Ex. 19–24); and before they entered the Promised Land, He reaffirmed that law and gave them the terms of the covenant they had to obey in order to possess and enjoy the land (Deut. 5–8; 27–30). It was because they violated the terms of the covenants that Israel suffered as she did.

Before we review the history of Israel and the lessons we can learn from it, we must deal with an important matter of interpretation. In chapter 18, Ezekiel taught that the children were not punished for the sins of the fathers, but in this chapter, he seems to say that the past sins of the nation (carefully documented) were the cause of Israel's failure and the Babylonian invasion. "Will you judge them, son of man, will you judge them? Then make known to them the abominations of their fathers" (20:4, NKJV). This statement from the Lord suggests that God was judging the Jews because of what their fathers had done.

But that wasn't what the Lord was saying to Ezekiel. By reviewing the history of the nation, God was judging that current generation *because they were guilty of the same sins of unbelief and rebellion*. Jeremiah said that his generation of Jews was *even worse than their fathers!* (Jer. 16:12) In this historical summary, God proved that He had been consistent in His dealings with the Jews. The exiles had complained that God had not treated Israel fairly (Ezek. 18:2, 19, 25, 29), but their national history proved that God was not only fair with them but also very long-suffering and merciful. God wasn't punishing the Jews in Ezekiel's day because of the sins their fathers committed centuries before but because Ezekiel's contemporaries had committed the very same sins! That's why God reviewed the history of Israel.

Israel in Egypt (Ezek. 20:5-8). God "chose" the nation of Israel when He called Abraham and Sarah to leave Ur of the Chaldees and go to the land of Canaan (Gen. 12), but the nation didn't even exist at that time. God built the nation in the land of Egypt.

When Jacob's family entered into Egypt, they numbered 66 people; Joseph's family was already in Egypt and they brought the total to 70 (Gen. 46). But when the Jews left Egypt at the Exodus, the fighting men alone numbered over 600,000 (Num. 1:46), so there may well have been over 2 million people in the nation. In Egypt, God revealed Himself to the Jews through the ministry of Moses and Aaron as well as through the terrible judgments He inflicted on the land of Egypt. He made it clear that the gods of the Gentile nations were only myths and had no power to do either good or evil. God reminded them of how He had judged these false gods in Egypt and proved them to be helpless nothings. (See Ex. 12:12; Num. 33:4.)

However, while living in Egypt, the Jews began secretly to worship the gods of the Egyptians. After all, if the Egyptians were masters over the Jews, then the gods of Egypt must be stronger than the God of Israel! The Jews defiled themselves with the gods of Egypt and grieved the heart of God. When God opened the way for Israel to leave Egypt, some of the Jews took their Egyptian gods with them! God had sworn by an oath ("lifted up my hand")[7] that He was Israel's God (v. 5) and that He would set them free and give them the Promised Land (v. 6). The true God set them free, but they carried false gods with them! The nation rebelled against God even after He demonstrated His grace and power in delivering them!

Israel's exodus from Egypt (Ezek. 20:9-10). The Lord had every reason to pour out His wrath on Israel, but for His name's sake, He rescued His people. God often worked on Israel's behalf, not because they deserved it but for the glory of His own name (vv. 14, 22, 44; see Isa. 48:9; 66:5), just as He has saved His church today "to the praise of His glory" (Eph. 1:6, 12, 14). The account of the Exodus did go before the Jews as they marched toward the Promised Land (Josh. 2:10), and it did bring glory to God's name.

Israel at Sinai (Ezek. 20:11-12). Israel tarried about two years at Sinai where God revealed His glory and gave them His laws. While they tarried there, Moses directed the construction of the tabernacle and its furniture. But even after seeing God's glory and hearing His voice, Israel rebelled against Him by making and worshiping a golden calf (Ex. 32). God gave them the Sabbath Day (the seventh day of the week) as a sign to remind them that they belonged to Him. By setting aside that one day each week to honor the Lord, Israel witnessed to the other peoples that they were a special nation, but they persisted in polluting the Sabbath and treating it like any other day (vv. 13, 16, 20).

The law that God gave Israel at Sinai consisted of statutes and ordinances governing every area of life: their civic responsibilities, the maintaining of courts and judges, the punishment of offenders, and the responsibilities of the people and their priests in the religious life of the nation. But because Israel was a theocracy and God was their King, every law had its religious implications. To break the law was to sin against the Lord, and the people did it frequently.

Those who obeyed God's law would "live" (Ezek. 19:11, 13, 21), an important word we considered in chapter 18 (vv. 9, 17, 19, 21, 28). It refers to physical life, not being subject to capital punishment because of deliberate disobedience to God statutes. But for the Jew who loved the Lord, trusted Him, and obeyed Him, it included the spiritual life that comes to all who believe. Romans 10:5 and Galatians 3:12 make it clear that nobody is saved simply by obeying the law; but those who trust the Lord will prove their faith by their obedience. Religious people like the Pharisees have a "law righteousness," but those who trust Christ have a "faith righteousness" that enables them to obey God's will (Phil. 3:1-16; Rom. 10). Salvation is always by faith (Heb. 11:6) and this faith always issues in good works and obedience.

Israel in the wilderness (Ezek. 20:13-26). After leaving Sinai, the Jews marched to Kadesh Barnea where the Lord told them to enter Canaan and claim their promised inheritance (Num. 13–14). He had already searched out the land (Ezek. 19:6), but the people insisted on sending in a representative from each of the twelve tribes to scout out the land. They searched the land for forty days, and all of the men agreed that the land was exactly as God described it; but ten of the spies said that God wasn't great enough to enable Israel to conquer it! This led to God's judgment that the nation would wander in the wilderness for forty years and that everyone twenty years old and older would die during that time (Num. 14). You would have thought that the Jews had learned their lesson by now, but even during the wilderness wandering, they rebelled against God and He had to punish them. Once again, it was for the glory of His name that He didn't destroy them and start a new nation with Moses as the father (vv. 11-21). At the end of the forty years, Moses prepared the new generation to enter the land by reviewing the law and the covenants, as recorded in Deuteronomy.

Israel in the Promised Land (Ezek. 20:27-30). Joshua brought the people into Canaan and led the Jewish army in the defeat of the enemy and the claiming of the land. Before he died, he directed in the assigning of the land to the various tribes, and he encouraged them to claim their land. Moses had commanded the people to wipe out the godless religion of the inhabitants of the land (Ex. 34:11-17; Deut. 7), and he warned them that if they failed to obey, their children would become idolaters and lose the Promised Land. Of course, that's exactly what happened. The people lusted after the gods of the land and participated in the filthy rites of heathen worship in the high places (Ezek. 19:28-29; see Deut. 18:9-14; Lev. 18:26-30).[8] Instead of winning the Canaanites to faith in the true and living God, the Jewish people began to live like their enemies and worship their gods! They even offered their children as sacrifices to the pagan gods (Ezek. 19:26, 31), something that was expressly forbidden in the Law of Moses (2 Kings 21:6; 2 Chron. 28:3; Lev. 18:21; Deut. 12:31; 18:10). Children are a gift from God, and His precious gifts must not be used as heathen sacrifices!

Israel in exile in Babylon (Ezek. 20:31-32). This is the practical application of the message to the people of Ezekiel's generation: they were living just like their fathers! "Even unto this day" they were sinning against the Lord! Ignoring their privilege of being God's special people (Num. 23:9), their fathers wanted to be like the pagan nations in their worship and in their leadership

(1 Sam. 8:5); and God let them have their way and then punished them. "When in Babylon, do as the Babylonians do" was the philosophy of the exiles, but they had been idolaters long before they went into exile.

Israel's future kingdom (Ezek. 20:33-44). Ezekiel had made it very clear to the elders why they weren't qualified to inquire of God, but he didn't end his message there. God in His grace gave him a message of hope for the people, though they certainly didn't deserve it. Ezekiel described a future "exodus" of the Jewish people from the nations of the world, a return to their own land which God swore to give them. He even used the same descriptive phrase Moses used when he spoke about the Exodus—"a mighty hand...an outstretched arm" (vv. 33-34; Deut. 4:34; 5:15; 7:19; 11:2). The "I will" statements of the Lord reveal both His mercy and His power.

"I will bring you out" (Ezek. 20:34) implies much more than the release of the exiles from Babylon. It speaks of a future regathering of Israel from the nations of the world to which they have been scattered (Deut. 30:1-8). God promises to bring them out, but He also says He will "bring them into the wilderness" (Ezek. 20:35-36) where He will deal with their sins and cleanse them of their rebellion (36:24-25; Hosea 2:14-15). His next promise is "I will bring you into the bond of the covenant" (Ezek. 20:37), teaching that Israel will be restored to her covenant relationship to the Lord and will experience the blessings of the New Covenant (18:31; 36:26-27). "I will purge out the rebels" (20:38) and they will not be allowed to enter the land of Israel and enjoy the blessings of the messianic kingdom.

As for the true believers who receive their Messiah, God declares, "I will accept them" (v. 40). God will establish a sanctified nation that will worship Him in holiness (v. 41). As the result of this New Covenant and new spiritual experience in their hearts, the people will come to know their God (v. 42) as well as know themselves and loathe themselves for the terrible sins they have committed (v. 43). No longer will they blame their fathers! They will come to know the grace of God, for all the blessing He showers on the nation will be for His name's sake and not because of any merit on their part (v. 44).

The experiences described in verses 33-44 cannot be applied to the return of the Jewish exiles to the land of Judah in 538 B.C. This was not an exodus from many countries nor did it result in the glorious restoration of the Jewish nation. We have to apply this paragraph to that time in the future that Ezekiel describes in chapters 33 to 48, when Christ will return and the promised kingdom will be established.

4. Divine responsibility (Ezek. 20:45–21:32)

In the Hebrew Scriptures, chapter 21 begins with 20:45, and this is the best arrangement, for 20:45-49 introduces the coming judgment on Judah and Jerusalem.[9] Ezekiel has explained the individual responsibility of the people and their leaders and the national responsibility of Israel. Now he focuses on the fact that God has a responsibility to punish His people when they rebel against Him. He must be true to His character and true to His covenant.

God identifies the target (Ezek. 20:45-49). Frequently in this book, God commanded His servant to "set his face" against something or someone (v. 46; 13:17; 21:2; 25:2; 28:21; 29:2; 35:2; 38:2). This was one way to point out the "target" at which His judgment would be hurled, in this case, Judah and Jerusalem (21:1-2). The prophet assumed a posture of stern judgment as he announced that threatened judgment was about to fall against "the south" (the Negev), and Judah and Jerusalem were in the territory south of Babylon. Using the image of a forest fire, he described the invasion of the Babylonians and the destruction of the Jewish nation. When you study chapter 21, you learn that the fire represents the deadly swords of the soldiers and that the "south" represents Judah and Jerusalem. According to Ezekiel 20:1, it was the year 591 B.C. when he gave these messages, so in five years, the Babylonians would set fire to the holy city and the temple. During Israel's wilderness wanderings, God didn't severely punish His people for their rebellion because He wanted to honor His name before the Gentiles (20:14, 22, 44); but now He would honor His name by burning their city and temple and sending them into exile.

God draws the sword (Ezek. 21:1-7). The word "sword" is used nineteen times in this chapter to represent the invasion and attack of the Babylonian army. God has His eye on three targets: the land of Judah, the city of Jerusalem, and the holy place of the temple. Unfortunately, some of the righteous would suffer along with the wicked, but this is often the case in times of war. Note that God declared that it was "My sword," because it was He who summoned the Babylonian army to punish His sinful people. If His own people won't obey Him, at least the pagan nations will!

At this point, God commanded Ezekiel to perform another "action sermon" by groaning like a man experiencing great pain and grief. When the people asked him why he was groaning so, he would tell them, "Because of the bad news that is coming," referring to the news of the fall of Jerusalem. The news didn't come until January 8, 585 B.C. (33:21-22), five months after the city had been burned, which was August 14, 586 B.C.; but the Lord told Ezekiel that the news was coming. The exiles nurtured the false hope that the Lord would spare the city and the temple, but everything the Lord had prophesied would come to pass.

God sharpens His sword (Ezek. 21:8-17). In this second "action sermon," Ezekiel not only cried and wailed (v. 12), but he smote his thigh and clapped his hands together (vv. 14, 17). It's possible that he was also brandishing a sword as he spoke, although the text doesn't state this. The Lord was preparing the Babylonian army to be effective and efficient in carrying out His plans. Despising the king of Judah (v. 13), the sword of Babylon would turn Judah's scepter into nothing but a stick! (v. 10) The invading soldiers would be so effective that one swordsman would do the work of three (v. 14), and for the Jews there would be no escape (v. 16). Even the Lord would applaud the soldiers as they executed the judgment that He had ordained (v. 17). Perhaps some of the Jews recalled Ezekiel's previous "action sermon" using the sword (5:1-4).

God directs the army (Ezek. 21:18-27). The pagan nations of that day used many forms of divination to discern the will of the gods, and Ezekiel pictured the Babylonian army at a fork in the road, trying to discover which way to go. Should they go to Rabbath, the capital of Ammon, and attack the Ammonites; or should they go to Jerusalem to attack the Jews? When the Lord told Ezekiel to "mark [appoint] two ways," he probably sketched on the ground a map of the roads looking like an inverted Y, and at the juncture stuck a "signpost" into the ground. (Remember his plan of Jerusalem drawn on a wet clay brick—4:1-8?) It was God's will that the army attack Jerusalem, so He overruled the soothsayers and diviners and made sure their decision was for Jerusalem. This doesn't mean that their system of divining was accurate or even proper, but that the Lord used it to accomplish His purposes.[10]

Nebuchadnezzar decided to attack Jerusalem, so he appointed his captains and made his plans. The people in Jerusalem were hoping he would attack the Ammonites, and when the word came that Jerusalem was his target, they hoped the diviners would say they had made a mistake. But God was in control and there had been no mistake. King Zedekiah had sworn an oath of allegiance to Nebuchadnezzar and had broken it (21:23; 2 Kings 24:20), and Nebuchadnezzar would not stand for this kind of rebellion from a weak vassal state. Zedekiah's sins had finally caught up with him (Ezek. 21:24).

Ezekiel paused to give a special message to Zedekiah, whom he refuses to call a king but refers to as a prince. He calls him profane and wicked, a man who has committed iniquity and will suffer because of it. He would lose his crown and his throne. The day had arrived when God would turn everything upside down. Those who were "great and mighty" would be humbled, and those who were humble would be exalted. The word translated "overturn" ("ruin," NIV) is *awwa*, and we can just hear Ezekiel lamenting: "Awwa—awwa—awwa!"

But once again, the Lord added a brief word of hope: the Messiah would one day come, the true Son of David and Israel's King, and would claim the Davidic crown and reign over His people (v. 27). The phrase "whose right it is" takes us back to Genesis 49:8-12, a messianic promise that we met in Ezekiel 19 when we studied the images of the lion and the vine.

God completes the task (Ezek. 21:28-32). But what about the Ammonites? When the Lord directed the Babylonian army to Jerusalem, did this mean He would not judge the Ammonites for their sins against Him and the Jewish people? They would rejoice to see Babylon ravage the land of Judah and set fire to Jerusalem and the temple. (See Ezek. 25.) Along with Judah and the other nations, Ammon had joined the alliance against Babylon (Jer. 27:1ff), so Ammon had to be punished. Their own false prophets and diviners would give them a false hope that they had been spared (Ezek. 21:29), but God hadn't told Nebuchadnezzar to put his sword in its sheath (v. 30). The message closed with another fire (see 20:47-48), but this time a furnace in which ore was smelted. God would "blow" against the furnace and make it hotter, and then He would pour out the molten metal on His enemies. The Ammonites would become fuel for the fire and the nation would disappear from the earth.

We come away from the study of chapters 18 to 21 with a fresh realization of the tragedy of rebellion against the Lord. Israel had a long history of rebellion, but the other nations weren't any better, except that Israel was sinning against the light of God's Word and His providential care over His people. If any people had the obligation to obey and serve the Lord, it was Israel, for the Lord had blessed them abundantly. Instead of becoming a holy nation to the glory of God, she became like all the other nations and failed to be God's light to the Gentiles.

And yet, woven throughout this series of messages is the theme of Israel's hope. The prophet reminded them that God had promised to regather them from the Gentile nations and give them their King and their kingdom. Historically speaking, weak King Zedekiah was the last ruler in the Davidic dynasty, but not prophetically speaking; for Jesus Christ, the Son of David (Matt. 1:1) will one day come and reign from David's throne. Ezekiel will discuss that theme in detail before he completes his book.

Under "Query 18" in his *Notes on the State of Virginia*, Thomas Jefferson wrote, "Indeed I tremble for my country when I reflect that God is just."[11] Ezekiel has defended the justice of God and magnified the mercy and grace of God. What more could he do?

SEVEN

See the Sinful City!

If you refer to the suggested outline of the Book of Ezekiel, you will see that these three chapters complete the second section of the book, "The fall of Jerusalem." Ezekiel focuses on *four final events*: the end of the city (chap. 22), the end of the kingdom (chap. 23), the end of a delusion (24:1-14), and the end of a marriage (vv. 15-27). Chapter 24 records two heart-rending announcements from the Lord: the beginning of the siege of Jerusalem (vv. 1-2) and the death of the prophet's wife (vv. 15-17). What a sobering way to climax Ezekiel's many messages to the spiritually blind Jewish exiles in Babylon!

1. The end of the city (Ezek. 22:1-31)

"David took the stronghold of Zion" (2 Sam. 5:7) and made Jerusalem his capital. Not only was the royal throne there but also the holy altar, for it was in Zion that God put His sanctuary. "For the Lord has chosen Zion; He has desired it for His habitation" (Ps. 132:13, NKJV). The Jews were proud of Mount Zion (Ps. 48) and claimed that the Lord loved Zion more than any other place (Ps. 87). But now the city of Jerusalem and the temple would be invaded by "unclean Gentiles" *who were brought there by the Lord!* Why would the Lord destroy His own beloved city and temple? Because His people had sinned and broken the covenant and they were beyond remedy. Ezekiel described the true character of the "beautiful city" and named some of the sins that the people in Jerusalem were committing even while he spoke. Ezekiel had exposed the past sins of the nation, but now he brought Jerusalem into the courtroom and brought the record up-to-date.

A defiled people (Ezek. 22:1-12). The words "blood" or "bloody" are repeated seven times in this paragraph and speak of death and defilement. The prophet named two grievous sins: the shedding of innocent blood (injustice) and the worship of foreign gods (see 7:23; 9:9). The officials in Jerusalem were accepting bribes and condemning innocent people to death so that others could claim their property (Amos 5:11-17; see 1 Kings 21). These judges had no respect for God or for man made in the image of God, and yet they were supposed to be honest men who upheld the law of the Lord (Ex. 18:21-26; Deut. 16:18-20). So evil was the judicial system in Jerusalem that the Gentile nations heard about it (Ezek. 22:4-5) and reproached the name of the Lord. Jerusalem was a "city infamous [defiled] and much vexed [full of confusion]" (v. 5).[1] But the time of their judgment was fast approaching. God had already declared the sentence but He had not yet begun the punishment. The princes had abused their power, but God would display His power.

Idolatry, injustice, and the abuse of power are rampant in our world today, and God in His mercy is holding back His hand of judgment to give sinners opportunity to repent and be saved. Divine truth and human rights are being ignored, but "the day of the Lord will come" (2 Peter 3:10) and sinners will be judged righteously by the all-knowing Lord.

Ezekiel named some of the sins that the people were committing, and he began with the abuse of people—parents, strangers and aliens, and orphans and widows (Ezek. 22:7). The Jews were commanded to honor their fathers and mothers (Ex. 20:12), and so are believers today (Eph. 6:1-3). God even attached a special promise to this commandment—"that your days may be long upon the land"—and now the Jews were about to be exiled from their land. The law also gave special consideration to widows, orphans, and aliens (Ex. 22:21-24; 23:9-11; Lev. 19:33-34; Jer. 5:28), and this commandment contained a warning. If these needy people were abused, the Jewish wives would become widows and the Jewish children would become orphans. Disobedience is a serious thing! The church today has a ministry obligation to strangers (Matt. 25:35, 43; James 2:1-13), widows, and orphans (James 1:27; 1 Tim. 5).

After dealing with the inhumanity of the people in Jerusalem, God condemned their idolatry (Ezek. 22:8). They defiled the temple with their idols (8:5ff) and by "worshiping God" hypo-critically, not worshiping with clean hands and obedient hearts (Isa. 1:10ff). Jeremiah told them that they had turned God's house into "a den of robbers" (Jer. 7:11), a place where thieves run to hide after they've broken the law. The Jews also polluted the Sabbath by treating it like any other day. The Sabbath was a special sign between God and Israel that they were His special people (Ezek. 20:12-13, 20; Ex. 31:13-17), and to violate this law was to defy the Lord's authority and deny Israel's calling and min-istry in the world.

But how could the people persist in these sins and not be judged by the courts? Because the courts were run by wicked men who had no desire to acquit the innocent or punish the guilty. The rich were set free and the poor were exploited. People accepted bribes and agreed to slander innocent people (Ezek. 22:9, 12), forgetting that the law prohibited slander and false witness (Ex. 20:16; 23:1-3, 6-8; Deut. 16:19; 27:25). According to the law, if someone were accused of a capital crime, at least two witnesses had to testify, and these witnesses would be the first to cast stones at the convicted guilty party (Num. 35:30-31; Deut. 17:6-7; 19:15).

In my years of pastoral experience, I have seen local churches torn apart by slander and false witness, in spite of the clear teach-ing in the New Testament about integrity in bearing witness

(1 Tim. 5:19; Matt. 18:16; 2 Cor. 13:1). It's a sobering thought that liars as well as murderers will have a place in the lake of fire and will not enter the heavenly city (Rev. 21:8, 27).

In Ezekiel 22:9b-11, God targeted the immorality of the Jewish people, starting with their participation in the unspeakably filthy "worship" at the pagan shrines. The tragedy is that these idolatrous men brought their immorality home with them! Sons had intercourse with their own mothers or stepmothers, fathers with daughters-in-law, and brothers with sisters or half-sisters! (See Lev. 18:6ff; 20:10ff.) Men were committing adultery with a neighbor's wife or with women having their monthly period (Ezek. 18:6; Lev. 18:19; 20:18).

How easy it is for us today to pass judgment on God's ancient people, but what about God's contemporary people? Sexual sins in the church and in so-called Christian homes have ripped churches and families apart, and many churches close their eyes to these offenses. Pornography—in print, on video, and on the Internet—is a common thing these days, and it's getting more and more daring on television. Unmarried people living together, "trial marriages," "gay marriages," and even "mate-swapping" have shown up in evangelical churches, and when faithful pastors have attempted to deal with such sin, they were told to mind their own business. The offenders simply left and starting attending other churches where they could live as they pleased. As Ruth Bell Graham said, "If God doesn't judge America, He will have to apologize to Sodom and Gomorrah."

"The love of money is a root of all kinds of evil" (1 Tim. 6:10, NKJV), so we aren't surprised that the business people in Jerusalem were charging exorbitant interest on loans and were practicing extortion rather than business (Ezek. 22:12). The Jews could charge interest to outsiders, but not to their own people (Ex. 22:25-27; Lev. 19:13; 25:35-38; Deut. 23:19-20), and they were to be fair in all their business dealings. The world's motto "Business is business" must never replace our Lord's commandment, "Give, and it will be given to you" (Luke 6:38, NIV).

Why were God's chosen people living such wicked lives?

Because they had forgotten the Lord (Ezek. 22:12), a sin that Moses had commanded them to avoid (Deut. 4:9, 23; 6:10-12; 32:18). They were admonished to remember their slavery in Egypt and God's grace in redeeming them (5:15; 15:15; 16:12; 24:18), and also remember the Lord their God (8:18). People who forget God gradually become their own god and begin to disobey God's Word, mistreat other people, and take God's gifts for granted. The Prophet Jeremiah in Jerusalem was accusing the people of the same sin (Jer. 3:21).

A *doomed people (Ezek. 22:13-22)*. God strikes His hands in angry response to the sins of His people (6:11; 21:14, 17),[2] and He announces that a day of reckoning is coming. The people of Jerusalem had the resolution to persist in their sins, in spite of God's warnings, but would they have the will and courage to endure God's day of judgment? His first act of judgment would be *dispersion (22:13-16)*; the people would be exiled to Babylon and others scattered to the surrounding nations (vv. 15-16), some of which had already occurred. The people should have known this judgment was coming, because in His covenant, God had promised this kind of judgment (Lev. 26:27-39; Deut. 28:64-68). The Jewish people wanted to worship the gods of the Gentiles, so why not live with the Gentiles and learn how to do it? God would humiliate His people before the eyes of the Gentiles and through this experience bring His people back to Himself.

The second judgment would be *fire (Ezek. 22:17-22)*, the destruction of their beloved city and temple. The prophet pictured a smelting furnace with different kinds of metals in it, and the dross (slag) being removed. That dross represented the people of Jerusalem who thought they were "the best" because they hadn't gone into exile. The image of the furnace is a familiar one in Scripture. Israel's suffering in Egypt was a furnace experience that helped to form the nation and prepare them for the Exodus (Deut. 4:20; 1 Kings 8:31; Jer. 11:4). But now, God's furnace was Jerusalem, and the fire would be divine judgment for the sin's of the people (Isa. 1:21-26; 31:9; Jer. 6:27-30). Two key words in this passage are "melt" and "gather." The people had gathered in

Jerusalem for safety, but it was the Lord who gathered them so He could melt them in His furnace as He poured His fury upon them. This same image will be discussed in Ezekiel 24:1-14.

A debased people (Ezek. 22:23-27). Ezekiel pointed the finger of accusation at the princes (vv. 25, 27),³ the priests (v. 26), the false prophets (v. 28), and the people of the land (v. 29), and each segment of society is found guilty. The princes were acting like animals, lions and wolves, hungry for their prey. Sin always debases people and turns them into beasts (Ps. 32:9; Prov. 7:21-23; 2 Peter 2:18-22), even into worse than beasts! These men abused their power and destroyed innocent people just to acquire more wealth. They manufactured poor widows by murdering innocent men and stealing their wealth.

You would think that the priests would have upheld the law and protested the evil deeds of the rulers, but instead they broke God's law (Jer. 32:32; Lam. 4:13). These men were given the sacred calling of explaining God's holy law (Mal. 2:6-8) so that the people could live holy lives and make a difference between holy things and common things (Ezek. 44:23; Lev. 10:10; 11:47; 20:25). But instead of teaching the law, the priests violated the law; and when others broke the law, the priests looked the other way. It was a situation not unlike that of Eli and his sons in the days of young Samuel (1 Sam. 2:12ff).

The people of the land (Ezek. 22:29) were the prominent land-owning citizens (12:19), often officers in the army, and they fell right in line with the princes and priests. They oppressed the poor when they should have aided them, and took advantage of the strangers instead of welcoming them and helping them. But everything they gained by their violence and abuse of power, they would lose when the day of judgment arrived.

A deceitful people (Ezek. 22:28). Along with the priests, the false prophets supported the evil political regime and encouraged the common people with lies. Instead of exposing sin, they whitewashed it! (See 13:10-16; Jer. 6:14; 8:11; 23:16-22.) They announced that God would never allow His holy city and temple to be trampled by the heathen, but that is exactly what the

Lord planned to do. The false prophets manufactured lies and the people gladly believed them.

A *disappointing people (Ezek. 22:30-31)*. God searched among His people for one person in authority who would stand in the gap so that the enemy wouldn't penetrate the wall and invade the city, but He found none. Of course, the Prophet Jeremiah was in Jerusalem, but he was a man with no authority who was rejected by the politicians, priests, and false prophets. Jeremiah himself had scoured the city, looking for a godly man (Jer. 5:1-6), but his quest was a failure. The Prophet Isaiah failed in a similar search (Isa. 51:18; 59:16). The Lord promised to spare Sodom and Gomorrah if He found ten righteous men in the city (Gen. 18:23-33), and He would have spared Jerusalem for one righteous man.

The Lord is still seeking men and women who will take their stand for the moral law of God, stand in the gap at the wall, and confront the enemy with God's help. As you read history, you meet godly men and women who had the courage to resist the popular evils of their day and dare to expose the breaks in the wall and seek to mend them. The Lord is looking for intercessors (Isa. 59:1-4, 16) who will cry out to God for mercy and for a return to holiness. Surely the Lord must be disappointed that His people have time for everything except intercessory prayer.

2. The end of the kingdom (Ezek. 23:1-49)

This chapter is a good deal like chapter 16 in that it depicts the history of the nation of Israel and its apostasy from the Lord. In both chapters, the image is that of prostitution, the nation breaking her "marriage vows" and like a harlot, turning to others for help.[4] However, in chapter 16, the sin is idolatry, trusting the false gods of the pagans, while in chapter 23, the sin is trusting other nations to protect her. In this chapter you will find both Israel (the Northern Kingdom) and Judah (the Southern Kingdom) playing the harlot and looking for help from Assyria, Babylon, and Egypt, instead of trusting Jehovah God to guide them and rescue them.

During the reign of Solomon's son Rehoboam, the Jewish

nation divided into two kingdoms, Israel and Judah. The Northern Kingdom of Israel (Samaria) almost immediately abandoned the true faith, started to worship idols, and eventually set up their own temple and priesthood; while the Southern Kingdom of Judah tried to remain true to the Law of Moses. Things got so bad in Samaria that in 722 B.C. God brought the Assyrians to conquer them and put an end to the nation. Judah had a few godly kings who sought to please the Lord, but the nation gradually disintegrated and was taken by the Babylonians (606–586 B.C.).

Oholah represents Israel whose capital was Samaria, while her sister Oholibah represents Judah whose capital was Jerusalem. Oholah means "her tent" while Oholibah means "my tent is in her." When hearing the word "tent," most Jews would immediately think of the tabernacle where God dwelt with His people. The Northern Kingdom of Israel had its own sanctuary and priesthood in Samaria, as well as idols and shrines throughout the land, but that was "her tent" and not "the Lord's tent." However, the Mosaic Law was still held in Judah, even though not always obeyed, and the levitical priests still served at the temple that Solomon built by God's direction and authority. Looking at Jerusalem, even with all of her sins, the Lord could still say, "My tent is in her." The glory had departed from the temple (9:3; 11:22-23), but the temple was still known as God's dwelling place.

With that background, we can now examine this parable and see how it applied to the Jews in Ezekiel's day as well as to God's people in our own day. The main message the Lord wanted Ezekiel to get across to the Jewish people was that He was perfectly just in punishing the kingdom of Judah because of the way they had behaved toward Him. The Lord made three declarations: Judah arrogantly ignored God's warning when He judged Samaria (23:5-13); Judah then went beyond the sins the Samaritans committed (vv. 14-21); therefore, the Lord had every right to judge Judah (vv. 22-35).

The people of Judah ignored God's warning (Ezek. 23:5-13). Both

Israel and Judah were positioned in such a way geographically that the political tensions among the larger nations and empires (Egypt, Assyria, Babylon) affected them drastically. Israel and Judah were often the "bridges" over which these nations marched their armies, and it was impossible for the Jews not to take sides. In the days when the nation was united, King David trusted the Lord to help him defend and deliver his people, but King Solomon's policy was to make political treaties to guarantee peace. This is why he married numerous heathen princesses so that their fathers wouldn't attack the Jewish nation.

Samaria had no true faith in the living God, so she looked to the Assyrians to help her. The picture here is that of a prostitute seeking a lover to care for her and the language is quite graphic. Samaria not only welcomed Assyria's soldiers but also Assyria's idols, and the religion of the Northern Kingdom became a strange mixture of Mosaic Law and Assyrian idolatry (2 Kings 17:6-15). So, to punish her, the Lord used the Assyrians—her "lovers"—to conquer her and put an end to the Northern Kingdom. The ten tribes that comprised the Northern Kingdom were mixed with other conquered nations and the land became part of the Assyrian Empire.

The leaders of Judah knew what had happened to their sister kingdom and why it happened, but they didn't take the lesson to heart. Judah also made alliances with Assyria and "fell in love" with the handsome soldiers in their beautiful uniforms (Ezek. 23:11-13). Instead of looking to the Lord to protect them, the people of Judah looked to their powerful neighbors for help, but they proved to be broken reeds. Assyria invaded Judah during the days of King Hezekiah, ravaged the land, and were stopped in their tracks at Jerusalem and slain by God's angel (Isa. 36-37; 2 Kings 18–19). This was God's warning to Hezekiah not to let the people follow the sinful example of Samaria.

The people of Judah sinned even more than Samaria did (Ezek. 23:14-21). God's punishment of Samaria and His miraculous deliverance of Judah should have brought the people of Judah to their knees in gratitude and dedication, but it didn't happen that way. Hezekiah began to fraternize with the Babylonians (Isa. 39), a nation that was growing in power. As they had admired the Assyrian armies (2 Kings 16:1-9), so the rulers of Judah began to admire the power of Babylon. King Jehoiakim asked Babylon to help him break the power of Egypt (Ezek. 23:35–24:7), and this only made Judah a vassal state of Babylon. The kingdom of Judah became more and more idolatrous as one weak king after another took the throne, some of them for only three months. Judah was actually more corrupt than her sister Samaria! (23:11)

The people of Judah will suffer the wrath of God (Ezek. 23:22-35). The logic is obvious: if God punished Samaria for her sins, and if Judah sinned worse than Samaria, then Judah must be punished also. In this section of his message, Ezekiel delivered four oracles from the Lord. First, God would bring the Babylonians to punish Judah just as He brought the Assyrians to punish Samaria (vv. 22-27). Ezekiel described in detail the officers in the army and the equipment they would carry. Using the image of punishing a prostitute, he described how the invaders would strip the nation, expose her lewdness, and mutilate her body. It isn't a very beautiful picture.

The second oracle (vv. 28-31) repeats some of the facts in the first one and reminded the people that this judgment was perfectly just. At one time, Judah courted the friendship of Babylon, but now they hated the Babylonians; yet God would allow the people they hated to ravage their land and destroy Jerusalem and the temple. The third oracle (vv. 32-34) uses the image of the cup, a familiar image in Scripture for experiencing suffering (Isa. 51:17, 22; Jer. 25:15-29; 49:12; Lam. 4:21; Hab. 2:16; John 18:11; Rev. 14:10). The cup He hands them will be large and deep and filled with the wrath of the Lord, and they will have to drink it.

The final oracle (Ezek. 23:35) explained why God had to judge His people: they had forgotten Him (22:12) and had cast Him behind their backs, that is, rejected Him and left Him out of their thinking and living. "There is no fear of God before their eyes" (Rom. 3:18). God's "wife" had become a harlot and abandoned her Husband. Jeremiah used a similar image (Jer. 2:1-8) and was astonished that a nation should change its gods (vv. 9-11). He said that Judah had rejected the fountain of living water and turned to broken cisterns that could hold no water (v. 13).

The two accused sisters have been presented to the court and their crimes have been explained. All that remains is for the judge to sum up the case and describe the sentence, which Ezekiel does in 23:36-49. Neither Samaria nor Judah has any defense and they can't take their case to a higher court. God's verdict is true and final. Ezekiel includes Samaria in this summation so that Judah can't say that God's judgment of the Northern Kingdom was unjust. All the evidence was presented and there could be but one decision: guilty as charged.

What were their sins? Idolatry, injustice, unbelief (depending on the heathen nations for help), followed by blatant hypocrisy. They worshiped idols and killed innocent people, and then marched piously into the temple to worship Jehovah! They prostituted themselves to heathen nations when, if they had trusted the Lord, He would have taken care of them and delivered them. In their idolatry, they even sacrificed their own children, sons and daughters who really belonged to God ("whom they bore to Me").

When Judah should have remained a separated people, declaring their faith in Jehovah, their leaders participated in an international conference against Babylon and allied themselves with the enemies of the Lord (v. 40; Jer. 27). The prophet described how the Jewish leaders at the meeting behaved like harlots preparing to serve a customer, but he compared the meeting to a drunken brawl,[5] a "carefree crowd" that didn't want to face the fact that Babylon was going to win.

From God's point of view, Judah was nothing but a worn-out adulteress soliciting "lovers," and their sin was something His heart couldn't accept. As Samaria had sinned by patronizing Assyria, so Judah was playing the harlot by seeking the help of pagan nations instead of trusting the Lord. That being the case, Judah would be treated like an adulteress and *even worse*. The Law of Moses called for the adulteress to be stoned (Lev. 20:10; Deut. 20:20), prostitutes to be burned (Gen. 38:24; Lev. 21:9), and murderers to be put to death, probably by stoning (Ex. 21:12-14; Lev. 24:17). Judah would be punished for adultery, prostitution, and shedding innocent blood (Ezek. 23:47).[6] Her sins would find her out.

3. The end of a delusion (Ezek. 24:1-14)

This chapter closes the section of the book that focuses on the destruction of Jerusalem (chapters 4–24) and it is divided into two parts: a parable about a boiling pot (24:1-14) and an "action sermon" involving the sudden death of the prophet's wife (vv. 15-27). After that, Ezekiel deals with God's judgment on the Gentile nations (chaps. 25–32) and His glorious promises for the people of Israel (chaps. 33–48).

God's message came to Ezekiel on January 15, 588 B.C., the date of the beginning of the siege of Jerusalem. So critical is this date that it's mentioned in 2 Kings 25:1-3 as well as Jeremiah 39:1-3 and 52:4-6. During their years of exile, the Jews observed four annual fasts to remember the painful events of the destruction of Jerusalem (Zech. 7; 8:18-23). They marked when the siege began (tenth month), when the walls were breached (fourth month), when the temple was burned down (fifth month), and when Gedaliah the governor was assassinated (the seventh month, Jer. 41:1-2).

God called Judah a "rebellious house" not only because they broke His laws and violated His covenant, but also because Zedekiah had broken his treaty with Babylon and incited the displeasure of Nebuchadnezzar. The image of the cooking pot takes us back to Ezekiel 11:1-13 where the Jewish leaders boasted that the Jews left in Jerusalem were better than the Jews taken off to Babylon. The Jerusalem Jews were the best "cuts of meat," while the Jews in Babylon were only the scraps! Of course, God contradicted that idea and made it clear that the exiles in Babylon would form a remnant with which He could rebuild the nation and the temple. Jeremiah had written to the exiles and instructed them to settle down, build houses, and raise families so that the remnant could continue the ministry for which the Lord had chosen Israel. God warned the Jewish leaders in Jerusalem that they weren't the "meat"—they were the butchers! They were guilty of shedding innocent blood, and God would judge them for their sins. If they weren't "cooked" in the cauldron of Jerusalem, they would eventually be slain by the swords of the Babylonian soldiers. Even if they escaped the city, they would be caught and killed.

In his parable about the cooking pot, Ezekiel used the image and vocabulary of the Jerusalem leaders. Yes, God would put "the best cuts of meat" into His pot (Jerusalem) and boil the meat and the bones (the Babylonian siege). He wouldn't "cook" the flesh; He would consume it! (Ezek. 10) Then He would pour out the burned mess *and burn the pot itself!* Jerusalem was an evil city, filled with sin like a filthy pot encrusted with rust and scum. She had shed innocent blood and hadn't even been decent enough to cover the blood (Gen. 4:10; Lev. 17:13; Deut. 12:16, 24; 15:23). The murderers left the evidence for everyone to see and didn't worry about the consequences! But God would avenge the inno-cent victims and expose the blood of their murderers for all to see.

The Jerusalem leaders were confident of deliverance because they were depending on a lie: "Our God will never allow His cho-sen people to be killed, His holy city and temple to be destroyed." This was a delusion, and Ezekiel put an end to it. It was *because* the Jews were His chosen people that God was punishing them, and *because* Jerusalem was His holy city that He couldn't allow it to continue wallowing in wickedness. The only way to purge the city was to burn it and make it a great funeral pyre (Ezek. 24:9-10). He judged the people in the city (the "select pieces of meat in the pot") and then burned the pot as well!

Both Jeremiah and Ezekiel had to deal with the false confidence of the people, a confidence based on a false interpretation of the-ology. Jeremiah warned Judah, "Do not trust in these lying words, saying, 'The temple of the Lord, the temple of the Lord, the tem-ple of the Lord are these'" (Jer. 7:4, NKJV). The presence of the temple in Jerusalem wasn't a guarantee that the city would be saved, especially when what was going on in the temple was contrary to the will of God. Any theology that makes sin easy and divine punishment unimportant is not biblical theology. God's judgment begins with His own people (2 Peter 4:17), and Hebrews 10:30 warns us that "the Lord will judge His people" (NKJV).

Our world today lives on delusions and myths because, like the Jews in Ezekiel's day, the world won't accept the authority of the Word of God. People still believe that might makes right, that money is the measure of worth and success, that the aim of life is to have fun and do what you want to do. You can believe whatever you please about God, yourself, and others, and everything will turn out fine because there are no consequences. But one day God will expose the stupidity of these delusions and the world will discover too late that there are consequences to what we believe and how we behave.

4. The end of a marriage (Ezek. 24:15-27)
It's interesting to study what is said in Scripture about the wives of the prophets. Abraham was a prophet (Gen. 20:7) who twice lied about his wife and got into trouble. Moses was criticized for the wife he chose (Num. 12:1), and Isaiah's wife was a prophetess (Isa. 8:3). She bore him at least two sons whose names were signs to the people of Judah. The Prophet Jeremiah wasn't allowed to have a wife (Jer. 16:1-4), and this was a sign to the Jews that judgment was coming and people would wish they had never married and brought children into the world. Hosea's wife became a prostitute and he had to buy her out of the slave market (Hosea 1–3). What a trial that must have been!

But Ezekiel paid a greater price than all these prophets. In order to give his message, Ezekiel had to see his wife die suddenly *and he was not to show great grief because of it!* God told him that she would suddenly die and that he was not to do what the Jews usually did in times of bereavement. He was allowed to groan quietly, but he was not permitted to weep or make the kind of lamentation that was typical of his people.

He gave his morning message to the elders, at evening his wife suddenly died, and the next morning he buried her. When the

Jews came to console him, they were shocked to see that he wasn't weeping aloud and displaying the usual signs of bereavement. Nor was he to eat the food that people would bring to help him in his sorrow. As they had done in the past, the people asked him for an explanation (Ezek. 12:9; 21:7), and the Lord gave him the message and opened his mouth so he could speak.

The prophet's wife was the joy of his life and the desire of his eyes (24:16), but the Lord took her away. The temple in Jerusalem was the joy of the Jewish people, for no other nation had such a sanctuary, but now the Lord would take the temple away. On August 14, 586 B.C., the Babylonians set fire to the temple in Jerusalem. Nothing is said about Ezekiel's children and we don't know that he had any, but God announced that, along with the destruction of the temple, the relatives of the exiles still living in Jerusalem would lose their lives. Once again, Ezekiel was a sign to the exiles of what the Lord was doing, and this was the most painful and costly of all his "action sermons." In order to preach one sermon, Ezekiel had to lose his wife. But Ezekiel commanded the Jewish exiles to mourn over the loss of the temple just as he had mourned over the loss of his wife, without loud wailing, copious weeping, or any change in their dress or eating habits. The death of the prophet's dear wife was an act of God, and so was the destruction of the temple. The woman who had died was innocent of any gross sin, but the temple had become a den of thieves. God gave Ezekiel only one day's notice that he would become a widower, but He had been speaking to sinful Judah for many years and they had not listened. The destruction of the temple and the city should not be a surprise to anybody.

But how did the people know that the prophet was telling the truth? They didn't have instant news service as we have today, so perhaps the whole thing was only Ezekiel's way of dealing with his wife's death. But God said that a messenger would arrive in Babylon with the news of the fall of the city and the destruction of the temple, and this occurred five months later, on January 8, 585 B.C. (33:21-22).

The next day, God opened the prophet's mouth and removed

the discipline He had imposed at the beginning of his ministry (3:25-27). From this point on, the prophet was free to speak as he felt led, and at the same time, the focus of his ministry shifted. He had exposed the nation's sins and announced her judgment. Now he would announce God's plans for the Gentile nations, including victorious Babylon; and then he would minister hope to the Jewish exiles and share with them visions of the kingdom yet to come.

Ezekiel has been a faithful servant of God, even to the point of sacrificing his beloved wife so he could declare the Word of God. What an example of dedication!

God Judges the Nations

The destruction of Jerusalem was welcomed by the Gentile nations that were located in the vicinity of the kingdom of Judah. During the great days of their nation, the Jews had been a separated people, and this irritated their neighbors. The Jewish claim that Jehovah was the only true and living God meant that the other nations worshiped only dead idols. Both Saul and David had met many of these nations on the battlefield, and the Gentiles remembered and resented those humiliating defeats. But as the kingdom of Judah drifted from the Lord, the Jewish people adopted the gods and the practices of the Gentiles, and to their neighbors, this looked like pure hypocrisy. After all, if Jehovah is the true and living God, why do the Jews need other gods? And why would the kings of Judah look to human allies for protection if Jehovah is able to care for them? Nothing pleased the Gentiles more than to be able to laugh at the Jews in their day of humiliation and claim that the gods of the Babylonians were stronger than the God the Jews worshiped.

What these nations didn't realize was that the destruction of Jerusalem wasn't just a punishment of the Jews; it was also a warning to the Gentiles. "If the righteous will be recompensed on the earth, how much more the wicked and the sinner?" (Prov. 11:31, NKJV) After all, if God first displays His wrath against His own people, "What shall the end be of them that obey not the gospel of God?" (1 Peter 4:17) There's a great difference between a loving parent chastening a child and a judge punishing a guilty criminal. Israel knew God's Word and therefore had sinned against a flood of light, but the Gentiles had the clear witness of creation (Rom. 1:18-32; Ps. 19) and conscience (Rom. 2:11-16) and were without excuse. But God was also judging the Gentiles for the way they had treated His people, because this was the covenant promise He had made with Abraham (Gen. 12:1-3).[1]

It's interesting that Ezekiel didn't have a message of judgment against the Babylonians, but God used Isaiah (Isa. 13:1–14:23; 21:1-9) and especially Jeremiah (Jer. 31; 40; 50–51) to do that job. God commanded Ezekiel to set his face against the nations (Ezek. 25:2; see 6:2; 13:17; 20:46; 21:2, 7) and declare that judgment was coming.

1. Judgment on nations related to Israel (Ezek. 25:1-14)

The Ammonites, Moabites, and Edomites were all blood relatives of the Jews. The Ammonites and Moabites were related to Israel through Lot, Abraham's nephew. Ammon and Moab were the two sons born out of the incestuous union of Lot and two of his daughters (Gen. 19:29-38). Edom is another name for Jacob's twin brother Esau (Ezek. 25:30; Edom means "red"), and Jacob fathered the twelve tribes of Israel. You would think that nations related by blood would be supportive of one another, but these three nations had a long-standing hatred against Israel and kept the feud going.

Note in these judgment messages that God gives the reason for the judgment ("because"—Ezek. 25:3, 6, 8, 12, 15; 26:2) and a description of the judgment ("therefore"—25: 4, 7, 9, 13, 16; 26:3).

Ammon (Ezek. 25:1-7). When Israel was marching toward the Promised Land, defeating one nation after another, God commanded them not to attack the Ammonites because He had given them their land (Deut. 2:19). They were a fierce people

(Jer. 40:14; 41:5-7), and both Saul and David had defeated them in battle (1 Sam 11; 1 Chron. 19-20). Ammon had united with Moab in attacking Judah but both were soundly defeated (2 Chron. 20). The Ammonites rejoiced at the destruction of Jerusalem and the temple (Ezek. 25:3, 6), and when Nehemiah went to Jerusalem to rebuild the walls, the Ammonites joined with Sanballat in opposing him (Neh. 2:10-19).

The Lord announced that He would deliver Ammon into the hands of "the men of the east" (Ezek. 25:4), meaning the Babylonian army. In his march, Nebuchadnezzar had paused at the juncture of two roads, one of which led to Jerusalem and the other to Rabbah, the capital of Ammon (21:18-24). There he sought guidance from his diviners, and God saw to it that he marched to Jerusalem. The Ammonites had breathed a sigh of relief and had been joyful when they saw Jerusalem ruined and the temple desecrated, but now their time had come. God would destroy Ammon and the nation would perish from the earth forever.

Moab (Ezek. 25:8-11).[2] It was Balak, king of Moab, who hired Baalam to curse Israel as they camped on the plains of Moab (Num. 22–24), and it was Baalam who taught the Moabites how to seduce Israel into sinning against God (Num. 25:1-9; 31:16). The sin of Moab was slander against Israel, a refusal to see the Jews as God's special people. To the Moabites, the fall of Jerusalem proved that the Jews were just like any other people. "If you are such a special nation," they argued, "why have you experienced such a humiliating defeat?" Even Baalam had admitted that Israel was a special people set apart from every other nation (Num. 23:8-10).

The Moabites were a very proud people because they thought their nation was impregnable (Isa. 16:6). Moab was located in the high mountains, with the Dead Sea on the west and the desert on the east. God told them He would bring invaders through their "inaccessible" northwest border ("flank," Ezek. 25:9, NIV), even though it was made up of sheer cliffs; and He did. It was the Assyrians who invaded and destroyed Moab, and today Moab is no longer remembered among the nations.

Edom (Ezek. 25:12-14). Edom's hatred of the Jews began when Esau foolishly sold his birthright to his brother Jacob, and when their mother schemed to secure the patriarchal blessing for her favorite son Jacob (Gen. 25:29-34; 27).[3] Jacob went to Haran to live with his uncle primarily to escape the anger and murderous intent of his brother. Esau's descendants became powerful tribal chiefs (Gen. 36), but Jacob's sons became the founders of the twelve tribes of Israel, the people God chose to accomplish His great purposes on this earth.

The Prophet Obadiah wrote that God would destroy Edom because of the way they treated the Jews (Obad. 10-14). When Jerusalem was being attacked, the Edomites cheered for the Babylonians (Ps. 137:7) and gave no help to the Jewish refugees who were trying to escape. Instead, the Edomites helped the Babylonians capture the fleeing people and rejoiced over the terrible calamities that had come to the Jews. Along with the Babylonians, they looted the city and robbed their own blood relatives. Sins against humanity are sins against God, because humans are made in the image of God. The day came when Edom felt the heavy hand of God's judgment (Lam. 4:21-22).

God's message to Edom reminds us that family feuds are costly and often lead to pain and tragedy. The Edomites sustained their hatred for the Jews from generation to generation. "[Edom] stifled his compassion; his anger also tore continually, and he maintained his fury forever" (Amos 1:11, NASB). "Let no man pull you so low as to make you hate him," said Booker T. Washington, and Jesus said, "Love your enemies, bless them that curse you, do good to them that hate you, and pray for them which despitefully use you, and persecute you" (Matt. 5:44). Edom's hatred and lust for revenge finally led to their ruin (Obad. 1-14). Ezekiel will have more to say about Edom in chapter 35.

2. Judgment on neighboring nations (Ezek. 25:15–26:21)

Having dealt with the sins of the nations related to Israel, Ezekiel then set his face against Philistia (25:15-17) and Phoenicia, especially the Phoenician cities of Tyre (26:1–28:19) and Sidon

(vv. 20-24). Once again, the themes of pride, hatred, and revenge come to the fore, sins that can motivate nations even today. It's very easy for arrogance to masquerade as patriotism, hatred as national zeal, and revenge as justice.

Philistia (Ezek. 25:15-17). After the Israelites entered and occupied the land of Canaan, the neighboring Philistines became serious enemies.[4] Among the judges, Shamgar (Jud. 3:31) and Samson (Jud. 13–16) attacked them, and both Samuel and Saul had to contend with them. It was David who finally defeated the Philistines, and they were kept under control throughout the reign of Solomon (2 Sam. 5:17-25; 21:15-22; 23:9-17). When the Jewish nation divided, the Philistines asserted their independence and became successful merchants and traders along with the Phoenicians.

The Philistines cultivated a national hatred for the Jews and seized every opportunity to harass and attack them. Ezekiel wasn't the only prophet who prophesied God's judgment on the Philistines (see Jer. 47; Amos 1:6-8; Zeph. 2:4-7). The Philistines allied with Egypt in an attempt to withstand Nebuchadnezzar; Babylon was too much for them and they were defeated and deported like the other vanquished nations (Jer. 25:15-32; 47).

Tyre (Ezek. 26:1-21). Ezekiel devoted four messages to the sins and the fate of the capital of Phoenicia (vv. 1-21; 27:1-36; 28:1-10, 11-19). During their reigns, both David and Solomon were friendly with Hiram, king of Tyre (2 Sam. 5:11; 1 Kings 5:1ff), and King Ahab's wife Jezebel was the daughter of Ethbaal, a later king of Tyre (1 Kings 16:31). The message in this chapter contains four parts, each beginning with a statement about the Word of the Lord (Ezek. 26:1-6, 7-14, 15-18, and 19-21).

Destruction announced (Ezek. 26:1-6). The image used here is that of a storm producing great destructive waves (vv. 3, 19). The city of Tyre was situated partly on the Mediterranean coast and partly on an island about half a mile from the coast, so Ezekiel's storm image was appropriate. God was angry at Tyre for rejoicing at Jerusalem's destruction and seeing it as an opportunity for Tyre to prosper even more. But the Lord announced that the nations would come like successive waves of the sea and bring Tyre to ultimate ruin. The name "Tyre" means "rock," so the statement "like the top of a rock" (vv. 4, 14) is significant. Tyre did become a bare rock and a place where fishermen dried their nets.

Tyre was able to survive the Assyrian conquest, but when Babylon came to power, Nebuchadnezzar besieged the coastal city for fifteen years (586–571 B.C.) and overcame it, but he did not conquer the island city. In 322 B.C., Alexander the Great besieged Tyre for seven months, built a causeway to the island and was able to conquer the city.

Destruction accomplished (Ezek. 26:7-14). He gives a description of the Babylonian siege of the part of Tyre that was on the shore of the Mediterranean. Nebuchadnezzar began his siege in 587 B.C., after the siege of Jerusalem, and though the coastal city was a formidable fortress, he managed to persevere and conquer. The Babylonians threw the timbers and stones into the water and claimed the spoils for themselves. God didn't think Nebuchadnezzar was "paid enough" for his efforts, so He gave him Egypt as an extra bonus (29:18-20).

Destruction lamented (Ezek. 26:15-18). Since Tyre was at the center of all merchandising along the Mediterranean coast and did business with every known country, her fall was devastating to the economy. There wasn't a "ripple effect"; there was a tidal wave! Their partners in business—called "princes" (v. 16) and "kings" (27:35)—had lost everything and could only lament the great tragedy that had struck. In 26:17-18 we have a brief lamentation over the fall of the city. Keep in mind that in ancient days, the prophets sometimes used funeral lamentations in a satirical manner to poke fun at the enemies of God. We will have examples in chapters 27 and 32.

People along the coast trembled as they wondered what would happen to the economy now that the great mercantile network was destroyed. Our world today is united in a series of electronic networks that can transfer information, money, and orders for merchandise with such speed that it's scarcely possible to register them. Imagine what would happen in the world's economy if all these electronic business connections in New York City alone were dissolved. This reminds us that in the end times, when the Antichrist has organized his great world network called "Babylon," the Lord will destroy the whole thing and leave the business people desolate and in mourning (Rev. 18).

Destruction forever (Ezek. 26:19-21). The prophet gives us insight into the full extent of Tyre's destruction by describing the victims' descent into "the pit" (v. 20). The Hebrew word *bor* means "a well, a pit, a cistern," but it also refers to the pit of death (Pss. 28:1; 88:4, 6) and sometimes is an equivalent of *sheol*, the realm of departed spirits. There were tragic consequences to the pride of Tyre and their evil attitude toward the Jewish people. "I will make thee a terror" (26:21, KJV) should read, "I shall bring terrors on you" (NASB). Note the statements the Lord makes about His actions toward the city of Tyre: He would make them desolate, cover them with water, bring them down into the pit, bring them terrors, and remove them from the earth. On the other hand, He promised Israel, their enemies, future glory and blessing!

3. Lament over Tyre's destruction (Ezek. 27:1-36)

The Old Testament prophets occasionally used "funeral dirges" in a satirical manner to ridicule their enemies, and you find something of that spirit in this lament over the fall of Tyre. Neither the prophet nor the Jewish nation was grieved over Tyre's destruction, but the event gave Ezekiel opportunity to express spiritual truth in this song. Since Tyre was a maritime city, the chapter compares the city and its business to a beautiful ship that eventually sinks and brings great grief to merchants and customers alike. This image is what is called "an extended metaphor," not unlike our "ship of state." A nation or a city isn't really a ship, but there are many points of comparison that can help us better understand the nation and the city. The words "merchant" and "merchandise" are used twenty-one times in this chapter, because Tyre was a mercantile city. The ship metaphor included all that was a part of the city of Tyre, its agents and customers, its business, and all the network it had developed in the Mediterranean world.

Building the ship (Ezek. 27:1-7). This was not only a useful ship that brought wealth to the city, but it was a beautiful ship that the nations admired (vv. 3, 11; see 28:12). Tyre was proud of its beauty and its success but didn't give any praise to the Lord for His goodness. The very best materials went into the building of the ship, starting with great fir timbers from Mount Hermon for the hull and deck, and cedars of Lebanon for the masts. They made the oars of oak from Bashan and the deck from pinewood from Cyprus, inlaid with ivory (see NIV and NLT). A large Phoenician ship would have as many as 50 oarsmen in a crew of 200. Egypt provided embroidered linen for the sail and banner, and from Cyprus came the cloth to make the beautiful awnings for the decks.

I once heard a sincere but ill-informed TV preacher declare that the United States should quit doing business with nations that espouse wrong political beliefs and the denial of human rights. His motives were right but his comprehension limited. He couldn't hear me, but I said out loud, "If we did, you wouldn't have either a microphone or a television camera!" I'm told that the familiar telephone has material in it from at least twenty different countries! Tyre's "ship of state" reminds us that the world is growing smaller and that nations that disagree still depend on one another for what they need. "Internet" is short for "international network," that invisible electronic system that ties together millions of computers and the minds and hearts of the people using them.

Manning the ship (Ezek. 27:8-11). In describing the ship's crew, Ezekiel was actually naming some of the nations that made it possible for Tyre to become such a great success. Oarsmen came from Sidon and Arvad, two other cities in Phoenicia, but the skilled mariners, the people who really managed things, came from Tyre. Veteran shipwrights from Gebal, another coastal city, traveled on board to caulk the seams and keep the ship in good repair.

Briefly, the image shifts from the ship metaphor to the actual city itself (vv. 10-11). Tyre had a paid army, mercenary soldiers from Persia, Lydia (Asia Minor), Libia (North Africa), Arvad (Phoenicia), Cilicia, and Gammad. These mercenaries sold their services to protect the city and its shipping enterprise. It doesn't appear that the soldiers anticipated any danger because they hung up their helmets and shields on the walls as decorations to add to the city's beauty. The coastal city of Tyre was a strong fortress, so much so that Nebuchadnezzar needed thirteen years to break through the defenses.

We shouldn't carry a metaphor too far, but it is significant that Ezekiel brought in the army and navy as necessary parts of the business enterprise of Tyre. Certainly national defense is as important to the success of business as it is to the safety of the private citizen, and sometimes "national interest" and "business" become intertwined. "Big business" always appreciates a foreign policy that opens new markets and protects them.

Sailing the ship (Ezek. 27:12-25). The beautiful and impressive ship of state was made for the waters, not for the wharf, so Ezekiel described how the city of Tyre did business along the Mediterranean coast. The word "merchant," used thirteen times in the *Authorized Version,* means "to do business, to trade." The nations named here bought merchandise from Tyre and sold products to Tyre. It was a business partnership that benefited all that were involved. Silver, iron, tin, and lead came from Tarshish, which was probably in Spain. Slaves[5] and bronze implements came from Greece and Turkey (Tubal). Also from Turkey came horses, chariot teams, and mules. But there were luxury items as well: ivory and ebony from Rhodes; and turquoise, coral, rubies, and fine fabrics from Jordan.

Tyre did business with the Jews and bought various foods from them. They also got wine and wool from Syria, and lambs, rams, and goats from Arabia. Also from Arabia came exotic spices, gold, and precious stones. Other nations supplied barks, perfumes, and manufactured products such as fabrics, wrought iron objects, and rugs. The people of Tyre would take the raw materials and manufacture various useful items and sell them to their agents and their customers. Along with bartering, money and credit were involved in these many transactions, so there were plenty of opportunities for moneylenders and brokers to make profits. Thanks to the business network of Tyre, luxuries and necessities, jobs and income were available to the nations of the known world.

Sinking the ship (Ezek. 27:26-36). Admiration turns to desolation. "But look! Your oarsmen are rowing your ship of state into a hurricane! Your mighty vessel flounders in the mighty eastern gale. You are shipwrecked in the heart of the sea!" (v. 26, NLT) The storm arrives that was promised in 26:3 and 19, and the great ship is shattered in the mighty waters. The "east wind" speaks of the invasion of the Babylonian army (17:10; 19:12). The valuable cargo, the beautiful ship, and the capable crew are all lost in the heart of the sea.

But that isn't all: Tyre's agents, brokers, traders, and customers will feel the repercussions of the sinking of the ship. People will stand on the shore and lament the end of the vast mercantile system that gave them jobs, income, and security. Some of the merchants will "whistle" or "hiss" when they hear the news (27:36), probably as a shocked response to the tragedy. However, the word can mean "to hiss in scorn or derision," suggesting that some of the leaders in the business network are happy to see Tyre fall. They cooperated in the system because they had to, but now perhaps they would have opportunity to build their own network and make a greater profit. This great lamentation is an advance demonstration of what the whole world will do when Satan's system "Babylon the great" collapses before the Lord returns to establish His kingdom (Rev. 18:17-19).

No matter how efficient, rich, and beautiful the "ship of state" might be, when the Lord decides to sink it, nothing can stay His hand. When Queen Victoria celebrated her "Diamond Jubilee" in 1897, Rudyard Kipling published his poem "Recessional" which sounded a quiet word of warning to a great nation somewhat intoxicated by their vast empire. When people read the third verse, we wonder if any of them thought of Ezekiel's description of "the ship of state,"

> Far-call'd our navies melt away—
>   On dune and headland sinks the fire—
> Lo, all our pomp of yesterday
>   Is one with Nineveh and Tyre!
> Judge of the nations, spare us yet,
>   Lest we forget, lest we forget!

4. Judgment of Tyre's ruler (Ezek. 28:1-19)

It appears that two different persons are addressed in these verses: the prince of Tyre (vv. 1-10) and the king of Tyre (vv. 11-19). The first speech is a declaration of divine judgment, while the second is more of a lamentation. Both of these persons were guilty of great pride because of their wisdom and wealth, and both abused their privileges and offended the Lord. In fact, the prince of Tyre even claimed to be a god! However, foreign invaders would destroy the prince of Tyre (vv. 7-10), while the Lord Himself would judge the king of Tyre (vv. 16-19). The prince is called "a man" (v. 2), but the king is called "the anointed cherub" (v. 14). More than one student has identified the prince of Tyre as the ruler of the city when Nebuchadnezzar invaded, but they see the king of Tyre as Satan, the enemy of God and of the Jewish people, who energized the prince and used him to accomplish his own evil purposes.[6]

Judgment on the prince of Tyre (Ezek. 28:1-10). The issue here is pride, a sin which God hates (Prov. 6:16-17). This ruler was proud of his wisdom and his wealth (Ezek. 28:3-5), and because of this pride, he exalted himself as a god. However, God would demonstrate that he was but a man, for the prince of Tyre would be slain and die like any other man. When you read Scripture, you find occasions when God judged arrogant rulers, such as Pharaoh, whom the Egyptians treated as a god (Ex. 5:2), Nebuchadnezzar (Dan. 4), and Herod Agrippa (Acts 12). World leaders who ignore the Lord and act as if they are gods will all be exposed and judged.

Judgment on the king of Tyre (Ezek. 28:11-19). The previous declaration was one of Ezekiel's "because...therefore" (vv. 6-7) statements, such as you find in chapters 25 and 26, but this paragraph is simply a statement of God's intention to judge the king of Tyre and destroy him. As you read these verses, you get the impression that this "king" is much more than a human regent and that this could be a description of Satan. That Satan wants to control nations and their leaders is clear from 1 Chronicles 21 and Daniel 9, and Matthew 4:8-10 states that he has delegated authority to dispose of the nations.

The use of the word "cherub" (Ezek. 28:4, 16) suggests that we're dealing here with an angelic creature, also the fact that he had been "upon the holy mountain of God" (v. 14). This sounds a great deal like the description in Isaiah 14:12ff. Satan began as an obedient angel but rebelled against God and led a revolt to secure God's throne. The text describes his great beauty and names nine jewels that were a part of that beauty. All of these jewels were also found in the breastplate of the Jewish high priest (Ex. 28:17-20). This suggests that in "Eden, the garden of God" and upon "God's holy mountain," this person had special priestly functions to perform for the Lord. The settings and mountings for these jewels were of the finest gold. His pride and selfish ambitions led him into sin and God judged him by casting him out. While the original description refers to the ruler of Tyre, it certainly applies to the god of this age, Satan, the enemy of the Lord.

The prince of Tyre, motivated and energized by the devil, engaged in business and also in violence (Ezek. 28:16), for he considered himself a god (v. 2). His way of doing business was also dishonest, for verse 18 speaks of "dishonest trade" (NIV). Satan's boast was, "I will be like the Most High" (Isa. 14:14), and his promise to Eve was, "[Y]ou will be like God" (Gen. 3:5, NKJV). The prince of Tyre accepted Satan's offer and it led to his downfall, just as it led to Satan's downfall. But during the career of the prince of Tyre, he was used of Satan to defile and destroy. The nations would be appalled at the judgment of the prince of Tyre and his city, but they had no idea that Satan was behind the city's success and Jehovah was behind the city's destruction. It reminds us of the ministry of the apostles in Luke 10:1-24. God used the apostles to heal the sick, cast out demons, and proclaim the message of the kingdom; but Jesus saw in their victories the fall of Satan (vv. 18-19).

5. Promises to Israel (Ezek. 28:20-26)
After delivering a message of judgment, Ezekiel sometimes "dropped in" a message of hope for God's hurting people. Even though the Lord was chastising His own people by destroying Jerusalem and the temple, He was still their God and had a loving concern for them. "But where sin abounded, grace abounded much more" (Rom. 5:20, NKJV).

Judgment on Sidon (Ezek. 28:20-24). Sidon was a rival city located about twenty-five miles north of Tyre. Usually the two cities are mentioned together (Isa. 23:1-4; Jer. 47:4; Joel 3:4), but here Sidon is singled out for judgment by the Lord.[7] The people of Sidon despised the Jews and often caused trouble for them, but now that opposition would end. "They shall know that I am the Lord God" (Ezek. 28:24). Ezekiel makes the startling statement that God would be glorified in the destruction of the city (v. 22; see 39:12-13). How could the Lord be glorified by such carnage? Because it would demonstrate His holiness in rejecting false gods and punishing sin. The swords of the Babylonian soldiers would kill many of the people, and those that escaped would die of the plagues that often accompany wartime slaughter.

The regathering of Israel (Ezek. 28:25-26). One of the major themes of this book is the deliverance of the Jewish exiles from Babylon and the future regathering and reuniting of the nation.[8] After the seventy years of exile and the Persian conquest of Babylon, God did cause Cyrus to allow the Jewish people to return to their land and rebuild the temple (2 Chron. 36:22-23; Ezra 1). But the return of about 50,000 people (2:64-65) in 538–537 B.C. didn't completely fulfill the promises in Ezekiel, for they have an application in the end times. Certainly the Jewish remnant that returned with Zerubbabel didn't "dwell safely" (Ezek. 28:26) because they had all kinds of problems with the people in the land. Furthermore, Ezekiel mentioned "nations" (plural) and not just the one nation of Babylon where the Jews were in exile.

There is coming a time when God will call His chosen people together into their own land, judge them, cleanse them, and establish His glorious kingdom (Zech. 10:8-12; 12:9-13:1; Matt. 24:31). God gave the land of Palestine to Abraham and his descendants (Gen. 13:14-18; 15:7-17) and He renewed the promise to Jacob (28:10-15; 35:12; Ps. 105:8-11). The Jews *owned* the land because God gave it to them, but they *possessed* the land only when they obeyed the terms of the covenant God gave them. During the exile in Babylon, they were out of the land because they had rebelled against the Lord.

Ezekiel will have more to say about Israel's future in chapters 37–48, but this brief promise must have brought encouragement to the faithful remnant among the exiles, just as the sure promise of Christ's return brings encouragement to His people today.

Egypt Will Fall!

Egypt is the seventh nation in Ezekiel's "judgment cycle" and receives more attention than any of the other nations the prophet addressed. Centuries before, Egypt had made the Jewish people suffer greatly as slaves, and even after the division of the Jewish kingdom, the Egyptians were a thorn in the flesh to the Jews and a most undependable ally. But the Jews were like their father Abraham (Gen. 12:10-20) and their ancestors (Ex. 14:10-12; 16:1-3; Num. 11:4-9, 18; 14:1-5) in that, whenever a crisis loomed, they were prone to look to Egypt for help. The longer the Jews were away from Egypt, the more they idealized their experiences there and forgot about the slavery and the toil. Of course, King Solomon had married an Egyptian princess and did a considerable amount of business with Egypt, but after he died, those bonds began to unravel. "Woe to those who go down to Egypt for help," warned Isaiah during an international crisis (Isa. 31:1, NKJV; see 30:1-2), and he would give the same warning to God's people today. Believers who look to the world for help, instead of trusting in the Lord, commit the same sin that the Jews often committed.

These four chapters are composed of seven messages (or oracles) that God gave to Ezekiel to deliver to the Egyptians and to the Jewish exiles. The phrase "the word of the Lord came," or a similar statement, marks off each message. Six of these seven messages are dated (the third one is not—30:1-19), so we are able to fit them into the chronology of the book. Each of the messages presents a picture—or metaphor—of the impending judgment of Egypt.

1. The monster slain (Ezek. 29:1-16)

The first message was given on January 7, 587 B.C., about seven months before Jerusalem was destroyed. The prophet set his face against Pharaoh Hophra, who ruled Egypt from 589 to 570 B.C. (See Jer. 44:30.) The picture here is that of killing a sea monster.[1]

Pharaoh's sins (Ezek. 29:1-7). The Lord compared Hophra to a monster that dwelt in the waters of the river and claimed the river for himself. The Nile River was so essential to the life of Egypt that it was treated like a god; but Hophra claimed that he was the one who made the river and that it belonged to him. In this oracle, Pharaoh was compared to a ferocious crocodile, guarding the waters of the land—the Nile and all the canals — and attacking anybody who dared to challenge his claims. His major sin was pride (vv. 1-5), taking credit for what the Lord God had done. Whatever greatness belonged to Egypt, it was because of the gracious gifts of God and not because of what Pharaoh and his people had accomplished.

But the Lord wasn't impressed by the crocodile or afraid of him! He promised to catch him, put hooks in his mouth, and drag him and the fish clinging to him (the people of Egypt) out to the fields where they would be exposed to the sun and die. They would become food for the beasts of the field and the carrion-eating scavenger birds. The Egyptian pharaohs were diligent to prepare their burial places, but Hophra would be buried like an unwanted dead animal. What a humiliating way to bury a man who claimed to be a god!

Hophra's second sin was his disloyalty to Israel (vv. 6-7). Egypt was like a weak reed that couldn't be trusted. The Jews should never have turned to Egypt for help, but when they did, the Egyptians should at least have kept their word. The Egyptians had a reputation for making promises and not keeping them (2 Kings 18:20-21; Isa. 36:6). It was Egypt who encouraged Judah to break their agreement with Babylon, and this foolish act on King Zedekiah's part is what incited the Babylonian attack against Jerusalem. While Nebuchadnezzar was attacking Jerusalem, the Jews negotiated with Egypt to send their army to deliver Judah, and for a short time, the Babylonians turned away from Jerusalem so they could deal with Egypt. But the scheme didn't work. The people in Jerusalem rejoiced that the siege was ended, but God warned His people that the army would return to Jerusalem to finish the job. (See Jeremiah 34:21-22; 37:8.)

Nebuchadnezzar's invasion (Ezek. 29:8-12). This is a prophecy of the coming of the Babylonian army to Egypt where they would fulfill God's Word and destroy man and beast as well as ravage the land (Jer. 43:8-13; 46). The people would either be slain or scattered and the land would be left "utterly waste and desolate" (Ezek. 29:10). The phrase in verse 10, "From the tower of Seveneh even unto the border of Ethiopia" is the Egyptian equivalent of Israel's "from Dan to Beersheba" and signifies the whole land, from top to bottom. The NIV translates it "from Migdol [in the north] to Aswan [in the south]."[2] Nebuchadnezzar would make a clean sweep of the land, and the desolation would last forty years (vv. 11-13). Nebuchadnezzar attacked Egypt in 568/67 B.C. and fulfilled that prophecy.

Divine mercy (Ezek. 29:13-16). After forty years, the Lord would (1) regather the scattered Egyptians to their land and permit them to establish their kingdom, but (2) their kingdom would not regain its former power and glory. It would become a "base kingdom." The Jews would learn that Egypt couldn't be trusted and would not put their confidence in Egypt. (Compare 28:24 and 29:16.) Note that the statement "they shall know that I am the Lord" is repeated three times in this message (vv. 6, 9, and 16). This statement is one of the key affirmations in the Book of Ezekiel and is used some sixty times. The Lord reveals

His attributes through His judgments just as much as He does through His blessings, and sometimes His judgments get our attention much more quickly.

2. The wages paid (Ezek. 29:17-21)

This second oracle was given April 26, 571 B.C., which is the latest date mentioned in the Book of Ezekiel. However, the prophet included it here because it related to Egypt. Since Nebuchadnezzar[3] was a servant of the Lord (Jer. 25:9; 27:6; and 43:19), he deserved his pay; but the spoils of war from the conquest of Tyre couldn't begin to compensate him for the time and work his army put into the siege. ("Great service" in Ezek. 29:18, NIV is "hard campaign.") They spent thirteen years building ramparts and attacking Tyre, but they couldn't prevent the city from using their large navy to transport their treasures elsewhere. Egypt had even assisted the people of Tyre in resisting the attack and relocating their wealth.

God determined that Egypt should provide the wages for the Babylonian army that had grown bald and bruised during the siege. God is sovereign over the nations and can accomplish His will without destroying either their freedom or their accountability to Him. In 568 B.C., Nebuchadnezzar did invade Egypt, sweeping through the country and leaving it desolate (see vv. 8-12). Thus God punished both Tyre and Egypt and rewarded Babylon.

But what does all this have to do with God's people Israel? The prophet added a word of promise for the Jews (v. 21), assuring them that there would come for them a time of restoration when He would give them new strength (the budding horn) for their new challenges. After the Medes and Persians conquered Babylon in 539 B.C. (Dan. 5), Cyrus issued the edict that permitted the Jews to return to their land and rebuild the temple (Ezra 1). Whatever the other nations may do, God sees to it that His people maintain their witness and accomplish their assigned work on earth.

The statement about opening Ezekiel's mouth doesn't refer to his enforced dumbness (Ezek. 3:26; 24:27), because that had been removed when the news arrived in Babylon that Jerusalem had been taken (33:21-22). That was on January 8, 585 B.C., but the prophecy in 29:17-21 was given on April 26, 571 B.C., which was fourteen years later. The promise to Ezekiel in verse 21 indicates that when his prophecy came true and the remnant returned to the land, they would respect Ezekiel's words and profit from them. The Jews in Babylon didn't take Ezekiel's ministry seriously (33:30-33), but the day would come when God would prove him right. "[T]hen at last your words will be respected" (29:21, NLT).

Ezekiel will return to the "monster" theme in 32:1-16.

3. The storm announced (Ezek. 30:1-19)

This third oracle isn't dated but was probably delivered about the same time as the previous one. It pictures the judgment of Egypt in terms of a great storm that shakes the very foundations of the land.

The storm is coming (Ezek. 30:1-5). "The day of the Lord" (v. 3) is a biblical phrase that describes any period of divine judgment, such as the judgment of Egypt. It particularly refers to the time of Tribulation in the last days when the Lord will punish the nations (Isa. 65:17-19; Joel 1–3; Zeph.1–2; Rev. 6–19) before He returns to earth to establish His kingdom. Whether this judgment is local, as with Egypt, or global, as in the last days, it is the Lord's work and nobody can stop it or control it. It is "a day of clouds, a time of doom for the nations" (Ezek. 30:3, NIV). In the end times, all the nations will experience this time of wrath, but in Ezekiel's time, judgment would fall on Egypt and her neighboring allies. This would include Ethiopia (Cush, the upper Nile region; see vv. 5 and 9), Put (an African nation), Lud (Lydia), the Arabian nations, Cub (Libya), and "the people of the covenant" (v. 5, NIV), who are probably Jews serving as mercenaries in the Egyptian army (see 27:10).

Egypt will be desolate (Ezek. 30:6-9). When the Babylon sword invades the land, not only with Egypt fall, but so will their allies. Those areas were desolate enough before, but now they would be even worse as the land is devastated. God will crush Egypt's allies and light a fire that will destroy the land. The people of Cush will think they are secure, so the Lord will send them messengers to wake them up, but it will be too late.

Babylon will do God's work (Ezek. 30:10-12). When the Lord punished Egypt during the time of Israel's slavery, He did the work Himself; but now He would use Nebuchadnezzar as His appointed servant to punish the proud Egyptians. His army would be ruthless (28:7, "terrible," KJV; see 31:12; 32:12) and fill the land with corpses. But His judgments would also affect the rivers and make them dry, a great catastrophe for such an arid land.

Nothing shall escape God's wrath (Ezek. 30:13-19). Ezekiel has told us what would happen and how it would happen, and now he reveals the vast scope of God's wrath. Note the repetition of the phrase "I will" as the Lord describes His work of judgment in both Lower Egypt ("Noph" = "Memphis," v. 13) and Upper Egypt (Pathros). Instead of a land of pride, Egypt will be a land filled with fear. "Zoan" is "Rameses," "No" is "Thebes," and "Sin" is "Pelusium." The verbs used make it clear that the Lord will permit total devastation: destroy, make desolate, set fire, pour fury, cut off, the day darkened. The Jews were led out of Egypt by a bright cloud (Ex. 13:21), but the Egyptians who once enslaved them will be under a dark cloud. As a result of God's judgment, the power and pride of Egypt will be destroyed, and the nation would never rise to its former heights again. The young men would be slain and the young women taken into slavery, so the future generation would be given into the hands of the enemy.

Nations never seem to learn that God is serious about what happens to His people Israel. The devastating judgment that God sent to Egypt before the Exodus should have taught the Egyptians a lasting lesson, but apparently they forgot it. In opposing God's purposes for Israel, Egypt invited God's judgments on their own nation, for the Lord always keeps His covenant promises.

4. The bones broken (Ezek. 30:20-26)

This oracle was delivered on April 29, 587 B.C. and refers to God's crushing the Egyptian military power. The arm is a symbol of power, but God would break both of Pharaoh's arms and leave

Egypt helpless. Nobody would apply splints or even bandage up the wounds to promote healing.

The first "breaking" took place at Carchemish in 605 B.C. when Nebuchadnezzar defeated Pharaoh Necho (2 Kings 24:7; Jer. 46:2). It was also at Carchemish that godly King Josiah was slain. The second "breaking" occurred when Pharaoh Hophra tried to help Judah when Nebuchadnezzar attacked Jerusalem (37:5ff). With both arms "broken," Egypt would not be able to wield a sword, and that would put an end to the battle. Pharaoh Hophra had a second title, "The Strong-Armed," but that title would not apply anymore.

While the Lord was permitting the Babylonians to break the arms of Egypt, He was also strengthening the arms of the Babylonians! He even put His own sword into the hand of Nebuchadnezzar! The Egyptians would be either slain or scattered and their land would be left desolate. "They shall know that I am the Lord" is repeated twice (Ezek. 30:25-26). During Israel's sojourn in Egypt, Pharaoh wouldn't recognize the Lord; but now the nation would learn that the Lord God of the Hebrews was indeed the only true and living God.

5. The tree felled (Ezek. 31:1-18)

The date of this message is June 21, 587 B.C., and the image in the message is that of a great tree that is cut down. In Scripture, a tree is sometimes used as the image of a nation or an empire (chap. 17; Dan. 4). The argument the prophet presented was simple. Egypt boasted in its greatness, yet Egypt wasn't as great as Assyria, and Assyria was conquered by Babylon. Conclusion: if Babylon can conquer Assyria, Babylon can conquer Egypt.

Assyria's greatness (vv. 1-9). Egypt boasted of its greatness, so the prophet asked Pharaoh to name a nation that compared with Egypt. "Who can be compared to Egypt?" Ezekiel asked, and then he answered his question: "Only Assyria!" The Egyptians would agree and be happy to have their country rated so high.

The cedars in Lebanon were widely known for their quality and their height. Assyria was like one of those cedars, impressive in height and expansive in growth. It was nurtured by many waters, which symbolize the nations under Assyria's control that contributed to her wealth. (These nations are also symbolized by the fowl and the beasts that had security because of the tree.) The Lord allowed Assyria to achieve greatness because He had a work for her to do. The northern kingdom of Israel had rebelled against the Lord, so He used the Assyrians to chastise them and conquer their land (722 B.C.). In the days of King Hezekiah, the Lord used the Assyrians to discipline the kingdom of Judah, but He didn't allow them to take Jerusalem (Isa. 37; 2 Kings 19; 2 Chron. 32). God is sovereign over the nations and is able to use even the pagan peoples to accomplish His purposes.

No other kingdom could compare with Assyria. In a burst of poetic exaggeration, Ezekiel said that even the cedars and other trees in the Garden of Eden paled into insignificance beside Assyria. But it was the Lord who made Assyria beautiful and great (v. 9), yet the Assyrians did not recognize or acknowledge this fact.

Assyria's fall (vv. 10-14). As we have seen before, God hates pride and judges it severely. He judged the pride of Judah and Samaria (chap. 16), Ammon, Moab and Edom (chap. 25) and expecially Tyre (23:3; chaps. 26–28), and also Assyria, and He would eventually judge Egypt. The logic of this judgment, what hope was there for a lesser kingdom like Egypt? God would call "the mighty one of the nations" (v. 10) to humble Assyria, and this is, of course, King Nebuchadnezzar (30:11).

The tree was very tall and stately, but it would be cut down and left on the land to decay. The smaller nations would abandon Assyria ansd seek help elsewhere. From the highest heights, Assyria would end up in the deepest depths of the underworld (sheol). From a position of great strength, the kingdom would fall into utter weakness, and from sustaining the lives of others to experiencing death and decay. Whereas once Assyria was admired and praised, it would end up being mocked. God had to teach Assyria a lesson (v. 14), that those who exalt themselves will eventually be abased, a lesson nations and individuals need to learn today (Prov. 29:23; Isa. 2:12; Mal. 4:1; Matt. 23:11-12; 1 Peter 5:5-7).

Assyria's burial (vv. 15-18). As with Tyre in chapter 28 and Babylon in Isaiah 14, Assyria was brought down to the under-world along with all the other rulers and nations that rebelled against God. When Assyria fell, a shock wave went through the nations, but the king of Assyria had this comfort: he wasn't any different from the rulers who had preceded him. They were all in the same place. In verse 18 the prophet addressed the ruler of Egypt: "To which of the trees in Eden will you then be likened in glory and greatness? Yet you shall be brought down…to the depths of the earth…" (NKJV).

The Egyptians were very careful in their practice of circumcision, but their ruler would be lying in sheol with the dead from nations that didn't practice it at all. What humiliation! (See 28:10.) He thought he and his kingdom was as great as Assyria, so God humbled him by putting him with the Assyrians in the world of the dead.

6. The monster trapped (Ezek. 32:1-16)

The date of this oracle is March 5, 585 B.C. two months after the exiles in Babylon received the news that Jerusalem had fallen (33:21-22). The "monster" theme was used in 29:1-16, but Ezekiel uses it again to bring out some additional spiritual truths.

The monster captured (vv. 1-10). This is an "official lamentation" for the king of Egypt who thought he was a great lion but in God's sight was only a crocodile.[4] Pharaoh thrashed about in the water and made a big scene, but all he did was muddy the waters and create problems by disobeying the Lord.

In chapter 29, God caught the Egyptian "crocodile" with a hook, but now Egypt is so weak, it can be easily caught with a net. (See 12:13; 17:20; 19:8.) God would take the crocodile to the land and leave him there to die, and the vultures would devour the carcass, reminding us of 29:3-5. But he adds two more images: the land drenched in blood and the heavens shrouded in darkness (vv. 6-8). These are reminders of the first and ninth plagues before Israel's exodus from Egypt, the turning of the water into blood and the darkness for three days (Ex. 7:20-24; 10:21-29). According to Revelation 8:8-9, a similar judgment will fall during the Great Tribulation.

The description of the signs in the heavens makes us think of the future day of the Lord described in Joel 3, Amos 5:18-20, and Matthew 24. It has well been said that past events cast their shadows before, and so it will be with the fall of Egypt. It was a dress rehearsal for the judgments of the last days. Once again, Ezekiel explained that just as the fall of Assyria caused a shock wave to go through the nations (30:16; see 27:35 and 28:19), so the fall of Egypt will frighten the nations (32:9-10). But will they learn from this experience and turn to the Lord? No, they will go right on sinning and rebelling against His truth.

The monster punished (vv. 11-15). Here the prophet repeated the prophecy that the sword of Babylon would leave Egypt desolate and that all of Egypt's pride and pomp would vanish. Even the animal life in the land would be destroyed as it was during the plagues of Egypt in Moses' time. With no people and animals available to work the land and draw the water, the streams and canals wouldn't be muddied and the water would "run like oil" with nothing to impede its flow. This is in contrast to Pharaoh's behavior described in verse 2. Ordinarily, the flowing of oil is a picture of peace and prosperity from God's blessings, but in this case, it speaks of peace because of God's judgment. No humans or animals are there to stir up the mud and defile the water. But the picture also reminds us that Egypt's defeat would help to bring peace to the "pool" of nations.

7. The corpse is buried (Ezek. 32:17-32)

This is the seventh oracle and since no other date is recorded, we assume it was given two weeks after the previous message— March 17, 585 B.C. It follows the style of 31:15-18 and describes the people of Egypt descending into sheol, the world of the dead. Ezekiel was instructed to wail because of the multitudes of people who would be slain by the swords of the Babylonians.

The picture is grim and almost macabre as the other nations welcome Pharaoh and his hosts and taunt them as they arrive in the underworld. We might paraphrase their words, "So you thought you were so beautiful and strong? Look at you now! You prided yourselves in being a circumcised people, but now you are lying down in death with the uncircumcised. Like us, you thought you were invincible, but now you have joined us in death and decay. You are no longer on a throne—you are in a grave! Your bed is a sepulchre."

Ezekiel named some of the nations, great and small, that welcomed Pharaoh and his people to sheol: Asshur (v. 22), which is Assyria; Elam (v. 24), an area in Iran; Meshach and Tubal (v. 26), probably located in Asia Minor; and Edom and the Sidonians, neighbors of Israel (vv. 29-30). Like the king of Assyria before him (31:16), Pharaoh would see all these princes and common people and be comforted that he wasn't the only one defeated and slain.

Death is the great leveler; and as John Donne reminded us, when the funeral bell tolls, "it tolls for thee." There are no "kings and commoners" in the land of the dead, and we can't enter that land in peace and safety without faith in Jesus Christ. "'O Death, where is your sting? O Hades, where is your victory?' The sting of death is sin, and the strength of sin is the law. But thanks be to God, who gives us the victory through our Lord Jesus Christ" (1 Cor. 15:55-57, NKJV).

INTERLUDE

Chapters 33 to 48 of Ezekiel focus on the hope of Israel as found in the promises God has made to His chosen people. In chapter 33, God reminds His prophet that he has been commissioned to be a watchman whose task it is to protect and inform the people by keeping his eyes open to what is happening and his ears open to what God is saying.

In the previous chapters, the Lord revealed His judgments on His own people and on the neighboring nations. Ezekiel told the exiles in Babylon that the city of Jerusalem would be taken by the Babylonians, the land would be ravaged, and the temple would be destroyed. But in this closing section of the book, he had the happy privilege of announcing a bright future for the people of God. The holy city and the Promised Land would be restored (chaps. 33–36), the divided kingdom would be united and protected (chaps. 37–39), and there would be a new temple in which the glory of the Lord would reside (chaps. 40–48). The glory that he had seen depart from the defiled temple (11:23) he saw return to the new temple (43:4-5; 44:4). The kingdom promised by the prophets would be established, and the Messiah, the Son of David, would reign from Jerusalem.

Some students prefer to interpret Ezekiel 33–48 idealistically or symbolically, applying these descriptions "spiritually" to the church today rather than literally to Israel in the future. But if we've been interpreting Ezekiel's prophetic word literally up to this point, what right do we have to change our approach and start interpreting his words symbolically? As Dr. David Cooper said, "When the plain sense of Scripture makes good sense, then we need no other sense." We must face the fact that both approaches—the symbolical and the literal—present problems to the interpreter, but taking Ezekiel's prophecies at face value seems to present fewer problems. Furthermore, seeing literal fulfillment of these prophecies accomplishes the purpose for which

God gave them, the encouragement of the people of Israel. Few nations if any have suffered as Israel has suffered, and to rob God's chosen people of their hope is to make their suffering meaningless.

Our approach will be to assume that these prophecies will have a literal fulfillment and that Israel will one day see her Messiah and share in the glorious kingdom promised by Ezekiel and the other prophets. At the same time, we will seek to apply the basic spiritual lessons taught in these chapters, truths that apply to God's people in the church today.

TEN

Warnings and Promises from the Watchman

It has well been said that the most important thing about prophets is not that they have hindsight or foresight but that they also have *insight*. Prophetic hindsight is important because it helps us deal with the past and understand better what God did and why He did it. Foresight helps us avoid trouble and have hope for the future. But insight helps us better understand ourselves and those around us, and what we must do to become better men and women who do the will of God. In these chapters, Ezekiel exercises all three gifts as he exposes sin, analyzes history, and gives promises for the future. He deals with the sins of the Jewish people (chap. 33), the sins of their leaders (chap. 34), and the sins of the neighboring land of Edom (chap. 35).

1. The sins of the nation (Ezek. 33:1-33)
This chapter reaches back into some of Ezekiel's previous messages and brings together truths that were important to Israel's understanding of God, their situation, and what God wanted them to do. You will find here references to 3:15-27; chapters 5 and 6; 11:14-21; 18:1-32; 20:1-8; and 24:25-27. It's as though the Lord led His servant to combine these basic spiritual truths in

one message so that nobody could say, "I didn't hear what the Lord said to us!" Ezekiel turned the light of God's Word on the nation as a whole (33:1-20), the people left in Judah and Jerusalem (vv. 23-29), and the exiles in Babylon (vv. 21-22, 30-33), and he revealed what was in their hearts and lives.

The entire nation (Ezek. 33:1-20). Every Jew who had ever lived in a walled city knew what Ezekiel was talking about when he referred to the watchmen on the wall, for these watchmen were important to the city's defense. Faithful watchmen kept their eyes focused on the horizon and gave the warning when they saw the enemy approaching. If the watchmen were alert and faithful and the people obedient, lives would be saved; if the watchmen were careless, or the people unconcerned, the city would be captured and people would die.

God had called Ezekiel to be His watchman (3:19-21) and it was his task to hear God's Word of warning and declare it to the people. The faithful watchman had clean hands, but the unfaithful watchman had hands that were stained by the blood of the victims who died because he didn't warn them. Isaiah compared unfaithful watchmen to blind men, dogs that can't bark, and people who can't stay awake (Isa. 56:10). Ezekiel was a faithful watchman who delivered God's message to the Jews in Babylon as well as those back in Judah, and that message was, "Repent—turn from your sins!" The word "turn" is used eight times in this chapter and it describes "repentance." The biblical words translated "repent" simply mean "to change your mind," but this change of mind also involves a change of life. If a thief truly repented, he or she would restore what had been stolen. The liars would confess their deception and ask for forgiveness, and the drunkards would stop their alcohol abuse.

The discussion in Ezekiel 33:10-20 reminds us of 18:1-32 where Ezekiel explained human responsibility before God. The Jews had blamed the older generation for what had happened to the nation, but Ezekiel made it clear that God didn't punish the children for the sins of their fathers. Each person was accountable for his or her own sins and couldn't blame somebody else.

But 33:10 suggests that some of the Jews were now feeling the pain of their sins like a heavy weight on their shoulders, and day after day were "wearing away." However, this feeling of remorse fell far short of real repentance.

We must correctly distinguish regret, remorse, and true repentance. Regret is an activity of the mind; whenever we remember what we've done, we ask ourselves, "Why did I do that?" Remorse includes both the heart and the mind, and we feel disgust and pain, but we don't change our ways. But true repentance includes the mind, the heart, and the will. We change our mind about our sins and agree with what God says about them; we abhor ourselves because of what we have done; and we deliberately turn from our sin and turn to the Lord for His mercy.

When Peter remembered his sin of denying Christ, he repented and sought pardon; when Judas remembered his sin of betraying Christ, he experienced only remorse, and he went out and hanged himself. "For godly sorrow produces repentance to salvation, not to be regretted; but the sorrow of the world produces death" (2 Cor. 7:10, NKJV). If the sinner turns *from* his sins and turns *to* the Lord in faith, he will be forgiven. Paul's message was "repentance toward God, and faith toward our Lord Jesus Christ" (Acts 20:21), and that message is still valid today.

As they did previously (Ezek. 18:21-29), the Jews debated with Ezekiel and affirmed that God wasn't being fair and that His ways were unequal. This response in itself proved that they had not really repented, because repentant sinners don't argue with God's Word. The Jews were saying, "God isn't using standard weights on His scales! He's got the scales fixed!" But their accusation against the Lord was false. As Ezekiel had already told them (vv. 21-29), it wasn't *God's ways* that were false but *their own ways!* It wasn't their responsibility to prove God wrong but to admit that they were wrong!

The people of the land (Ezek. 33:23-29). The Babylonians had left some of the poor people of the land to take care of the fields and the ruins (Jer. 52:16), while the rest who survived the siege were taken to Babylon. The Lord heard what these people were saying: "We have a right to this land because the Lord spared us to live here." After all, when Abraham was just one man,[1] God gave him the land; but the survivors were many and had lived on the land a long time. The very fact that they had survived proved that they were special to the Lord. Therefore, they could claim the land for themselves because the former owners were either dead or in exile.

They had forgotten that Jeremiah had already settled the question of which group was God's choice people, the exiles in Babylon or the survivors in Judah. As recorded in Jeremiah 24, God showed Jeremiah two baskets of figs, one filled with very good figs and the other with very bad figs. The very good figs represented the exiles in Babylon, the remnant God would use to rebuild the temple and restore the nation. The very bad figs were King Zedekiah and the leaders in Jerusalem who disobeyed the Lord by breaking the treaty with Babylon. It's obvious that the remnant in Judah was not considered "special" or "choice" by the Lord.[2]

But Abraham was a righteous man, and the people left in Judah had been living in defiance of God's law! In Ezekiel 33:25-26, Ezekiel listed some of the sins they were committing: eating meat with the blood still in it (Deut. 12:16, 23; Lev. 17:10); worshiping idols (Ex. 20:4-6); murder (v. 13); relying on violence ("stand upon your sword," KJV); and doing abominable things, like committing adultery (v. 14). No, instead of inheriting the land and becoming rich, the people would be slain by the sword, the beasts of the field, or the pestilence that often accompanies war (Ezek. 33:27; see 5:12; 7:15; 12:16; 14:12-21). Instead of the land becoming their prize possession, it would become desolate and enjoy its Sabbath rest (Lev. 26:32-35, 43; 2 Chron. 36:21).

The exiles in Babylon (Ezek. 33:21-22, 30-33). The Babylonian army set fire to Jerusalem on August 14, 586 B.C., and about five months later—January 8, 585 B.C.—a fugitive arrived in Babylon to announce the sad fact that Jerusalem and the temple had been destroyed. This validated the prophecies of Ezekiel and proved that he was indeed the prophet of God (Deut. 18:20-22). The night before he received this news, Ezekiel had been in a prophetic state with God's hand upon him, so he knew that something special was about to be revealed. The hearing of this news brought about the opening of Ezekiel's mouth so that he was no longer mute when he wasn't declaring the message of God (Ezek. 3:26-27). He was now able to converse with people and have a "pastoral" ministry among them apart from his prophetic preaching. For about seven and a half years, Ezekiel had been under this constraint, but now he was free to speak. Certainly the exiles noticed this and would be curious to know what had happened to him.

But Ezekiel knew that the people who came to his house to hear him speak didn't appreciate his ministry or obey what they heard. As the exiles met one another during the day, they would step out of the hot sunlight and discuss the prophet's ministry (v. 30). They even invited people to come with them to hear the preacher! But going to hear the Word of God wasn't a serious thing to them. "Come on, let's have some fun! Let's go hear the prophet tell us what the Lord is saying" (v. 30, NLT). But they weren't concerned about God's truth or their personal responsibility; all they wanted to do was get up-to-date information so they could make money! They listened to God's preacher but refused to obey what God told them to do (James 1:22-25; Ps. 78:36-37; 1 John 3:18). They saw Ezekiel as an entertainer who sang love songs, not as an exhorter who sought to convey God's love to them.

This information could have discouraged the prophet, but the Lord added a message of faith and hope: The day would come when the fulfillment of God's prophetic Word would convince careless people that a prophet had truly been among them. This would mean personal privilege (hearing the Word), personal responsibility (obeying the Word), and personal accountability (being judged by the Word that they had heard, John 12:48).

Believers today have the Word of God readily accessible not only in public meetings, but also in literature, on the Internet, over radio and television, as well as on video and audio tapes and CDs, and we will have much to answer for when we see the Lord. The important thing at the Judgment Seat of Christ won't be how much Bible we studied or learned, but how much we loved and obeyed.

2. The sins of the leaders (Ezek. 34:1-31)

Ezekiel had already exposed the sins of the nation's leaders (chap. 22), but he returned to this theme because it had a bearing on Israel's future. While this message applied to Israel's current situation in Ezekiel's day, it also had application in that future day when the Lord gathers His scattered people back to their land. This message certainly must have brought hope to the exiles as they realized the Lord has not forsaken them but would care for them as a shepherd for his sheep.

When the Lord spoke about "the flock," He was referring to the nation of Israel (34:31). "We are His people, and the sheep of his pasture" (Ps. 100:3; see 77:20; 78:52; 80:1). Moses saw Israel as a flock (Num. 27:17; see 1 Kings 22:17) and so did Jeremiah (Jer. 13:17) and Zechariah (Zech. 10:3). Jesus spoke of "the lost sheep of the house of Israel" (Matt. 10:6; 15:24). Because Jesus called Himself "the Good Shepherd" and "the door of the sheep" (John 10:7, 11), the image of the flock carried over into the church (Acts 20:28-29; 1 Peter 5:2-3). Our English word "pastor" comes from the Latin and means "shepherd."

Exploiting and abusing the sheep (Ezek. 34:1-10). Kings and officers in government were referred to as "shepherds" (2 Sam. 7:7-8; Ps. 78:70-71; Isa. 56:10-11; 63:11; Jer. 23:9-11; 25:18-19). It was their responsibility to care for the people, protect them, and see to it that their needs were met. But the selfish leaders of the kingdom of Judah had abused and exploited the people because they thought only of themselves. They milked the sheep and ate the curds, fleeced the sheep and made garments of the wool, and butchered the sheep and enjoyed the meat, but they failed to care for the sheep and meet their needs. Whenever leaders *take* from their people but don't *give* them something in return, they are exploiting them. But true leaders don't exploit their people—they sacrifice for them. Jesus the Shepherd set the example by laying down His life for His flock (John 10:10).

The leaders not only exploited the sheep but they also abused them by neglecting to meet their needs. Sheep require constant care, but the leaders didn't manage the nation's affairs for the sake of the sheep but for their own profit. They didn't care for them at all. If the leaders' sins of commission were bad, their sins of omission were worse. They didn't minister to the sick and injured, nor did they seek for the lost and scattered sheep. They ruled only with force and cruelty. Three times Ezekiel accused them of allowing the sheep to be scattered, and a scattered flock without a shepherd is vulnerable and easily attacked by beasts of prey (Jer. 50:6). Because the leaders made selfish and unwise decisions, the nation fell apart and the flock was scattered.

Rescuing the flock (Ezek. 34:11-22). Was there any hope for God's scattered people? Yes, because the Lord would come to deliver His flock from their oppressors and gather them to Himself. In Ezekiel's time, the Lord brought His people back from Babylon; but the picture here is certainly much broader than that, for the Lord spoke about "countries" (v. 13). Ezekiel promises that in the end times, the Lord will gather His flock "from all places where they have been scattered" (v. 12) and bring them back to their own land where He will be their Shepherd (Matt. 24:31).

It's difficult to apply this prophecy to the return of the remnant after their exile in Babylon, and even more difficult to "spiritualize" it and apply it to the church today. The prophet is speaking about a literal future regathering of Israel, a topic that is mentioned frequently in Ezekiel's book (Ezek. 11:17; 20:34, 41-42; 28:25; 36:24; 37:21-25; 38:8). This promise of regathering is a part of God's covenant with the Jews (Deut. 30:1-10), and the Lord always keeps His promises. (See also Isa. 11:11-12; Jer. 23:3-8; and Micah 2:12; 4:6-8.) After He gathers His people, He will see to it that none of the "fat cattle" who preyed on the weaker ones will push them around, muddy their drinking water, or tramp down their pastures. The "fat [sleek] and strong" in Ezekiel 34:16 refer to the leaders who took advantage of the people. Don't read into "rams and he-goats" (v. 17) the New Testament image of "sheep and goats" as found in Matthew

25:31-46, because in Bible times, it was customary for shepherds to have both sheep and goats in the flocks.

Protecting the flock (Ezek. 34:23-31). This is definitely a prophecy of future events, because the returned remnant didn't have an august ruler caring for them, nor did "showers of blessing" come to the land. The economic situation at the beginning was difficult, the harvests were poor, and the peoples of the land were opposed to any Jewish presence there. But when Israel is regathered to her land in the end times, the Messiah will rule over them and be their Shepherd-King. The "prince" (v. 24) will not be King David, resurrected and enthroned, but the Lord Jesus Christ whom Israel will receive and trust when they see Him (Zech. 12:9-13:1; see Jer. 23:5; 30:8-10; Hosea 3:5). Ezekiel mentions "David the prince" in 37:24-25; 45:22; 46:4, and these references point to the Messiah.

Agriculture in the land of Israel depended on the early and latter rains from the Lord, and He promised to send the rain faithfully if the people honored His covenant (Lev. 26:1-5; Deut. 28:9-14). But if they disobeyed Him, the heavens would turn to brass and the ground to iron (Deut. 11:13-17; 28:23-24). If the people repented and sought His forgiveness, He would send the rain and heal the land (Deut. 30; 2 Chron. 7:12-14).

The Lord also promised that the people would be safe in the land and not be oppressed by the peoples around them. Except during the reigns of David and Solomon, the nation of Israel has been attacked, conquered, and ravaged by one nation after another, but this will cease when Messiah is on the throne. A "covenant of peace" would govern the land (Ezek. 34:25; see 37:26), which probably refers to the New Covenant that Jeremiah promised in Jeremiah 31:31-34. The law of God would be written on the hearts of the people and they all would know the Lord and obey His will.

Neither the pain of scarcity nor the shame of defeat will rob the Jewish people of the blessings the Lord has planned for them. In the past, their sins forced the Lord to turn His face against them; but in the future kingdom, He will smile upon them and dwell with them. Ezekiel had watched the glory of God leave the temple (Ezek. 11:22-23), but he would also see God's glory return (43:1-5). The name of the holy city would become "Jehovah Shammah—the Lord is there" (48:35).

3. The sins of Edom (Ezek. 35:1-15)

The Lord had already pronounced judgment on Edom through Isaiah (Isa. 34; 63:1-6), Jeremiah (Jer. 49:7-22), and Ezekiel (25:12-14), but now He did it again and added some details. Mount Seir is another name for Edom, the nation founded by Esau, Jacob's twin brother. "Edom" means "red" and was a nickname given to Esau (Gen. 25:30). Esau was a man of the world who had no spiritual desires and willingly sold his birthright to his brother Jacob. Esau fought with his brother even in their mother's womb (vv. 21-26) and hated his brother because the Lord had chosen Jacob to receive the blessings of the covenant. This hatred was passed on from generation to generation and the Edomites maintained what God called "a perpetual hatred" (v. 5; 25:15; Amos 1:11-12; Obadiah). This hatred was no doubt like some of the "ethnic wars" that the world has seen today.

Once again, the Lord reminded the Edomites of their great sin against their brethren when they assisted the Babylonians in attacking the Jews during the siege of Jerusalem. What their founder Esau vowed to do in his day, they accomplished in their day when they killed their own blood relatives (Gen. 47:41). In Ezekiel 35:6, the word "blood" in the KJV should read "bloodshed." The Edomites pursued the Jews to kill them, so bloodshed would pursue them. The Edomites carried on a perpetual hatred against Israel, so the land of Edom would receive a perpetual desolation. Edom would be no more.

Was this a just judgment? Yes, it was, and the prophet gave the reasons why the destruction of Edom was an act of righteous judgment. For one thing, the descendants of Esau were greedy and wanted to claim the conquered nations of Judah and Samaria for themselves, completely ignoring the will of the Lord. God had given the land of Canaan to Abraham and his descendants, and that meant Jacob and not Esau. During Israel's march to Canaan, they were warned not to meddle with the Edomites because God had assigned their land to them and they would not inherit any land in Canaan (Deut. 2:1-7). But the Edomites wanted to change God's plans and annul God's covenant and take the land for themselves. When the Babylonians invaded Judah in 606 B.C., the Lord was there fulfilling His own purposes (Ezek. 35:10) and He saw what the Edomites did.

The Lord also saw their anger (v. 11) and promised to repay them in kind, for nations as well as individuals reap what they sow. He heard their blasphemous words against their brothers the Jews, how they rejoiced because the land of Israel was being ravaged and plundered by the Babylonian invaders. But they weren't blaspheming men, they were blaspheming God and boasting in their pride as though they would escape judgment. In their arrogance, Edom rejoiced over the fall of Israel; but one day, the whole earth would rejoice over the fall of Edom!

God's promise to the Jews was that one day they would no longer be a prey to the other nations (34:28), and this chapter explains why: God will deal with their enemies and remove them from the face of the earth. "You will be desolate, O Mount Seir, you and all of Edom" (35:15, NIV).

ELEVEN

From Restoration to Reunion

Our hope is lost!" That's what the Jewish exiles were saying to each other as they "pined away" in Babylon (37:11; 33:10), and from the human point of view, the statement was true. But if they had listened to their prophets, they would have had hope in the Lord and looked forward with anticipation. Jeremiah had written to them that they would be in Babylon for seventy years, and that God's thoughts toward them were of peace and not of evil (Jer. 29:10). Ezekiel had given them God's promise that He would gather His people and take them back to their land (Ezek. 11:17; 20:34, 41-42; 28:25). A Latin proverb says, "Where there is life, there is hope," but the reverse is also true: where there is hope, we find reason to live. Swiss theologian Emil Brunner wrote, "What oxygen is to the lungs, such is hope for the meaning of life."

In his previous messages, Ezekiel looked back and reproved the people because of their sins. Now he looks ahead and encourages the people by telling them what the Lord will do for Israel in the future. These promises go beyond the ending of the Babylonian Captivity and anticipate the end times. The Jewish people will be gathered to their land, the land will be cleansed and restored, and the nation will have a new temple and the presence of the glory of the Lord. The future of Israel can be summarized in four words: restoration, regeneration, resurrection, and reunion.

1. Restoration: the land healed (Ezek. 36:1-15)

God gave the land of Israel to the Jews as a part of the Abrahamic Covenant (Gen. 12:1-3; 13:14-18; 15:7-21). That settled their *ownership* of the land, but their *possession* and *enjoyment* of the land depended on their faith and obedience (Lev. 26). The Christian life is similar. We *enter* God's family by trusting Jesus Christ (John 3:16; Eph. 2:8-9), but we *enjoy* God's family by believing His promises and obeying His will (2 Cor. 6:18–7:1). Disobedient children have to be chastened (Heb. 12), and God often had to chasten the people of Israel because of their rebellion and disobedience.

Ezekiel had set his face against Mount Seir, which represented the land of Edom (Ezek. 35), but now he addressed "the mountains of Israel" as representative of the land of Israel. The Babylonians had ravaged and plundered the Promised Land and the neighboring nations (especially Edom) had tried to possess the land (36:10). Instead of assisting the Jews, the neighbors had ridiculed them and even helped the Babylonians loot the city of Jerusalem. Why? Because of their long-standing hatred of the Jews and a desire to possess the land of Israel. "Aha, even the ancient high places are ours in possession" (v. 2).

But the Lord knew what the enemy was saying and doing, and He determined that there would be serious consequences because of their decisions. That's why you find the word "therefore" six times in this section (vv. 3-7, 14). First, the fire of God's jealous love would burn against Israel's enemies because of the way they had treated His people and His land (vv. 4-6; Lev. 25:23). He even took an oath (Ezek. 36:7) that the nations would be repaid for the way they treated the Jews. They had taunted and ridiculed the Jews, but now they themselves would be put to shame.

Ezekiel described that future day when the land would be healed and once again produce abundant flocks, herds, and harvests (vv. 8-9). This was a part of God's covenant with Israel

(Lev. 26:3-5). The land would not only be fruitful, but it also would be safe and secure (Ezek. 36:10-12). The combination of war, pestilence, and wild beasts had decreased the Jewish population (6:1-8; 7:15; 12:16), but God had promised they would be as numerous as the dust of the earth and the stars of the heavens (Gen. 13:16; 15:5). If the nation was to fulfill its divine purposes on earth, the people had to multiply.

God accused the mountains of Israel of depriving the Jews of their children (Ezek. 36:12-14, see NIV). This may refer to the fact that the pagan shrines were in the high places, and there some of the Jews offered their own children to the heathen gods. But that would end, because the exile in Babylon cured the Jews of their idolatry, and in the future kingdom, only the true and living God would be worshiped. In Ezekiel 40–48, Ezekiel will have more to say about the restored land of Israel when Messiah reigns on the throne of David in Jerusalem.

Since the founding of the nation of Israel in 1948, great progress has been made by the Jewish people in reclaiming the land. There has been a great deal of reforestation and irrigation, and the waste places are being transformed. As wonderful as this is, it is nothing compared with what the Lord will do when His people are gathered back to their land from the nations of the world. "Even the wilderness will rejoice in those days. The desert will blossom with flowers. Yes, there will be an abundance of flowers and singing and joy! The deserts will become as green as the mountains of Lebanon, as lovely as Mount Carmel's pastures and the plain of Sharon. There the Lord will display His glory, the splendor of our God" (Isa. 35:1-2, NLT).

2. Regeneration: the people cleansed (Ezek. 36:16-38)

The Jewish people forgot that the land belonged to the Lord, for He said, "The land is Mine" (Lev. 25:23). In fact, the whole earth belongs to the Lord (Ex. 19:5; Ps. 24:1), and we have no right to abuse the natural resources He shares with us.

God's indictment against His people (Ezek. 36:16-23). Israel was guilty of two great sins, the first of which was *polluting God's land* (*vv. 16-19*). Long before the Babylonians had swept through the kingdom of Judah, the sins of the leaders and the people had polluted the so-called "holy land." When God's people disobeyed God's law and behaved like the heathen nations around them, they defiled the land and broke the covenant (Lev. 18:26-30). Not only did they worship idols and sacrifice their children's innocent blood, but they also shed blood when they falsely accused the poor and needy in court and led them out to die. Each act of disobedience only polluted the land more, until the Lord was so grieved by their rebellion that He had the land vomit them out, and He sent them to Babylon. In our contemporary world, we wonder how much land is being polluted by the destruction of innocent babies, the murders of innocent people, including children in school, and the general disregard for both the laws of man and the law of God.

Their second sin was that of *profaning God's name before the Gentiles (Ezek. 36:20-23)*. It was bad enough that they had polluted the land God allowed them to enjoy, but they also profaned God's holy name instead of being godly witnesses in the Gentile lands where He sent them (vv. 20-23). They had imitated the pagans for so long that they felt right at home among them and adopted more of their ways. During the exile, there was a godly remnant that remained true to the Lord, but in general, the Jews tended to forget their calling as the people of God. Five times in this paragraph we're told that the Jews profaned the name of God before the pagans before whom they had been sent to be a light (Isa. 42:6; 49:6). In spite of their disobedience, what an opportunity the Lord gave the Jews to introduce the Gentiles to the true and living God!

The Jews were separated from their temple, now destroyed, and from the things necessary for Jewish worship, but the Lord was still with them and could see their hearts. The Jews had profaned God's name by defiling the sanctuary (Ezek. 5:11; 22:26), but He had promised to be "a little sanctuary" for them there in Babylon (11:16). They had profaned the Sabbaths (22:8; 23:38), but they knew what day it was in Babylon and could still seek to obey God. The still had the Law and the Prophets and could meditate on the Word and praise the Lord. Instead of the Jews sanctifying God's name among the heathen, they profaned His name by their lack of separation and godly witness; but is the church today any different? Do we live in such commitment to Christ that the world sits up and takes notice and wants to hear what we have to say?

The Lord promises to change the people only because He desires to sanctify and glorify His great name (36:22). In the last days, when the Lord gathers His people back to their land, everything the Lord will do for them will be because of His grace and not because they deserve it. God didn't give them the land because of their righteousness (Deut. 9:6), and He won't restore the land because of anything good they have done. God in His grace gives us what we don't deserve, and in His mercy He doesn't give us what we do deserve! All that we have in Christ comes from God's grace (Eph. 1:7; 2:8-10) and was designed for God's glory (1:6, 11, 14).

God's transformation of His people (Ezek. 36:24-38). In the last days, when God brings His chosen people back to the Promised Land (v. 24), He will change them spiritually; for, after all, only a transformed people can enjoy a transformed land. The spiritual experience described in this section illustrates what happens to every sinner who trusts Jesus Christ.

First, God will *cleanse them from their sins*, and this is pictured by "sprinkling" (vv. 25, 29; 37:23). According to the Mosaic Law, every Jew who became defiled[1] had to be cleansed before he or she could return to the camp and the blessings of the covenant community. This was accomplished either by bathing in running water or by being sprinkled with water prepared for that purpose (Lev. 14:1-9; Num. 19; 8:5-7; Heb. 10:22). Of course, water can never change the heart, but this is only a picture of the gracious forgiveness we have through faith. God forgives trusting sinners because of the death of Jesus on the cross (Eph. 1:7). When believers confess their sins to the Lord, they are cleansed because of Christ's blood (1 John 1:9).

Second, the Lord will *give them a new heart (Ezek. 36:26)*. Ezekiel had already spoken about this inward change (11:18-20; 18:31), the kind of change that the Lord yearned for Israel to experience before they entered the Promised Land. "Oh, that they had such a heart in them that they would fear Me and always keep all My commandments"(Deut. 5:29, NKJV). The Prophet Jeremiah shared the same promise that Ezekiel gave: "Then I will give them a heart to know Me, that I am the Lord; and they shall be My people, and I will be their God" (Jer. 24:7, NKJV). Jeremiah spoke about the New Covenant God would make with the Jews, a covenant not written on stones but on their hearts and in their minds (31:31-33; 32:29; see Isa. 59:21; Heb. 8:8-13). A "stony heart" is a hard heart, one that doesn't receive God's Word and nurture spiritual growth (Ezek. 2:4; 3:7).

Third, the Lord will *give them the Holy Spirit within (Ezek. 36:27)*. It is the Spirit who accomplishes these divine miracles in the hearts of those who trust the Lord for salvation. He gives us a new heart and a new spirit and also a new desire to love the Lord and obey Him. The Holy Spirit is given like refreshing water upon parched ground, and this produces the "fruit of the Spirit" in our lives (Isa. 44:3; Gal. 5:22-23). The witness of the Spirit in the heart is proof that the person has been born of God (Rom. 8:9, 14-17; Eph. 1:13-14). Because you have God's Spirit within, you share in the divine nature (2 Peter 1:1-4) and therefore want to obey the divine will. It is nature that determines conduct. Dogs act like dogs because they have a dog's nature, and God's people act like they belong to God because they have God's nature within (1 John 3:9). Ezekiel will deal again with this gift of the Spirit in Ezekiel 37:14 and 39:29.

Fourth, the Lord will *claim them again as His people (Ezek. 36:28)*. It will be like a renewal of the covenant, for they will live in the land, He will be their God and they will be His people. This will be a permanent arrangement, for they will no longer rebel against the Lord and disobey His will.

Fifth, the Lord will *cause the land to flourish (vv. 29-30, 33-35)*. Under the covenant God made with Israel before they entered

Canaan, He agreed to bless them and meet their needs if they would obey Him (Lev. 26:1-13; Deut. 28:1-14). When you read these promises, you are amazed at what the Jews gave up when they turned from serving God to serving idols. But when Israel enters into the promised kingdom, God will bless them and make the land like the garden of Eden (Ezek. 36:35). The land will yield its harvests and the people will be enriched by the blessing of the Lord. The cities will be rebuilt and the ruins removed. It will be a wonderful new land for the new people of God. The beauty and fruitfulness of the land will be a testimony to the nations (v. 36).

Sixth, the people *will abhor their sins (Ezek. 36:31-32)*. When some people remember their sins, they enjoy them again in the dirty depths of their imagination. This is evidence that they really haven't judged them and repented. When true children of God remember their past disobedience, they're ashamed of themselves and abhor themselves because of what they have done to the Lord, themselves, and others. "You who love the Lord, hate evil" (Ps. 97:10, NKJV). "Abhor that which is evil; cleave to that which is good" (Rom. 12:9). One of the evidences of the Spirit's presence within is a growing sensitivity to sin and a strong desire to turn away from it.

A seventh blessing will be *fellowship with the Lord (Ezek. 36:37)*. In Ezekiel's day, the people couldn't inquire of the Lord or pray and be heard because they had sin in their hearts (14:1-5; 20:1-3, 30-31). God even told the Prophet Jeremiah not to pray for the people (Jer. 7:16; 11:14; 14:11). But under the New Covenant, the people will have fellowship with the Lord and be able to pray to Him.

The eighth blessing will be *the multiplication of the population (Ezek. 36:37-38)*. As in chapter 34, God pictures His people as a flock of sheep, and every shepherd wants to see his flock increase. The Jewish population was greatly reduced during the Babylonian invasion, but the Lord will bless His people and cause them to be fruitful and multiply (see 36:12-13). The picture here is of the men going to Jerusalem for the annual Passover feast, bringing animal sacrifices with them. The number of animals in Jerusalem would increase greatly, and that's the way the Jewish people will increase in their kingdom.

Finally, as the result of all these blessings, *the Lord will be glorified*. Israel didn't glorify God in their land or the temple, nor did they glorify Him in the countries to which they were scattered. But the day will come when God will be glorified by His people and the glory of the Lord will return to the land.

Every born-again believer sees a parallel here with their own experience of faith in Christ. The Lord has washed us (1 Cor. 6:9-11), given us new hearts and His Holy Spirit within, and because of this, we should have a holy hatred for sin. We have the privilege of communion with God and prayer for our needs, plus a desire within to do His will. God wants to make our lives abundantly fruitful so we will glorify His name. The Lord has made us a part of His New Covenant (Heb. 8; 10) so that our union with Him through Christ is eternal and unchanging. Hallelujah, what a Savior![2]

3. Resurrection: the nation reborn (Ezek. 37:1-14)

Ezekiel has told the people the Lord's promise to restore the land and regenerate His people. But what about the nation itself, a nation divided (Israel and Judah) and without a king or a temple? The remnant would return to the ravaged land and rebuild the temple and the city, but none of the blessings Ezekiel promised would come to them at that time. No, the Prophet Ezekiel was looking far down the corridor of time to the end of the age when Jesus the Messiah would return and claim His people. Ezekiel told the people that the dead nation would one day be raised to life, and the divided nation would be united![3]

The dry bones (Ezek. 37:1-3). At the beginning of Ezekiel's ministry, the Spirit transported him to sit among the discouraged exiles by the canal (3:14ff). Later, the Spirit took him in visions to Jerusalem (8:3ff), to the temple gate and then back to Babylon (11:1, 24). Now the Spirit brought him in a vision to a valley filled with many bleached bones, scattered on the ground, the skeletons of corpses long ago decomposed and devoured by carrion-eating birds and animals. These people were slain (37:9), and they may have been soldiers in the Jewish army (v. 10).

It was a humiliating thing for the body of a dead Jew not to be washed, wrapped, and buried with dignity in a grave or a tomb. These bodies were left on the battlefield to become food for the vultures to eat and objects for the sun to bleach. But the Lord had warned Israel in the covenant He made with them that their sins would lead to just that kind of shameful experience. "The Lord will cause you to be defeated before your enemies....Your carcasses shall be food for all the birds of the air and the beasts of the earth, and no one shall frighten them away" (Deut. 28:25-26, NKJV). Jeremiah was preaching this same message in Jerusalem: "I [the Lord] will give them into the hand of their enemies and into the hand of those who seek their life. Their dead bodies shall be for meat for the birds of the heaven and the beasts of the earth" (Jer. 34:20, NKJV).

The Lord told Ezekiel to walk around among the bones so he could appreciate their vast number and see how dry they were. As a priest, Ezekiel was never to be defiled by the dead, but this was a vision and the bones were not toxic. The prophet must have been wondering why the Lord gave him this vision, but the Lord's question gave him the answer: "Can these bones live?" From the human point of view, the answer is no, but from the divine point of view, nothing is impossible. It is God who "gives life to the dead and calls those things which do not exist as though they did" (Rom. 4:17). Ezekiel's reply didn't question the power of God; it only expressed the prophet's conviction that God knew what He was going to do and was able to do it.

The dead army (Ezek. 37:4-8). Ezekiel had prophesied to the mountains (6:2; 36:1) and to the forests (20:47), and now he is commanded to prophesy to the dead bones. The Word of the Lord is "living and powerful" (Heb. 4:12); it not only *has* life but it *imparts* life (1 Peter 1:23). "The words that I speak to you, are spirit, and they are life" (John 6:63, NKJV). God's word of command in Ezekiel 37:4 is followed by His word of promise in verses 5 and 6. Ezekiel believed the promise and obeyed the command, and the bones came together. Then the skeletons were covered with flesh and skin so that what was lying there in the valley looked like a sleeping army. The bodies lacked only one thing: life.

The living army (Ezek. 37:9-14). God commanded Ezekiel to prophesy to the wind and told him what to say. In the Hebrew language, the word *ruah* can mean wind, breath, spirit, or Spirit. Jesus made use of this when He spoke to Nicodemus about the blowing of the wind and the new birth through the Spirit (John 3:5-8). There's also a reference here to the creation of Adam in Genesis 2. At his creation, Adam was complete physically, but he had no life until the breath of God entered into him (v. 7). When Ezekiel spoke the living Word of God, the breath from God entered the dead bodies and they lived and stood to their feet.

The Lord then explained to His servant the meaning of the vision. The dead dry bones represent the whole Jewish nation, both Israel and Judah, a divided nation and a dead nation, like bleached bones on a battlefield. Israel's situation seemed hopeless, but "with God, all things are possible" (Matt. 19:26). There will come a day when God's living Word of command will go forth and call His people from their "graves," the nations to which they have been scattered across the world (Ezek. 37:21; Jer. 31:8; Matt. 24:31). The children of Israel will come together, but the nation will not have spiritual life until they see their Messiah, believe on Him, and receive the gift of the Holy Spirit of life (Ezek. 39:29; Zech. 12:9–13:1). The nation will be born—and born again—"in a day" (Isa. 66:7-9).[4]

Of course, there's a spiritual application in this vision for any individual or ministry that is in need of new life from God. Too often God's people are like that standing army, lifelike but not alive. How does the life come? Through the Holy Spirit using the faithful proclamation of the Word of God. Said Charles Spurgeon, "Decayed churches can most certainly be revived by the preaching of the Word, accompanied by the coming of the heavenly breath from the four winds."[5] From time to time, in response to His people's prayers, the Lord has seen fit to send a new "breath of life" to His church and His servants, and for that blessing we should be praying today.

4. Reunion: the kingdoms united (Ezek. 37:15-28)

The nation of Israel was a united people until after the death of Solomon. His son's unwise and arrogant policies divided the kingdom in 931 B.C., with ten tribes forming the Northern Kingdom of Israel, also called Ephraim or Samaria, and the tribes of Judah and Benjamin forming the Southern Kingdom of Judah. The Northern Kingdom soon went into idolatry and apostasy and in 722 B.C. was taken by Assyria, but the kingdom of Judah had some unusually good kings and maintained the Davidic line and the ministry at the temple. However, toward the end of Israel's political history, some very weak kings reigned and the nation drifted into idolatry and unbelief. The Lord finally brought the Babylonians to chasten His people. There is a political Israel today, but the majority of the Jewish people are scattered around the world.

This is the last of Ezekiel's "action sermons." He took two sticks, each one to represent one of the divisions of the Jewish nation. One he labeled "For Judah" and the other "For Joseph." Like a performer before an audience, the prophet announced that the two sticks would become one in his hands—and they did! The people saw what he did but they didn't understand what he meant by it. He explained that the Lord would gather the people together to one place, their own land of Israel. He would make them one nation, obedient to one king, and (most important) worshiping one God. There would be no more idols or disobedience to the law of the Lord.

But what would maintain the unity of the people? For one thing, the Lord would cleanse them and renew spiritual life within them so that they no longer had any ambitions to compete with one another. Old jealousies and enmities would be gone (Isa. 11:13) and Israel and Judah would together humble themselves and seek the Lord (Jer. 50:4; Hosea 11:1). Another factor is that their one king would be the Messiah, and He would shepherd them with love and grace. He would be their "prince forever" (Ezek. 37:25) and serve as the Prince of Peace (Isa. 9:6).

Third, the Lord would so order and bless the land that the nation would be one (Ezek. 37:25). This will be further explained in chapter 45. The nation would be governed by a "covenant of peace" (37:26; 34:22-25), which is the "New Covenant" that Jeremiah wrote about in Jeremiah 31:31-34. But central to the nation's unity will be the new temple (Ezek. 37:26-28) where the glory of God will dwell. In their wilderness days, Israel had the tabernacle to unite the camp of Israel, with each tribe assigned a specific place to pitch their tents. The temple in Jerusalem was also a source of unity, for three times a year the men had to go to Jerusalem to celebrate feasts, and the people were allowed to offer sacrifices only at the temple.

In chapters 40–48, Ezekiel will go into detail describing this future temple and its ministries. God called it "my tabernacle" (37:27) because the Hebrew word means "a dwelling place."[6] God's presence with His people will sanctify the land, the temple, and the nation, just as He promised in His covenant (Lev. 26:11-12). The nations of the earth will come to worship the Lord with His people Israel (Isa. 2:1-5) and "the earth shall be filled with the knowledge of the glory of the Lord, as the waters cover the sea" (Hab. 2:14).

Whether it's the children of Israel or the saints in the church today, the Lord wants His people to be united. "Behold, how good and how pleasant it is for brethren to dwell together in unity" (Ps. 133:1). Paul appealed to the believers in Corinth to cultivate unity in the church (1 Cor. 1:10), and he exhorted the Ephesian believers to "make every effort to keep the unity of the Spirit through the bond of peace" (Eph. 4:3, NIV). Sometimes it takes prayer, sacrifice, and patience to maintain the unity of God's people, but it's important that we do so. Jesus prayed that His people might be one and manifest to the lost world the living unity between Christ and His church and among believers and local churches (John 17:20-23). A divided church is not a strong church or a church bearing witness to the grace and glory of God. God's people today need the fresh wind of the Spirit to give us new life from God and new love for one another.

TWELVE

God Protects the Nation

M any Bible scholars consider this section of Ezekiel to rank among the most difficult prophetic passages in Scripture and they don't all agree in their interpretations. Some have identified this invasion with the Battle of Armageddon, described in Revelation 16:13-16 and 19:11-21, but the contrasts between these two events are too obvious.[1] Others see Ezekiel 38–39 as a description of an "ideal battle" that assured the Jews in exile of God's power to protect His people. While the assurance is certainly there, this approach doesn't explain the many details recorded in these two chapters. We will approach these chapters assuming that they are describing actual events.

The reference to "Gog and Magog" in Revelation 20:7-9 has led some students to place this invasion *after* the millennium, but this interpretation also has its problems. The army described in verse 8 will come from the four corners of the earth, while Gog's army will be comprised of men from six nations and will invade from the north. Also, if fire from heaven devours the army mentioned in verse 8, why would it be necessary to spend seven months burying the bodies and seven years (into eternity?) burning the weapons? The words "Gog and Magog" are probably used to relate the two prophetic events but not to equate them. Both Ezekiel and John describe attacks against Jerusalem and the Jews, and in both events, the Lord miraculously delivers His people.

A suggested scenario. Before we examine Ezekiel 38–39, we should review the "prophetic situation" prior to this invasion of the Holy Land. From our present point of view, the next crisis event on God's prophetic calendar is the rapture of the church, an event that can occur at any time (1 Thes. 4:13-18). Jesus Christ will come in the air and call His people to be with Him in heaven. According to Daniel 9:24-27[2], the nation of Israel will make an agreement with the head of a ten-nation European coalition to protect them for seven years so they can rebuild their temple in Jerusalem. *We don't know how much time elapses between the rapture of the church and the signing of this covenant.* It's the signing of the covenant that triggers the start of the seven-year Tribulation period described in Matthew 24:1-28 and Revelation 6–19.

After three and one-half years, this European leader will emerge as the Antichrist (the Beast). He will break the covenant with Israel, set up his own image in the Jewish temple, and try to force the world to worship and obey him (Dan. 9:27; 2 Thes. 2:1-12; Matt. 24:15; Rev. 13). During the last three and one-half years years of the Tribulation period, the world will experience "the wrath of God," and the period will climax with the return of Christ to the earth to defeat Satan and the Beast and establish His kingdom. That's when the Battle of Armageddon will be fought.

If this is the correct sequence of prophetic events, then during the first half of the Tribulation period, Israel will be in her land, protected by the strongest political leader in the world. It will be a time of peace and safety when the other nations won't threaten them (Ezek. 38:8, 11, 14). Since we don't know how much time will elapse between the rapture of the church and the signing of the covenant, it's possible that the Jews and this powerful European leader will complete their negotiations very soon after the saints have been taken out. We don't know how long it will take for Israel to rebuild the temple, but it will be complete by the middle of this seven-year period. That's when this powerful European leader will break the covenant, reveal himself as the man of sin, and set up his own image in the temple.

With this suggested scenario in mind, perhaps we can better understand the invasion described in these two chapters.

1. Before the invasion (Ezek. 38:1-13)
The leader of this army is named Gog, ruler of "Magog," which means "the land of Gog." It was located between the Black Sea and the Caspian Sea. The title "chief prince" can be translated "prince of Rosh," a place that hasn't been located yet on the map of the ancient world. But if "prince of Rosh" is the correct translation, then this man will rule over Rosh, Meshech, and Tubal. The latter two places are located in eastern Asia Minor along with Gomer and Beth-Togarmah.[3] Prince Gog's allies will be Persia (Iran), Cush (ancient Ethiopia), Put (Libya), Gomer, and Beth Togarmah, both located near the Black Sea.

Since all these nations except Put, Cush, and Persia are located north of Israel, it's tempting to identify Rosh with Russia and therefore Meschech with Moscow and Tubal with Tobolsk, both cities in Russia; but we would have a hard time defending this on linguistic grounds. This doesn't rule out the participation of modern Russia, since it is located in the north (vv. 6, 15; 39:2), but neither does it demand it.

The prophet encourages his listeners (and readers) by telling them the end of the story even before he begins: God will defeat this vast coalition army and rescue His people Israel in their land (38:3-4a). This invasion won't occur until "after many days…in the latter years" (v. 8), at a time when Israel is enjoying peace and security under the protection of the political leader who signed the covenant. Prince Gog and his allies will think that Israel is an easy target, but they forget the protection of the God of Jacob.

This raises the perplexing question: Why would Gog and his allies want to attack Israel at all, knowing that a powerful ten-nation European alliance had promised to defend the helpless

Jews? The overt purpose stated in verses 12-13 is to seize the wealth in the land of Israel, a purpose that the other nations understood. But if our suggested scenario is correct, perhaps these nations also want to prevent the rebuilding of the Jewish temple. The nations named are identified with Islam, and they would want to protect the "Dome of the Rock," a revered Muslim monument[4] which has stood on the temple site for centuries.[5]

Whatever Prince Gog's thinking might be, it's clear that it is the Lord who brings this army out (v. 4, NASB; vv. 16-17). Prince Gog thinks he has worked out the whole scheme (vv. 10-11), but it is God who is in charge. The northern coalition comes into the land of Israel confident of victory, but they are walking into a trap.

2. During the invasion (Ezek. 38:14–39:8)
Enemies have frequently attacked Israel from the north, including Assyria, Babylon, and the Hittites. Prince Gog and his horde will swoop down from the north, "like a cloud to cover the land," totally ignorant that the God of Israel intended their destruction. The decisions made in the war room of Magog will conform to the will of the Lord who planned this invasion for His own purposes.[6] God in no way violated their own freedom to think and decide, but He overruled Gog's decisions for His own purposes, just as He did with Babylon (21:18-24). "The lot is cast into the lap, but its every decision is from the Lord" (Prov. 16:33, NKJV). "The king's heart is in the hand of the Lord, like the rivers of water; He turns it wherever He wishes" (Prov. 21:1, NKJV).

What does the leader of the European coalition think when this undeclared war begins? Surely a man of his intelligence would have known that these nations were mobilizing.[7] Having just entered into the seven-year covenant with Israel, he had to act to protect them; but he would also want to make the best use of the crisis to promote his own agenda. After all, he had agreed to protect Israel so that he might one day use their temple for his own evil purposes. Perhaps he could use Gog and his allies to hasten the day when he would become world dictator.

But before the European leader has time to act, God will intervene in His jealous wrath and wipe out the invading forces! First, He will cause an earthquake that will be felt around the world (Ezek. 38:19-20). This earthquake doesn't seem to fit any of the earthquakes mentioned in the Book of the Revelation (Rev. 6:12; 8:5; 11:13, 19; 16:18), but in some places on the earth, the damage will be terrible. The shaking of the land of Israel will throw the invading army into panic and the men will begin to slaughter one another. Then God will send rain, hailstones, and fire and brimstone (sulfur) from heaven as well as a plague on the army, and this will end the invasion, leaving so many corpses that it will take seven months to bury all of them (Ezek. 39:12).

The description of the defeat in chapter 38 focuses on the army, but in 39:1-8, the focus is on the leader of the army, Prince Gog of Magog. In the *Authorized Version*, verse 2 gives the impression that one sixth of the invading army will be spared and sent home humiliated. However, the verse is stating that it is God who brings Prince Gog into the land and allows him to try to attack the people of Israel. "And I will turn you about, and will lead you on, and will cause you to come up from the uttermost parts of the north, and will lead you against the mountains of Israel" (AMP).

God not only leads the prince, but He also disarms him so that he is helpless before his enemy (v. 3). Instead of slaughtering the Jews, his soldiers will themselves be slaughtered and become food for the vultures and the beasts of the field. But the Lord won't stop with His judgment of the armies that invade Israel; He will also send a fiery judgment on the land of Magog! (v. 6)

In verse 23, the Lord gives three reasons for bringing Gog and his armies to Israel and then defeating them so dramatically. First, this victory will reveal the *greatness* of the Lord as He displays His power before the nations (v. 23). There is no evidence that the Israelite forces ever confronted the invading army. The Lord intervened and used weapons that no general on earth could use—rain, hailstones, and fire and brimstone from heaven! In fact, the invading army will get out of control and destroy itself! This victory will also reveal *His holiness* as He judges the sins of the leader from Magog and deals with his enmity against the Jews. The wealth of the Holy Land belongs to the Lord, and He has shared it with His people Israel, and the other nations have no right to exploit it.[8] Third, the victory will *make Jehovah known to the Gentile nations*, and the world will see that the God of Israel is the only true and living God.

But perhaps the most important reason is given in 39:7, that *Israel will recognize the holiness of God and be convicted of her own sins*. During their time of dispersion in the other nations, the Jews had profaned the name of the Lord (36:19-23). Now God has gathered them back into their own land, but they are still not a converted people; otherwise they would confess God's holiness and greatness. It will not be until they see their Messiah that they will loathe their sins, put their trust in Christ and become a regenerated people (37:25-38). But this great victory will be the beginning of their spiritual experience with the Lord. Both Israel and the nations will know that Jehovah is the Lord, the Holy One of Israel. During the difficult Tribulation period, did the Jewish people remember God's great victory over the invaders? Did it encourage their faith? Did any of the Gentiles remember and turn to God?

We're tempted to speculate on how the European leader responded to this remarkable series of events. No sooner did he guarantee his protection to Israel than a coalition of nations invaded Palestine and he couldn't do anything about it. Perhaps he said that the "forces of nature" were under his control! At least the Jews could build their temple without interference from the neighboring nations. The Lord will give Antichrist what he wants, but in the end, it will all combine to lead to his destruction.

3. After the invasion (Ezek. 39:9-29)

The sudden destruction of this great army will leave behind a multitude of corpses as well as a huge amount of military materiel. We aren't told how much other damage was done by the storm God sent, but it's clear that the land needed cleaning up.

The cleansing of the land (Ezek. 39:9-16). People from the cities of Israel will go out and gather and burn the weapons and supplies left by Gog's defeated army. The ancient military equipment listed here includes hand shields and body shields (bucklers), bows and arrows, and clubs and spears. These are not the weapons of a modern army, but Ezekiel used language the people could understand.[9] If he had written about jet planes and rockets, he would have been a poor communicator. So large will be the collection of unused equipment that the people will use it for fuel for seven years.

But supposing these were actually wooden weapons, would they last that long? Could that many people heat their homes, factories, and businesses for seven years by burning bows and arrows, clubs and spears and shields? And will the people in Israel at that future time be heating the buildings with fireplaces and wood-burning stoves? Wouldn't the dead soldiers ceremonially defile most of this equipment? The burning of the equipment simply says that the Jews didn't keep it to use themselves and they destroyed it so nobody else could use it. Gog and his army came to spoil Israel, but Israel spoiled them!

But the land also had to be cleansed of the corpses. The fact that the Jews show respect for their enemies and give the dead decent burial is a testimony to their kindness. Of course, exposed corpses defiled the land, so it was necessary to remove them as soon as possible; but it will take seven months to finish the job. And even then, a special crew of workers will continue searching for bodies or bones that may have been overlooked. It's likely that the city called Hamonah ("horde," referring to the "horde" of soldiers slain) will be established as a headquarters for this mopping-up operation. The nation of Israel will remember this great day of deliverance and perhaps make it an annual day of celebration to the glory of God (v. 13, NIV).

Where is the cemetery for this vast horde of dead soldiers? The graves are in Israel in a location where people travel (v. 11). In fact, there will be so many corpses that the burial operation will block the traffic.[10] Some students believe this burial place will be east of the Dead Sea in an area known as "The Valley of the

Travelers." The new name will be "The Valley of Gog's Hordes."

The call to the feast (Ezek. 39:17-20). Not all the corpses can be buried immediately, so the carrion-eating birds and beasts will enjoy a feast at the invitation of the Lord. (The bones left behind will be buried; see v. 15.) This invitation to a feast is a frequent biblical image for the judgment of God and His victory over His enemies. Isaiah uses it for God's victory over Edom (Isa. 34:6), Jeremiah for God's victory over Egypt (Jer. 46:10), and Zephaniah for the Lord's dealing with Judah (Zeph. 1:7-8). A similar invitation will be given out after the great Battle of Armageddon (Rev. 19:17-21). So humiliating is this defeat of Gog and his allies that the Lord refers to their officers as rams, lambs, goats, and bullocks! They arrogantly entered Israel as proud soldiers but would be buried like slaughtered animals. Such is the fleeting greatness of man.

The compassion of the Lord (Ezek. 39:21-29). God destroyed the invading army not only for the protection of His people but also for the demonstration of His glory before the Gentiles. This miracle was also a reminder to the Jews, newly returned to their land (vv. 27-28), that Jehovah alone is the Lord. The fact that the Jews rebuild their temple is evidence they have faith in the ancient religious system, but that isn't the same as saving faith in their Messiah, Jesus Christ. This experience of deliverance will remind them of the many times their ancestors were miraculously delivered by the Lord, as recorded in their Scriptures.

But the victory over Gog and his hordes will say something to the Gentile nations about Israel (vv. 23-24). It will tell them that the Jews are indeed the people of God who were chastened by God in the past but now are destined for a kingdom. There will come a day when this rebellious nation will be cleansed and forgiven, and the Lord will pour out His Spirit on His people. That will happen when they see the Messiah, repent of their sins, and trust Him for their salvation.

The Gentile nations and the people of Israel will experience great suffering during the seven years of Tribulation. But the Lord in His mercy will seal 144,000 Jews to be the nucleus of the promised kingdom, and will also save a great multitude of Gentiles to share that kingdom with them (Rev. 7). The last temple the Jews ever build will be defiled by Antichrist and ultimately destroyed. But God has promised His people a new land and a new temple, and Ezekiel will describe these to us in the closing chapters of his book.

THIRTEEN

EZEKIEL 40–48

Glory in the Temple

Ezekiel has described the return of the Jewish people to their land, the cleansing of the nation, and the restoring of the land to productivity and security. But for the picture to be complete, he must give them assurance that their beloved temple and its ministries will be restored, for the presence of God's glory in the temple was what set Israel apart from all the nations (Rom. 9:4). In the last nine chapters of his book, Ezekiel will describe in detail the new temple and its ministry, the new boundaries of the tribes in the land, and the return of the glory of God to Israel.

1. The interpretation of the new temple

For centuries, devout and scholarly Bible students, both Jewish and Christian, have struggled to interpret the vision described in these chapters, but they have by no means reached a satisfactory agreement. At least four views have emerged from these studies, and all of them have their strengths and weaknesses.

Ezekiel described "ideal worship" for God's people. Rejecting the idea that a literal temple will be built in Israel, this view spiritualizes the vision God gave Ezekiel and seeks to apply it to the church today. The temple represents the glorious presence of

God among His people, and the gates speak of the open access the people have to the Lord. The river from the temple pictures the flowing forth of God's blessing from the church to the world, getting deeper and deeper and turning the desert into a garden. The arguments for this view center on the finished work of Christ and the end of the Old Covenant. Because of the death, resurrection, and present ministry of Christ our High Priest, we no longer need earthly temples, priests, or sacrifices. The New Covenant of grace has superseded the Old Covenant of law, and to go back to the Old Covenant is to reject the messages of Galatians and Hebrews. This interpretation is presented primarily by those of the amillennial school who also spiritualize the Old Testament promises to Israel. They believe there is no future for Israel as a nation, and this includes the establishing of an earthly kingdom.[1]

But this approach has its problems, not the least of which is the presence of so much detail in these chapters. If the Lord wanted Ezekiel simply to describe "ideal spiritual worship" for the church today, He didn't have to give us the measurements of the walls, gates, courts, and buildings. The prophet's use of temple imagery is no problem to us because he was a priest and the Jewish people understood this language; but why all the details? Do we ignore them or seek to understand and apply them? If so, what do they mean for spiritual worship today? Furthermore, why would Ezekiel leave out so many important elements from the Old Testament pattern of worship? Ezekiel's temple has no ark, golden altar of incense, lampstand, table of bread, veil, or high priest. He includes only three of the five levitical sacrifices, and two of the seven annual Jewish feasts, and yet none of these omissions is explained. (I will have more to say about the Old Covenant issue later in this chapter.)

When we start to spiritualize the Scriptures, every interpreter does that which is right in his own eyes and the results are confusing. We can't deny that the temple is used as an image of both the church universal (Eph. 2:19-22) and the local church (1 Cor. 3:9ff), but similarity of image is no proof that what the Bible says about a Jewish temple should be applied to the church. The idea that the river from the sanctuary pictures the worldwide blessings of the Gospel (or the church) is a bit hard to accept in the light of church history. Instead of the pure river of blessing flowing out from the church to the world, it appears that the dirty river of sin is flowing from the world into the church!

However, the "spiritual" approach does emphasize an important point. The Jewish people had defiled their temple and the glory of the Lord had departed, and Israel needed to return to holy worship and abandon their routine of empty religious activity. In fact, it's a lesson the church needs to recover today. Too much so-called worship is only a demonstration of man-centered religious activity that fails to bring glory to the Lord.

Ezekiel gave the plans for the post-captivity temple. If this is true, then the Jewish remnant didn't know it when they returned to their land, because they built the second temple according to the plans Moses gave in Exodus. The old men in the group wept, not because the second temple wasn't like Ezekiel's vision but because it was so unlike the magnificent temple Solomon built (Ezra 3:10-13). Perhaps the vision of the new temple may have encouraged the Jewish remnant in their difficult work, but that wasn't the reason God gave Ezekiel this glorious vision. The Jewish remnant had Joshua the high priest with them, but Ezekiel said nothing about a high priest, and nowhere is it recorded that the glory of the Lord filled the second temple. The "second temple" interpretation falls short of dealing honestly with the biblical text.

Ezekiel's vision anticipated John's vision in Revelation 21. Yes, there are some similarities. Both men were taken to high mountains (Ezek. 40:10) and both saw the glorious city of God. In both visions, a man was measuring the city (vv. 15-17), and both visions describe a life-giving river (Rev. 22:1). Ezekiel and John both emphasized the exclusion of defilement from the city (21:27). However, John's vision says nothing about worship; in fact, he states clearly that there will be no temple in the city he described (v. 22). Ezekiel's temple is designed in a square and is made from ordinary materials (stone abounds in Israel), while John's city appears to be a cube (v. 16) and is made out of precious metals and jewels. The heavenly city will be comprised of believers from the whole world (vv. 24-27), while Ezekiel's temple is emphatically Jewish, including the offering of levitical sacrifices.[2] While this doesn't exclude believing Gentiles, it does mark the worship as Jewish. It doesn't appear that God had John's vision in mind when He showed Ezekiel the temple.

Ezekiel described a temple to be used during the millennial reign of Christ. This interpretation takes the prophetic Scriptures at face value and tries not to spiritualize them. Ezekiel described the design of a literal temple that will be the center for worship during the kingdom of Christ, a worship based on the levitical order in the Mosaic Law. According to Ezekiel 43:6-12, the Lord gave all the details in order to focus the Jews' attention on God's holiness and thus bring them to repentance. The Lord wanted them to treat His temple with respect and not like any other building in the neighborhood, and He especially wanted them to abandon their idolatry.

To this present day, Israel has had four different sanctuaries: the tabernacle of Moses, the temple of Solomon, the second temple after the Captivity, and Herod's temple in the time of Jesus. God's glory left the tabernacle (1 Sam. 4:19-22) which was eventually replaced by Solomon's temple. Before the temple was destroyed by the Babylonians, Ezekiel saw God's glory leave the temple (Ezek. 9:3; 10:4; 11:22-23). There is no evidence that the glory of God ever resided in either the second temple or Herod's temple. The Son of God ministered in Herod's temple and in that sense brought back the glory (John 1:14; Hag. 2:7). But Jesus abandoned the temple in a manner similar to the way the glory left Solomon's temple: He went to the Mount of Olives (Ezek. 11:22-23; Matt. 23:38; 24:3). When at His return, Jesus brings the glory to the millennial temple, He will come from the Mount of Olives (Ezek. 43:1-5; Acts 1:9-12; Zech. 14:4). The Jews have not had a temple since Herod's temple was destroyed by the Romans in A.D. 70.

There are two temples in Israel's future: the Tribulation temple, which will be taken over by the Antichrist (Dan. 9:24, 26-27; Matt. 24:15; 2 Thes. 2:1-4; Rev. 11:1; 15:5), and the millennial temple that Ezekiel described in these chapters. But Ezekiel isn't the only prophet who said there would be a holy temple during the Kingdom Age. You find a kingdom temple and kingdom worship mentioned in Isaiah 2:1-5, 60:7, 13; Jeremiah 33:18; Joel 3:18; Micah 4:2; Haggai 2:7-9; and Zechariah 6:12-15, 14:16, 20-21. Ezekiel 37:24-28 records God's promise to His people that He would put His sanctuary among them. "My tabernacle also shall be with them; indeed, I will be their God, and they shall be My people" (v. 27, NKJV).

God gave the plans for the tabernacle to Moses, a prophet (Ex. 25:8-9, 40), and the plans for Solomon's temple to David, a king (2 Chron. 28:11-19). Now He reveals the plans for the glorious millennial temple to Ezekiel who was a priest as well as a prophet. These plans had a direct bearing on the people to whom Ezekiel was ministering, discouraged Jews who in the Babylonian siege had lost their land, their holy city, their temple, and many of their loved ones. In these closing chapters of his prophecy, Ezekiel assured them that God would keep His covenant promises and one day dwell again with His chosen people.

As we study these difficult chapters, we will discover other reasons why the literal interpretation of this vision yields the best understanding and application of the Word that God gave Ezekiel.

2. The plan of the new temple (Ezek. 40:1–46:24)
It was on April 28, 573 B.C.—the first day of Passover—that God gave Ezekiel the vision recorded in chapters 40–48. The Jews had been captives in Babylon for twenty-five years, and Passover would only remind them of their deliverance from Egypt. Passover was also the beginning of the religious year for Israel (Ex. 12:2), and the Lord chose that significant day to tell His servant about the glory that Israel would share when Messiah established His kingdom.

In a vision, Ezekiel visited the land of Israel, but unlike his

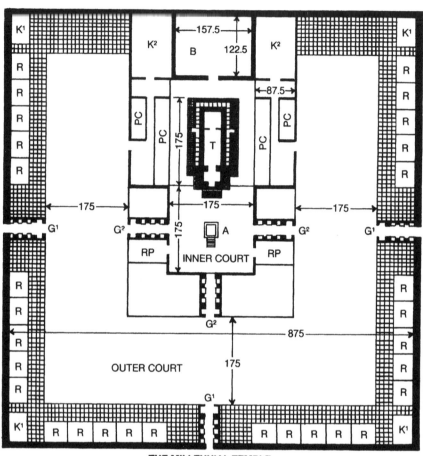

THE MILLENNIAL TEMPLE
(Dimensions are in feet.)

A	Altar (43:13-17)
B	Building (function not explained) (41:12)
G¹	Outer gates (40:6-17, 20-27)
G²	Inner gates (40:28-37)
K¹	Kitchens for people's sacrifices (46:21-24)
K²	Kitchens for priests (46:19-20)
PC	Priests' chambers (42:1-14)
R	30 rooms in outer court (40:17)
RP	Rooms for ministering priests (40:44-47)
T	Temple proper (40:48-41:11, 13-14, 16-26)

previous "visits," he didn't see sinful people, a devastated land, or a defiled temple. This time he saw a new land and a glorious new temple. Just as Moses received the tabernacle plans while on a mountain, so Ezekiel received the plans for the temple while on a mountain. Moses wasn't allowed to enter the Promised Land, but he saw it from a mountain (Deut. 34:1-4) and from a high mountain Ezekiel saw the land and its new tribal divisions.

It's unlikely that the new temple would be on any other site than Mount Zion, but critics of the literal interpretation of this vision point out that Zion is not really a "very high mountain." However, they may be overlooking the geographical changes that will occur in the land of Israel when the Lord returns to deliver His people and establish His kingdom (Zech. 14:4, 10). God promised that the Jews would worship and serve Him on a high mountain (Ezek. 20:40) and that Messiah would rule from a high mountain (17:22-23), and He will keep that promise. Both Isaiah and Micah speak of the high mountain (Isa. 2:1-2; Micah 4:1). Zion will not only be elevated physically, but it will become the center of the worship of the Lord for the whole earth.

In his vision, the prophet saw a man colored like bronze, which suggests he was an angelic visitor, standing just outside the eastern gate of the temple. He held a linen cord and a reed (rod), both of which were used for taking measurements, the line for long distances (Ezek. 47:3) and the rod for shorter measurements. The rod was probably a little over ten feet long (40:5).[3] To measure property is symbolic of claiming it for yourself. During those years when the Jewish remnant was trying to rebuild their temple, the Prophet Zechariah saw a man measuring the temple, and this was a sign that the temple and the city would one day be restored (Zech. 2). God commanded the Apostle John to measure the temple in Jerusalem before it was trampled down by the Gentiles (Rev. 11). This was evidence that no matter what happened, Jerusalem and the temple belonged to God and would one day be restored and sanctified.

The man would give Ezekiel a guided tour of the temple precincts, starting from the eastern gate and then returning there at the end of the tour. But before they walked up the seven steps that led through the eastern gate into the outer court, the guide gave Ezekiel some solemn counsel (Ezek. 40:4). The prophet was to pay close attention to what he saw and heard because he would have to tell everything he learned to the exiles in Babylon. Of course, through his book, he would tell generations of people what he learned from the Lord during his tour of the temple. This means that the facts recorded in these chapters contained truths that Jews in Ezekiel's day needed to know and believe. These truths are needed today by both Jews and Gentiles, if we are to understand God's plan for the future. If all God wanted to do was impress Ezekiel with "spiritual worship," the angel would have told him so.

The outer court (Ezek. 40:5-27). The entire sacred area was 875 feet square, including a wall 10 feet high and 10 feet thick (v. 5). The temple area itself was on the west side of the enclosure, 175 feet from the walls, and the back part reached to the edge of the sacred area. Behind the temple were two kitchens for preparing sacrificial meals, plus a third building whose purpose was not explained. At each corner of the walls, there was a kitchen; in the center of the east, north, and south walls there was a gate; and on either side of these three gates, built right into the walls, were five special rooms for the worshipers, making a total of thirty rooms. They were used for eating the meals associated with the sacrifices. As you walked through any of the three outer gates, you passed six rooms where the temple guards were stationed, and each of the chambers was about ten feet square and decorated with images of palm trees.

The outer court covers nearly 400,000 square feet, but it will not have a court of the Gentiles with the all-important separating wall (Eph. 2:14)[4], nor will it have a separate court of the women. In the millennial temple, our Lord's desire will be fulfilled that His house be a house of prayer for men and women of all nations (Mark 11:17; Isa. 56:7; Jer. 7:11). The size of the outer court and the accessibility of so many rooms suggest that the area will be a place for fellowship, where people can meet and enjoy sacrificial meals together.

The inner court (Ezek. 40:28-47; 43:13-17). Walking straight across the outer court from any of the three gates in the outer wall, you would come to one of the three gates leading into the inner court. Eight steps will take you through the gate (40:31), past the rooms for guards, and into the inner court. The walls containing these inner gates will contain chambers for the priests and for the preparation of offerings. The inner court is 175 feet square and the altar of sacrifice is placed in the center of the court (43:13-17).

The brazen altar in the Old Testament tabernacle was a "box" made of acacia wood covered with bronze. It was seven and one-half feet square and four and one-half feet high. About two and one-half feet from the top was a grating on which the sacrifices were laid and a fire was kept burning. The altar in Solomon's temple was thirty feet square and fifteen feet high and was approached on all four sides by steps (2 Chron. 4:1; 1 Kings 8:64).[5] The altar in the millennial temple will be about twenty feet tall, with a stairway on the east side. The altar will be tiered, with the base thirty-one and one-half feet square, the next level twenty-eight feet square, the third twenty-four and one-half feet square, and the top level (the "altar hearth") twenty-one feet square.

The sanctuary (Ezek. 40:48–43:12). Like the inner court where the altar will stand, the area containing the sanctuary will be 175 feet square. The portico leading to the sanctuary is quite elaborate with pillars on each side of the door. This reminds us of the two large pillars in Solomon's temple that stood before the entrance to the holy place (1 Kings 7:15-22). The angelic guide showed Ezekiel the various rooms adjacent to the inner court and the temple proper, all of them set aside for the ministering priests (Ezek. 41:5–42:20).

Nothing is said about a veil between the holy place and the holy of holies, but since the Messiah will be present with His people, the veil is not necessary. He wants His glory to be revealed to all. There is also no mention of the ark of the covenant or the mercy seat on which the blood was sprinkled on the annual Day of Atonement. There is mention of a wooden altar or table that probably stood before the entrance to the holy of holies (41:21-22). Made completely of wood, it will stand about five and one-half feet high and be three and one-half feet square. Nothing could be burned on it, so perhaps it will be used to display the bread that formerly stood on the table in the tabernacle and the temple.

In the millennial temple, there is nothing said about a golden altar of incense or the seven-branched golden lampstand. The altar of incense symbolized the prayers of God's people ascending to the Lord (Ps. 141:2; Rev. 8:3), but since the Lord is present with them, there is no need for symbolic prayer. As for the lampstand, which symbolized the light of God's truth through the nation of Israel, the Shekinah glory was present in the temple of the Lord.

Ezekiel had seen the glory depart from the temple, but now he saw the glory return (Ezek. 43:1-12). His guide took him back to the eastern gate in the outer court, and when the prophet looked out, he saw the glory approaching from the east. Along with the sight of the glory came the sound of the Lord's voice "like the noise [roar] of many waters" (v. 2; see 1:24; Rev. 1:15; 14:2; 19:6). The whole land of Israel was enlightened by the radiance of God's glory, and Ezekiel fell to the ground as he did when he saw the glory throne at the beginning of his ministry (Ezek. 1:28; 3:23; 9:8; 11:13). Then the temple was filled with God's glory, and the Spirit transported Ezekiel back into the inner court. When Moses dedicated the tabernacle (Ex. 40) and Solomon the temple (2 Chron. 5:11-14), the glory of God moved in, signifying that the Lord had accepted their worship and approved of their work.

In both the tabernacle and the temple, God's glory was "enthroned" on the mercy seat in the holy of holies (Ex. 25:22; Ps. 80:1; 99:1), but the millennial temple will have no ark and no mercy seat. However, the temple will still be God's throne (Ezek. 43:6-7) and the Messiah will reign as both King and Priest (Zech. 6:9-13). Today, Jesus Christ is enthroned in heaven as our "high priest after the order of Mechizedek" (Heb. 6:20; Ps. 110:1). It was the king-priest Melchizedek who met Abraham after the battle of the kings and blessed him with bread and wine (Gen. 14:17-24), and the spiritual significance of this event is explained in Hebrews 7. In Jewish history, prophets, priests, and kings were all anointed for their offices, but the offices were kept separate. Priests like Jeremiah, Ezekiel, and John the Baptist were called to be prophets, but no priest would dare to take the throne. The one king who tried to serve as a priest was smitten with leprosy (2 Chron. 26:16-23).

The presence of God's glory and God's throne will so sanctify the temple that the people will approach the sanctuary with awe and not treat it like any other building, nor will they repeat their heinous sin of defiling the temple with their idols. God spoke to the prophet and told him to tell the Jewish people what he saw and heard so they would be ashamed of their past sins and turn from them. He must describe the glory of the temple in detail and write it down so they will get the message and want to obey the Lord. You find a similar admonition in Ezekiel 44:4-8 when Ezekiel was at the north gate. This passage reminds us that people who frequent "holy places" ought to be "holy people." The Jewish remnant that returned to their land to rebuild the temple would need to take this message to heart, and we need to take it to heart today.

The altar and sacrifices (Ezek. 43:13-2; 45:13–46:24). We have already dealt with the brazen altar and we must now consider the perplexing problem of the sacrifices. The Lord instructs the priests in how the altar should be dedicated by the offering of a series of sacrifices during the week of consecration (43:18-27). In the dedication of the tabernacle (Ex. 40:29) and Solomon's temple (2 Chron. 7:1-10), sacrifices were offered and the blood applied to the altar.

When the millennial temple is discussed, the question is frequently asked, "Since Jesus has died for the sins of the world, fulfilled the law, and brought in the New Covenant, why would believing Jews want to return to the Old Covenant? What need is there to go back to animal sacrifices when Jesus has made one perfect offering for all time?" This is one of the major arguments used by some students against taking Ezekiel 40–48 literally. But if we understand the role of the sacrifices under the Old Covenant, it will help us see their significance in the millennial temple.

The sacrifices mentioned in this section of Ezekiel are: the burnt offering (40:38-39, 42; 43:18, 24, 27; 44:11; 45:15, 17, 23, 25; 46:2, 4, 12, 13, 15); the trespass or guilt offering (40:39; 42:13; 44:29; 46:20); the sin offering (40:39; 42:13; 43:19, 21, 22, 25; 44:27, 29; 45:17, 19, 22; 23, 25; 46:20); the peace or fellowship offering (43:27; 45:15, 17; 46:2, 12); the meal (grain) offering (42:13; 44:29; 45:15, 17, 24, 25; 46:5, 7, 11, 14, 15, 20); and the drink offering (45:17).[6] For the Mosaic regulations for these offerings, see Leviticus 1–7.

The burnt offering speaks of total dedication to the Lord, "all on the altar" (1:9; Rom. 12:1-2). The sin offering (Lev. 4; 6:21-30) and the tresspass or guilt offering (Lev. 5; 7:1-10) deal with the sinner's offenses against God and people. The sin offering was brought by those who sinned through ignorance, for there was no sacrifice available for high-handed deliberate sin (Num. 15:30-36; Ps. 51:1, 11, 16-17). The trespass offering dealt with offenses for which some kind of restitution should be made. The offerer was required to restore the amount of the property plus a fine of about 20 percent of its value. Sin is not a cheap thing—nor is God's forgiveness!

The peace or fellowship offering (Lev. 3; 7:11-38) was given to the Lord as an expression of praise and thanksgiving or perhaps as the indication of the completion of a special vow to the Lord. Part of the meat from the sacrifice was given to the worshiper, and he could cook it and enjoy a feast with family and friends. Except for weddings and other high occasions, the Jewish people rarely killed their animals just to have a meal. Meat was an occasional luxury. Therefore, the fellowship offering was an occasion for worshiping the Lord and enjoyment with His people. The grain or meal offering involved presenting sheaves, the roasted kernels of grain, fine flour, or various kinds of baked cakes. It was the acknowledgment that God is the source of the food that sustains life (1 Chron. 29:10-14). The drink offering was a portion of wine that was poured out along with another sacrifice. It symbolized life poured out wholly to the Lord (Phil. 2:17).

All of these offerings in some way pointed to Christ and His sacrifice of Himself for our sins (Heb. 10:1-18). God forgave the sins of the worshipers if they brought the sacrifice by faith and trusted the Lord, because the blood of animals can never remove the guilt of human sin (v. 4). God's forgiveness was declared (Lev. 4:20, 26, 31, 35; 5:10, 13, 16, 18; 6:7), but only because of the work of Jesus Christ which was pictured by the sacrifice. Old Testament believers weren't forgiven because animals died, but because they put their faith in the Lord (Heb. 11; Ps. 51:16-17; Hab. 2:4). Therefore, the use of animal sacrifices in the millennial temple no more minimizes or negates the finished work of Christ than these sacrifices did before Jesus died. It appears that the sacrifices will be offered in a memorial sense and as expressions of love and devotion to the Lord (Isa. 56:5-7; 60:7). They will also bring people together for fellowship and feasting to the glory of the Lord.

The temple will be a place of learning for both Jews and Gentiles (Isa. 2:1-3), and no doubt the worshipers will study the Old Testament law and learn more about Jesus. They will study the New Testament as well and see the deeper significance of the sacrifices and the feasts. The only "Bible" that the early church possessed was the Old Testament, and the Christians were able to lead sinners to faith in Christ without John 3:16 or "The Roman Road." Of the seven feasts that the Jews celebrated (Lev. 23), it appears that only Passover (Ezek. 45:21-24) and Tabernacles (v. 25; Zech. 14:16-19) will be observed in the Kingdom Age. Passover speaks of the Lamb of God and the deliverance of the Jews from bondage in Egypt, and Tabernacles was a joyous harvest feast that anticipated the coming kingdom and reminded the Jews of their wilderness journeys.[7] Ezekiel 44:24 indicates that the weekly Sabbath will also be observed.

Will the Lord's Supper also be observed in the Kingdom Age? The words of Jesus after He instituted the Lord's Supper seem to suggest that it will. "But I say to you, I will not drink of this fruit of the vine from now on until that day when I drink it new with you in My Father's kingdom" (Matt. 26:29, NASB; see Mark 14:25; Luke 22:18). If the saints in the church can remember Christ by breaking bread and drinking the cup, why can't the Jewish believers remember Him by bringing sacrifices? Neither remembrance has any atoning value.

The priests (Ezek. 40:44-49; 42:1-14; 43:19-27; 44:9-31). God's desire was that the entire nation of Israel be "a kingdom of priests" (Ex. 19:6), but this was never fulfilled. Believers today are part of "a holy priesthood" and "a royal priesthood" (1 Peter 2:5, 9) through Jesus Christ their High Priest. In the millennial temple, the priests and Levites will minister to the people and to the Lord. There will be singers (Ezek. 40:44) to give a "sacrifice of praise" as well as priests to offer the sacrifices brought by the people. No high priest is mentioned because Jesus Christ, the King-Priest, is on the throne and reigning from the temple.

Three times we're told that the descendants of Zadok will be the priests (v. 46; 43:19; 44:15). Zadok was related to Aaron through Aaron's third son Eleazar (1 Chron. 6:1-8, 50-53) and served during David's reign along with Abiathar (2 Sam. 8:17; 1 Chron. 15:11). However, Abiathar defected from David and joined the party that promoted Adonijah as David's successor to the throne (1 Kings 1), and this cost him and his descendants the priesthood (2:26-27). This act fulfilled the prophecy given concerning Eli the high priest and his wicked sons (1 Sam. 2:27-36). The name Zadok means "righteous," and in his book, the Prophet Ezekiel emphasizes separation and holiness.

We have already seen that special chambers will be set aside in the temple for the use of the priests (Ezek. 40:44-46; 42:1-14). Some will be residences while other rooms will be used for daily ministry, such as changing garments, preparing the sacrifices, and cooking the meat for the meals. (See verses 13-14.) When the temple is dedicated, the priests will offer the sacrifices (43:18-27), just as the priests did when the tabernacle and the temple were dedicated (Num. 7:2; 2 Chron. 7:1-11).

The Lord will be very particular about the way the sanctuary is used (Ezek. 44:5-9). He warns the future priests that they must teach the people to make a difference between the clean and the unclean (v. 23; see 22:26) and not to permit outsiders to defile the temple. Many of the Mosaic regulations for the priests are summarized in 44:10-31. The Levites will be disciplined because they didn't stand for what was holy and right in the years before the Captivity. They will be allowed to kill the sacrifices, assist the worshipers, serve as gatekeepers, and help in the temple, but they will not have priestly privileges.[8] The priests will be permitted to offer the sacrifices and draw near to table (44:16), which may refer to the altar or to the table standing before the holy of holies (41:22).

The Lord will also be particular about the conduct of the priests (44:17-31). He tells them what to wear (vv. 17-19), how to groom themselves (v. 20), not to drink wine while ministering (v. 21), who not to marry (v. 22), and at all times to show and teach the difference between clean and unclean (v. 23), even if a relative dies (vv. 25-27).[9] They will act as judges and see to it that the law was honored and obeyed (v. 24). Like the Old Testament priests, the kingdom priests will not have an inheritance of land but will have the Lord as their inheritance and be able to live from the temple offerings (vv. 28-31; see Num. 18:20; Deut. 18:1-2; Josh. 13:33).

3. The logistics of the new temple (Ezek. 45:1–48:35)

The closing chapters of Ezekiel's prophecy explain how the land of Israel will be divided during the Kingdom Age, with a section assigned to the Lord, another to the prince, and then one to each of the twelve tribes. The first assignments of the Promised Land were made after the conquest of Canaan, with Joshua, Eleazar the high priest, and the heads of the twelve tribes casting lots before the Lord to determine the boundaries (Num. 26:52-56; 34:16-29; Josh. 13–22). During his reign, King Solomon divided the land into twelve "royal districts," and required each district to provide food for the king and his household for one month (1 Kings 4:7-19), but no actual boundary lines were changed. However, the plan wasn't popular with the people (1 Kings 12:1-19).[10]

The Lord's portion (Ezek. 45:1-6; 48:8-9). Between the areas assigned to Judah and Benjamin will be a section reserved for the Lord and the prince. The Lord's section will be 8.3 miles square, which equals about 55 square miles. The area will be divided horizontally into three sections, each section 8.3 miles long. The top section (3.3 miles wide) will be the sacred area for the temple and the priests. The priests will not be permitted to own land but will be allowed to live there near the sanctuary (44:28). Like the Old Testament priests, the Lord will be the portion of their inheritance (Num. 18:20; Deut. 10:9; Josh. 13:14, 33). The center area will be the same size as the top area and will belong to the Levites. During the old dispensation, the Levites were allowed to own land but were scattered throughout Israel so they could minister to the people (Josh. 21). Genesis 49:5-7; 34:25-31 suggests that this scattering was also a form of discipline.

The bottom area (1.75 miles wide) will be assigned to "the city" and the free land around it. The city is first mentioned in Ezekiel 40:2 and is probably Jerusalem with a new name "Jehovah Shammah—the Lord is there" (48:35). The area assigned to the city will belong to the whole house of Israel (45:6) and will be at the center of the lower strip of land. The "common lands" on either side of that section will be available to all the people of Israel (48:15) and will also be used for growing food to feed the inhabitants of the city. The suggestion seems to be that a "staff" of people from the tribes will work this land so that the "staff" in the city can take care of civil affairs and host visitors who come to worship at the temple.

The prince's portion (Ezek. 45:7–46:18; 44:1-3; 48:21-22). Without explaining who he is, Ezekiel introduces "the prince" in 44:1-3 and mentions him at least sixteen times in the rest of the book. He is not to be confused with "David...their prince" (34:24; 37:24-25) whom some see as the Messiah, the heir to David's throne (Luke 1:30-32); nor should he be confused with the Messiah. The prince will be a married man and will have sons who can inherit his land (Ezek. 46:16-18), which is located on

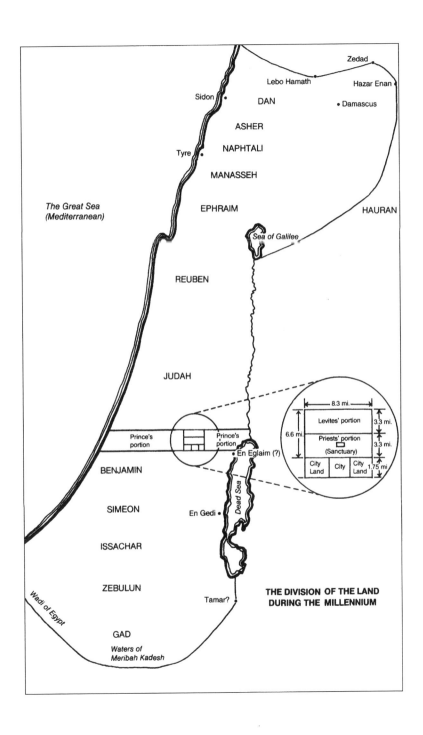

Zedad

Lebo Hamath

Hazar Enan

Sidon

DAN

Damascus

ASHER

NAPHTALI

Tyre

MANASSEH

The Great Sea
(Mediterranean)

EPHRAIM

HAURAN

Sea of Galilee

REUBEN

JUDAH

8.3 mi.

Prince's
portion

Prince's
portion

Levites' portion

3.3 mi.

6.6 mi.

Priests' portion

3.3 mi.

(Sanctuary)

En Eglaim (?)

City
Land

City

City
Land

1.75 mi

BENJAMIN

Dead Sea

SIMEON

En Gedi

ISSACHAR

ZEBULUN

THE DIVISION OF THE LAND
DURING THE MILLENNIUM

Tamar?

Wadi of Egypt

GAD

Waters of
Meribah Kadesh

either side of the central sacred area. Nowhere is he identified as a member of the royal family, a priest, or a Levite. We aren't even told what tribe he will come from. Apparently he will be a civil ruler, a vice-regent under the authority of the Messiah, and yet most of his functions will be religious.

He will offer sacrifices for himself (44:3; 45:22)[11]—something Messiah would not have to do—and will receive gifts from the people to be used for the worship of the Lord (45:13-16). The prince will provide sacrifices for special occasions (vv. 17-25), including the dedication of the sanctuary, the Sabbaths, Passover, Tabernacles, and at new moon. On the Sabbath and at new moon, he will present his offerings before the people are permitted to worship (46:1-8). During the week, the eastern gate into the inner court will be closed, but it will be opened for the prince on the Sabbath and at new moon, or whenever he wants to present a voluntary burnt offering or peace offering (v. 12). He will be allowed to come as far as the eastern gate but not to the altar in the inner court. He will present his sacrifices, watch the priests prepare them, and when they are offered, will prostrate himself before the Lord (v. 2). After the sacrifice, he will leave the sanctuary just as he came in. When the people come in to worship on the special feast days, they must exit by the gate opposite the one by which they entered (v. 9). The prince will not isolate himself from the people on the feast days but be a part of the crowd (v. 10). The prince must see to it that the daily burnt offerings are presented on the altar, just as they were in the tabernacle and temple (Ex. 29:42; Num. 28:6).

The Year of Jubilee will be celebrated during the Millennial Age (Ezek. 48:16-18). This was the fiftieth year during which the land was not farmed, slaves were set free, and property reverted back to the original owners (see Lev. 25). During the 1,000-year reign of Christ, there will be time for twenty such celebrations. Ezekiel makes the special point that during the Kingdom Age, the prince would not oppress the people or confiscate their land as the rulers did during the last days of the kingdom of Judah. The people of Israel failed to obey the laws relating to the

Sabbatic Year and the Year of Jubilee, so God had to send them into exile so that His land could enjoy the rest it needed (2 Chron. 36:14-21; Lev. 26:14ff; Jer. 25:9-12; 27:6-8; 29:10).

The river of life (Ezek. 47:1-12). After seeing the kitchens in the temple (46:19-24), the prophet noticed a trickle of water issuing from the holy of holies, past the altar on the south side. The guide led him out the north gate (the eastern gate was closed) and around the temple to the eastern gate where he saw the water coming out from under the building on the south side of the gate. (See Pss. 36:8; 46:4.) The guide measured the depth of the water four times and the river became so deep you could swim in it. Ezekiel learned that the river flowed to the Dead Sea where it brought new life to that forsaken area. The water from the temple would heal the Dead Sea as well as the rivers, and the water creatures would multiply wherever the waters came. The trees on the banks of the river would provide food each month and the leaves would be used for healing. Life comes from the temple of God, not from a palace or a government building!

Jerusalem is the only great city of the ancient world that wasn't located on a river, and in the east, a dependable water supply is essential for life and for defense. During the Kingdom Age, Jerusalem shall have a river such as no other nation ever had. But is this a literal river or merely a sacred symbol of the life-giving power of the Lord? Perhaps it is both. Joel 3:18 and Zechariah 13:1 and 14:8-9 speak of this river as a literal entity, so the river both illustrates and accomplishes the life-giving work of God. Jesus saw such a river as a symbol of the Holy Spirit (John 7:37-39), and the Apostle John saw a similar scene in the heavenly city of God (Rev. 22:1-2). A river played an important role in the Garden of Eden (Gen. 2:10-14).

The portions for the tribes (Ezek. 47:13–48:7, 23-29). In the millennial kingdom, the boundaries of the tribes will be altogether different from what they were before Israel fell to Assyria and Judah to Babylon. The boundaries of the land (47:13-23) will be about what Moses described in Numbers 34, but each tribe's allotment will cut straight across the land. From north to south, the tribes will be Dan, Asher, Naphtali, Manasseh, Ephraim, Reuben, and Judah. Next is the land assigned to the Lord, the prince, and the city, followed by the tribes of Benjamin, Simeon, Issachar, Zebulun, and Gad. It appears that all of the tribes will have access to the Mediterranean Sea except Zebulun and Gad. Judah, the royal tribe (Gen. 49:10) will be located adjacent to the temple area from which Jesus will reign. The tribes descended from sons born of Jacob's wives' maids, Zilpah and Bilhah—Dan, Asher, Naphtali, and Gad—are located the farthest north and south. We aren't told how much land each tribe is given, but only where they will be located. There will be peace among the tribes as they submit to the kingship of their Messiah, Jesus Christ.

The portion for the city (Ezek. 48:30-35). This will be a "kingdom Jerusalem," a new city for the new nation and the new era. Jerusalem's gates have always been significant (Neh. 3; Pss. 48; 87:2; 122:2), but now the city will have twelve gates, each one named after one of Jacob's twelve sons. Instead of "Ephraim" and "Manasseh" (two gates), there will be "Joseph" (one gate), and Levi will have a gate. Any Gentile coming to the city to learn about the Lord will have to enter the city through one of these gates and be reminded that "salvation is of the Jews" (John 4:22). The city will be about 1.6 miles square. These gates, of course, remind us of the gates to the holy city that John described in Revelation 22:10-13, 21.

But the most important thing about the new city will be the presence of the Lord among His united people (Ezek. 35:10). The new name will be "Jehovah Shammah—the Lord is there." This is one of seven compound names of Jehovah found in the Old Testament: Jehovah Jireh—"the Lord will provide" (Gen. 22:13-14); Jehovah Rapha—"the Lord who heals" (Ex. 15:26); Jehovah Shalom—"the Lord our peace" (Jud. 6:24); Jehovah Tsidkenu—"the Lord our righteousness" (Jer. 23:6); Jehovah Shammah—"the Lord is present" (Ezek. 48:35); Jehovah Nissi—"the Lord our banner" (Ex. 17:8-15); and Jehovah Ra'ah—"the Lord our shepherd" (Ps. 23:1).

4. The meaning of the new temple

In examining all the information Ezekiel recorded for us, we must be careful not to lose the major messages among these important details. There is a sense in which the messages of the entire book are wrapped up in one way or another in chapters 40 to 48. The spiritual lessons are as meaningful to us today as they were to Israel in Ezekiel's day, or as they will be to the Jewish people in Messiah's day.

Separation from sin. Ezekiel was a priest as well as a prophet, and it was the responsibility of the priests to teach the people the difference between the holy and the unholy and the clean and the unclean (Lev. 10:10-11; Ezek. 44:23). Israel drifted into sin because they began to erase these differences and became like the pagan nations around them. The temple in Jerusalem, with its special courts and holy chambers, reminded the people that God put a difference between the holy and the profane. For people to "call evil, good, and good, evil, [and] put darkness for light, and light for darkness" (Isa. 5:20) is to violate the basic principle of holy living. (See Ezek. 40:5; 42:14-20; 43:7.)

Worship. The temple was a place of worship, but the heart of the worshiper was far more important that his or her gifts. The Jews in the Southern Kingdom of Judah had defiled the holy temple of God and dared to worship Jehovah along with the idols of the nations around them! God's people don't decide how they are going to worship the Lord; they simple obey what He has told them in His Word.

Fulfillment. One of the purposes of the millennial kingdom is that God might fulfill His promises to His people, promises He couldn't fulfill because of their rebellion and unbelief. In His grace and mercy, God gave Israel a wonderful land, a perfect law, and a glorious Lord. They defiled the land by their terrible crimes; they disobeyed the law by adopting pagan practices; and they defied their Lord and tempted Him by resisting His calls to repentance. But during the kingdom, Israel will trust the Lord, obey His Word, worship in His temple as they should, and bring delight to the Lord who will rule from David's throne.

But there's a further fulfillment, for the Kingdom Age will "wrap up" all the previous ages in God's revelation of Himself and His purposes. The land will be like the Garden of Eden (36:35), complete with a river of life and trees of life. The promises made to Abraham will be fulfilled and his descendants will possess and enjoy their land. The Law of Moses will be obeyed from the heart, and the Lord will be worshiped and glorified. The Messiah that Israel rejected at His first coming will be received and honored and will reign over them (43:6-7). God will fulfill every kingdom promise found in the pages of the prophets![12]

God's glory and God's name. If the Book of Ezekiel teaches us anything, it teaches us that we must honor God's name and magnify His glory. The glory of God departed from Israel because they defiled the temple. The glory of God returned to the new temple because it was holy and a place where God could dwell. "They shall know that I am the Lord" is a statement found at least sixty times in Ezekiel's book. While God's glory doesn't dwell in our church buildings, God can be glorified or disgraced by what we do in those buildings we have dedicated to Him. As His people, we must be reverent and honor His name.

The sovereign rule of God. The first vision God gave Ezekiel was that of His glorious throne, moving quickly here and there so that His angelic creatures could accomplish His purposes in the world. Today, the church of Jesus Christ is left in this world not just to pray "Thy will be done on earth as it is in heaven," but to help accomplish that will in the power of the Holy Spirit. God is still on the throne and Jesus Christ has "all authority in heaven and on earth" (Matt. 28:18). Need we ask for more?

Chapter One

From Priest to Prophet
(Ezekiel 1–3)

1. Ezekiel became a prophet to his countrymen. Who would you say are our prophets today?

2. What would you list as the top two reasons that prophets are resented in whatever culture they appear?

3. Ezekiel experienced a vision full of images that related to God's sovereignty, starting with a powerful storm. What images represent God's sovereignty to you?

4. Describe a time when you felt God calling you to do something, even if it wasn't as dramatic as Ezekiel's call.

5. What kinds of things might Ezekiel have been afraid of as he considered the truth God had called him to tell?

6. In what ways can we receive the Word, take it in, almost like the food we eat?

7. Name someone you look to as a "watchman on the wall."

8. If we are the people of God, and God's prophets among us are the watchmen who warn us of danger, what are the enemies or dangers that we need to be warned about?

9. Ezekiel's message to his people was a message of God's sovereignty and of Israel's responsibility. Describe Israel's responsibility to God.

10. What should be our response to Ezekiel's message reminding us of God's sovereignty over us?

Chapter Two

The Death of a Great City
(Ezekiel 4–7)

1. The Jews were exiles far from home. Describe the feelings you would have about "home" if you were in their situation.

2. Wiersbe says that Ezekiel became a curiosity, a kind of celebrity, because of his unorthodox methods of communication. What kinds of things does that tell you about the prophet?

3. Putting yourself again in the shoes of the exiles, how do you suppose they responded to Ezekiel's message that God would allow their homeland to be destroyed?

4. How do you respond to the concept of God turning His face away from His people, which was part of Ezekiel's message?

5. In what ways do you think Ezekiel's "mime" kind of messages would have been more effective than mere spoken words?

6. In what ways do you think Ezekiel's self-imposed silence affected his message once he did speak out?

7. Of all the sins of Israel, why was idolatry the one God spoke of most through the prophets?

8. What are some examples of "false idols" that our culture highly values that God sees as no better than waste?

9. In discussing "the morning has come," Wiersbe's explanation almost sounds like the proverb, "what goes around comes around." How do you find that phrase pertinent to sin in the life of Old Testament Israel and of us today?

Chapter Three

The Glory Has Departed
(Ezekiel 8 – 11)

1. Israel's sin caused God's glory to depart from the temple. How does our sin affect God's glory and presence with us?

2. Describe a time in your own life when, like Ezekiel, you needed a refresher of God's original call.

3. What comes to your mind when you think of God's jealousy?

4. In what ways today do we ask God's glory to abide amid the false idols we worship?

5. How would you describe the line we cross where God says, "Judgment will come no matter what you do"?

6. Wiersbe writes, "Often in Scripture you find God sending judgment, not because unbelievers have sinned, but because His own people have disobeyed His law!" Where do you see this truth lived out in our world today?

7. There were many false prophets in Ezekiel's day. What labels would you give the godless philosophies or world views that you see around you today?

8. God Himself was the temple for the exiles in Babylon. How is God a temple for us today?

9. How do you envision what it will be like when God's glory returns at the second coming of Christ?

10. What do you think it was like for Ezekiel to hear that God's judgment of destruction had begun in Jerusalem?

C h a p t e r   F o u r

The Truth About the False
(E z e k i e l   1 2 – 1 4)

1. What sometimes causes us, like the Israelites, to believe that we will not suffer consequences for our actions?

2. What would be some everyday terms we use to describe spiritual blindness and deafness?

3. What would you say is the cure for spiritual blindness and deafness?

4. The Jews had difficulty believing that God's judgment was imminent. How near do most of us today feel God's judgment is?

5. Explain your perspective on the relationship between our belief in God's judgment and our obedience to God's commands.

6. If someone asked you for the top three ways to identify a false prophet, what would you tell them?

7. If you were asked to compare "truth" to a building, what kind of building would it be?

8. Ezekiel confronted the false religious leaders. What makes it difficult to confront hypocritical leadership today?

9. If faith can't be "borrowed," how does the presence of righteous people benefit a city or a culture?

10. What do you see around you every day that reminds you that God's judgment is coming?

Chapter Five

Pictures of Failure
(Ezekiel 15 – 17)

1. The people of Ezekiel's day did not take the Word of the Lord seriously. What evidences do you see today that our countrymen do not take God's Word seriously?

2. Describe the most unusual methods you've seen used to communicate God's truth.

3. The Bible often uses a vine as imagery for the church. In what ways do you see the church function as a living vine?

4. Explain how idolatry in our lives is like adultery in our relationship with God.

5. Why do you think our adoption into God's family sometimes becomes a point of pride rather than privilege?

6. If we know our blessings come from God, why is it so easy to stray from Him in the midst of them?

7. Some of the difficulties that Israel experienced were disciplinary actions from God. Describe a time you were disciplined by God.

8. What results (from our perspective and from God's perspective) when we don't take our own sin seriously?

9. In what ways does God deal with His church through national leadership as He did in Ezekiel's day?

10. Why do you think Ezekiel, and many other prophets, taught through parables and images as well as sermons?

Chapter Six

God Is Just!
(Ezekiel 18–21)

1. How do you describe the balance between understanding your family's influence and taking responsibility for your own life as an individual?

2. What is the relationship between responsibility and accountability?

3. What examples have you seen where children suffer as a consequence of their parents' sin?

4. What examples have you seen where people blame their sin on their personality? ("It's just who I am!")

5. In what ways do we sometimes blame God for our bad choices?

6. What would you say are the top three reasons it is difficult to repent of sin and choose a different life?

7. What kind of correlation do you see today between the morals of our national leaders and the morals of our nation?

8. Ezekiel talks a lot about the covenant that Israel had with God. What kind of covenant do we have with God?

9. List some ways that we have not learned from the past and thus repeat the mistakes of our ancestors.

10. As we take responsibility for our own sinfulness, what does Christ's sacrifice mean to that process?

Chapter Seven

See the Sinful City!
(Ezekiel 22–24)

1. What modern city would you compare to Jerusalem?

2. What do the social manners of a civilization (how people treat each other) reveal about the morals of that civilization?

3. Describe the role you believe pornography has played in the moral makeup of our country.

4. Ezekiel prophesied against the extortion-like business practices of the Jews. Where do you draw the line between running a profitable business and taking advantage of people?

5. Ezekiel described God's judgment in terms of doom and fire. What kinds of judgment from God do you see in the world?

6. The people of Judah are described as blatantly hypocritical. What are the dangers of hypocrisy?

7. Ezekiel leans heavily on the imagery of adultery to describe the Jews. In what ways do you compare your relationship with God to a marriage in which you should be faithful?

8. The Jews believed nothing bad could happen to them because they were chosen. Name some other reasons why people at times think they are "untouchable."

9. What kinds of places today represent God's presence to you the way the temple of Jerusalem did to the Jews?

10. What kinds of things keep us from repenting of sin even when we hear about God's judgment?

Chapter Eight
God Judges the Nations
(Ezekiel 25-28)

1. The Gentile nations surrounding Judah were enemies who delighted in Jerusalem's downfall. Who would delight in Christianity's downfall today?

2. List some reasons why God punishes His own children before He punishes unbelievers who disobey Him more openly.

3. Many of the enemy nations of Israel were actually extended family. In what ways are family disputes often hotter and longer standing than non-family disputes?

4. Ezekiel began to speak God's judgment against Judah's enemies. In what ways, if any, do you see God standing today against the enemies of His children?

5. In what ways do you think God holds people groups or nations accountable for their actions today as He did in proclaiming the judgments on the nations through Ezekiel?

6. What is our national responsibility in terms of doing business with nations that deny human rights and espouse immoral political beliefs?

7. Today we often boycott nations or businesses to affect their behavior. How effective do you think boycotting is?

8. In what ways do you believe God still regards those who help or hurt the Jewish nation?

9. In what ways do you think God protects and defends Christians today as He did the Jewish nation in Ezekiel's day?

Chapter Nine

Egypt Will Fall!
(Ezekiel 29-32)

1. In what ways do we "look to the world for help" rather than trusting God?

2. Pharoah Hophrah's sin was pride. What are the dangers, for any of us, in the sin of pride?

3. Often through God's judgment, Ezekiel tells us, people come to "know that I am the Lord." What kinds of things happen in your life that renew your belief that God is the one true God?

4. God worked through the national conflicts between Tyre, Egypt, and Babylon to accomplish His plan. In what ways do you see God working at an international level today?

5. Describe the ways (if any) that we, like the ancient nations, are used to accomplish God's purposes even when we are unaware of it.

6. In what ways do you agree or disagree with the quote, "Those who cannot remember the past are condemned to repeat it"?

7. In Ezekiel's prophecy, the king of Egypt is compared to a crocodile. To what animal would you compare the leaders you see in the world today?

8. If Ezekiel were here today to prophesy about the fate of our country, what do you think he would say?

Chapter Ten

Warnings and Promises from the Watchman
(Ezekiel 33-35)

✱ 1. Think about someone you believe has the gift of prophecy. Describe that person's insights into life.

2. List the benefits of each: hindsight, foresight, insight.

3. Describe someone who has been a watchman in your life and called you to repent and restore your relationship with God.

4. In your own words how would you distinguish among regret, remorse, and repentance?

5. Describe a time when you struggled, as the Jews of Ezekiel's day, with God's fairness.

6. Ezekiel's preaching took on a kind of entertainment value. In our current culture, does the church have any kind of entertainment value?

7. What are the dangers or benefits of part of God's business on the earth being seen as entertainment?

8. Describe your response to this quote: "The important thing at the judgment seat of Christ won't be how much Bible we studied or learned, but how much we loved and obeyed."

9. If you had to make a short list of the sins of our national leaders, what would be the top three?

10. What words would you use to describe the peaceful state of the world Ezekiel promised when Jesus comes back to reign?

Chapter Eleven

From Restoration to Reunion
(Ezekiel 36–37)

1. Based on your life experience, describe the power of hope.

2. Describe in your own words the relationship between the faith that adopts us into God's family and the obedience that allows us to enjoy our place there.

3. One way Ezekiel described the future kingdom was as safe and secure. In what ways would our everyday lives be different if security and safety weren't issues?

4. What keeps us, like the Jews, from feeling accountable to God about how we care for the earth?

5. Explain what it means to "profane God's name" before unbelievers?

6. What does it feel like to be forgiven of our sins, as God said He would do for the Jews?

7. One of the blessings God promised the Jews was fellowship with Him. Describe what it is like to be out of fellowship with God.

8. In what way does God breathe life into us as He did in Ezekiel's vision of the dead bones?

9. What do you look forward to most in the coming kingdom of God?

10. How should our hope of God's eventual restoration of our world affect the way we "do church" today?

Chapter Twelve

God Protects the Nation
(Ezekiel 38-39)

1. How do you respond to the fact that there are passages, such as the one in this chapter, upon which even the most knowledgeable scholars can't agree?

2. If you had to give one reason why end-time prophecies are so difficult, what would that reason be?

3. For what reasons is it important to study Scripture passages that are difficult, even impossible, to understand definitively?

4. Name some reasons that you think God gave us details about the end times beyond the fact that He is victorious.

5. What events have you seen that cause you to believe the stage is being set for the end-time prophecies of Ezekiel?

6. In the end, when God defeats all the forces of the earth, everyone will know that He is the "only true and living God." Describe a world where everyone knows that.

7. How do you interpret prophecies written in ancient times but describing the future? For instance, how do you interpret the weapons of battle: bows, clubs, and spears as today's weapons?

8. What kinds of reasoning do you think keep Satan believing that he has a chance to defeat God in the end?

9. What do you fear most about the war Ezekiel describes?

10. Knowing what Ezekiel tells us about the end of the world, what should we do to be ready?

Chapter Thirteen

Glory in the Temple
(Ezekiel 40–48)

1. How do you think God would describe "ideal worship"?

2. In what ways do you agree or disagree with the statement, "Too much so-called worship is only a demonstration of man-centered religious activity that fails to bring glory to the Lord."

3. Wiersbe talks about the difference between interpreting prophecies literally or symbolically. List some principles that can help us decide which way to interpret prophecies.

4. In what ways did the temple function for the Jews similarly to how our church buildings function for us today?

5. Many of the sacrifices reminded the Jews of the total devotion that God wanted from them. What rites do we maintain today that remind us to be devoted followers of God?

6. God was specific in His instructions about the rituals that would be maintained in the temple. What are the spiritual rituals that you maintain today that are most meaningful to you?

7. In what ways do you think we will experience the Lord's presence differently in His future kingdom than we do now? How will worship be different?

8. List the people today who fulfill the role of priest as Ezekiel represented it.

9. The Book of Ezekiel reminds us to revere God's name. As you look around you, what places do you see where an increased reverence for God would make a difference?

N O T E S

Chapter 1

1. Numbers 8:23 states that the priests began their work at age twenty-five, but during the first five years, they were "learning the ropes" in preparation for their twenty years of ministry (thirty to fifty). According to our calendar, Ezekiel was called on July 31, 593 B.C. He had spent his first five years as an exile in Babylon and was now ready for service.

2. Some students see some significant parallels between Ezekiel and Jeremiah: Ezekiel 2:8-9—Jeremiah 1:9; Ezekiel 3:3—Jeremiah 15:16; Ezekiel 3:8—Jeremiah 1:8, 17; 15:20; Ezekiel 3:14—Jeremiah 6:11; 15:17; Ezekiel 3:17—Jeremiah 6:17; Ezekiel 4:3—Jeremiah 15:12; Ezekiel 5:6—Jeremiah 2:10-13; Ezekiel 5:11—Jeremiah 13:14; Ezekiel 7:26—Jeremiah 4:20. There are numerous parallels between the Book of Ezekiel and the priestly code in the Pentateuch, as well as the Book of Revelation.

3. The Hebrew word *ruah* means spirit, Spirit, or wind, and in his book, Ezekiel uses the word in all three senses.

4. The theme of Israel's rebellion and hardness of heart is found often in the Book of Ezekiel: 2:3-7; 3:26-27; 5:6; 12:2-3, 9, 25; 17:12, 15; 20:8, 13, 21; 21:24; 24:3; 44:6.

5. The Lord used this image to describe the heathen people left in the land of Canaan (Num. 33:55). Once again, God classified His rebellious people with the pagan Gentiles.

6. Was this experience a vision or did God actually transport Ezekiel to Tel-Abib? The scholars are divided in their interpretation. That this was a literal moving of the prophet and not merely a vision seems to be the plain reading of the text. The fact that the prophet sat among the exiles for seven days suggests a physical move. (See 8:1; 11:1, 24; 43:5.)

7. The suggestion here is that Ezekiel was silent for those seven days. Under the levitical law, it took seven days for a priest to be ordained and installed into his ministry (Lev. 8:35). Ezekiel the priest spent seven days being ordained as a prophet.

8. The symbolic "action sermons" are found in 3:22-26; 4:1-3, 4-8,

N O T E S

9-11, 12-14; 5:1-3; 12:1-16, 17-20; 21:6-7, 18-24, 15-24; 37:15-28.
9. A.W. Tozer, *The Pursuit of God* (Tyndale House), 102.

Chapter 2

1. Samuel Heilman, *A Walker in Jerusalem* (Summit Books, 1986), 15.

2. The phrase "bear the iniquity" can mean to suffer for one's own sins (Lev. 17:15-16) or to take to oneself the sins of others (10:17; 16:22). Since the high priest represented the people before God, and the priests offered the sacrifices for sin, they were "bearing" the nation's sins in a symbolic sense. Without their ministry, there could be no forgiveness.

3. The subject of the length of the reigns of the Jewish kings is sometimes puzzling, so we shouldn't look for absolute figures. Fathers and sons were sometimes coregents, and at least two kings of Judah reigned for only three months each.

4. As far as the trade routes were concerned, there is a sense in which the land and the city were centrally located. The land was a "bridge" over which the nations trod as they attacked one another, and the Jews suffered the consequences.

5. In Ezekiel 25 and 26, God promised to punish the Ammonites and the people of Tyre because they laughed at the plight of Israel and took advantage of it. Indeed, the Jews were put to shame before the very people whose sins they practiced and thus brought judgment on themselves.

6. "Behold, I am against you" (v. 8) is a frequently repeated statement in the Book of Ezekiel: 13:8, 20; 21:3; 26:3; 28:22; 29:3, 10; 30:22; 34:10; 35:3; 36:9; 38:3; 39:1.

7. See 6:12; 7:8, 12, 14, 19; 9:8; 13:13, 15; 14:19; 16:38, 42; 20:8, 13, 21, 33-34; 21:17, 31; 22:20-24, 31; 24:8, 13-14, 17; 30:15; 36:6, 18-19. Ezekiel has much to say about the wrath of God.

8. This is another phrase found often in the Book of Ezekiel: 17:21; 21:17, 32; 23:34; 24:14; 26:5, 14; 28:10; 30:12; 34:24; 39:5. Ezekiel spoke by the authority of the Lord God.

9. Early in Israel's history, before worship was centralized at the tabernacle in Jerusalem, the "high places" were sometimes used for worshiping the Lord (1 Sam. 9:11-25; 10:5; 1 Kings 3:4). Then they

were used to worship both the Lord and a false god, and finally they were dedicated totally to the idol. The Lord commanded all the high places and the idols to be destroyed when Israel entered the land (Deut. 12).

10. The phrase "set your face against" is found also in 13:17; 20:46; 21:2, 7; 25:2; 28:21; 29:2; 35:2; 38:2.

11. Some scholars translate this word (*gillulim*) to mean "logs" or "blocks of wood." No matter how the people decorated their idols, these false gods were still only "hunks of wood." But the word can mean "pellets of dung."

12. The word "sword" is used eighty-six times in the Book of Ezekiel.

13. Ezekiel will take up this theme of adultery again in chapters 16 and 23.

14. In 25:6, these same actions were Ammon's gleeful response to the destruction of the land of Israel, but the Lord certainly would be happy to see His people suffer and His land devastated.

15. Some expositors see here the image of a ropes "woven" around the prisoners as they are led away to Babylon.

Chapter 3

1. It's interesting that the name Jaazaniah in verse 11 means "the Lord hears."

2. These angels remind us of the seven "trumpet angels" in Revelation 8–9.

3. The word "shekinah" come from a Hebrew word that means "to dwell." God's glory had dwelt in the holy of holies in the temple, but now it would be taken away.

4. Before ushering in the great day of His wrath, God showed John the holy of holies in heaven and the ark of the covenant (Rev. 11:15-19). One reason the world resists the idea of divine judgment is because they divorce it from the holiness of God and the glory of God. God was "enthroned" on the mercy seat (1 Sam. 4:4; 2 Sam. 6:2; Pss. 80:1; 99:1, NIV). His throne is a holy throne.

5. Naaman took a load of soil from Israel to Syria so he could still be close to the Lord (2 Kings 5:17), and David complained that Saul had driven him away from his own land and therefore from the Lord

(1 Sam. 26:17-20).

Chapter 4

1. *The Life and Selected Writings of Thomas Jefferson*, edited by Adrienne Koch and William Peden (The Modern Library, 1993), 255.

2. When the prophet covered his face and kept his eyes to the ground, it suggested the great humiliation God had brought upon the king. Had he obeyed God's message from Jeremiah, he and his family and staff would have been spared. The covering of the face also suggests the impending blindness of the king.

3. Whenever we use drama to convey God's truth to people, we still need the Word of God to make the message clear and authoritative. The spiritually "blind" and "deaf" will be attracted by drama and pantomime, but not everybody will accurately interpret what they see. Ezekiel preached a message after his "action sermons" because it's the Word of God that brings conviction and conveys faith (Rom. 10:17).

4. Ezekiel uses this image again in 22:28.

5. Some students think that the sorceresses used the barley and bread in their magical incantations to determine the future, and this is possible. It does seem like a small fee for their services.

Chapter 5

1. Parables and allegories are given primarily to elucidate one main truth, and it's dangerous to build one's theology on imagery that is supposed to *illustrate* theology. The major truth in John 15 is the believer's need to abide in Christ, through prayer, meditation in the Word, worship, and obedience. Our union with Christ never changes, because the Holy Spirit abides with us forever (John 14:16), but our communion with Him does change.

2. The Hebrew word for "professional prostitution" (*zana*) is used twenty-one times in this chapter. God considered Israel to be His wife, and her idolatry was the equivalent of adultery and harlotry (Hosea 2; Jer. 2:20-25; 3:1-13).

3. It was believed that the salt had an antiseptic power and would also help strengthen the skin.

4. On the practice of sacrificing children to idols, see 2 Kings 21:6;

23:10; Jeremiah 7:31; 19:5. The Law of Moses prohibited such an evil practice (Lev. 18:21; 20:2; Deut. 12:31; 18:10).

5. See Isaiah 20:5-6; 30:1-5; 31:1; Hosea 7:11; 12:1.

6. The Hebrew verb describes the changes in the woman's genital area when she is sexually aroused.

7. Sodom and Gomorrah are frequently named in Scripture as examples of the judgment of God against sin. See Genesis 18:16–19:29; Deuteronomy 29:23; 32:32; Isaiah 1:9-10; 3:9; 13:19; Jeremiah 23:14; Lamentations 4:6; Amos 4:11; Zephaniah 2:9; Matthew 10:15; 11:24; Mark 6:11; Luke 10:12; 2 Peter 2:6; Jude 7.

8. The word "daughters" (vv. 46, 48-49, 55) refers to smaller cities around a larger city, i.e., "daughter cities."

9. In Scripture, a tree can represent a ruler, a kingdom, or a dynasty (Jud. 9:8-15; Isa. 10:33; Ezek. 31:1-18; Dan. 4; Zech. 11:2).

Chapter 6

1. The guilt and condemnation for a parent's sin could not be passed on to the children, but the *consequences* of parental sin could bring suffering to the family. In Old Testament days, the Jewish people lived in extended families, and often four generations lived together. This meant that younger generations were influenced by the bad examples of their relatives as well as their good examples. Hereditary tendencies could be passed along as well as social diseases. But at the same time, a godly relative's example, teaching, and prayers could bring blessing to his or her descendants for years to come. Neither Ezekiel nor Jeremiah denied that innocent people were suffering because of the sins of the godless Jewish leaders (Lam. 5:7). The thing they opposed was that the people were using the proverb as an excuse for their own sins, claiming that their generation wasn't guilty of disobedience.

2. Idolatry and adultery were capital offenses (Deut. 13; 22:22; Lev. 18:20; 20:10). Offenses relating to material goods (stealing, exploiting, charging interest, etc.) were usually punished by restoration of an equal amount plus a fine.

3. The case described in verse 24 isn't that of a righteous man who commits one trespass, but it describes a righteous man who adopted a sinful lifestyle and repeatedly defied God's law. Certainly he could have

repented and returned to God, even as King Manasseh did (2 Chron. 33:11-19); but the man Ezekiel described persisted in his sins. It's possible to have an outward behavior that appears righteous and still not have saving faith in the Lord.

4. It's interesting that the images of the lion and the vine are found in Genesis 49:8-12.

5 King Zedekiah tried the same approach with Jeremiah, but it didn't work (Jer. 37).

6. *Peter's Quotations: Ideas for Our Time*, 244. This is a version of George Santayana's famous saying, "Those who cannot remember the past are condemned to repeat it."

7. The phrase "lifted up my hand" means to make a solemn oath and is used seven times in chapter 20. God swore that He was their God (v. 5) and would deliver them and give them their land (v. 6). At Kadesh Barnea, He swore that the older generation would not enter the land (v. 15), and in verse 23, He swore to disperse them if they disobeyed Him (v. 23). He swore to give them the land of Israel (v. 28), and He swore to bring them back to the land after their dispersion (v. 42).

8. The word "Bamah" (v. 29) means "high place." In the question "What is the high place to which you go?" the word "go" is *ba* in Hebrew and "what" is *ma*.

9. Note the repetition of "the word of the Lord came" in 20:45 and 21:1, 8, and 18. This phrase introduces a new portion of God's message to the people.

10. Several kinds of divination are mentioned in verse 21: selecting an arrow from the quiver, as if drawing straws; consulting small images of the gods; and inspecting the entrails of an animal sacrifice. Perhaps verse 22 is describing the casting of lots (see NIV).

11. Adrienne Koch and William Peden, eds., *The Life and Selected Writings of Thomas Jefferson* (The Modern Library, 1993), 258.

Chapter 7

1. For a graphic description of what happens to society when officials break the law and are not punished for it, read Isaiah 59.

2. Of course, God is spirit and therefore doesn't have literal hands; but the Bible uses human terms to explain spiritual truths.

3. The KJV reads "prophets" in verse 25, but the word refers to the nobility in the city, the people with authority.

4. You find a similar image and message in Jeremiah 3. The Book of Hosea is an exposition of the image of religious and political prostitution.

5. The word "Sabeans" in verse 42 could refer to the nomadic desert tribes who were invited to the conference, but the word may also mean "drunkards" (see NIV margin).

6. Who are the "righteous men" who sentence Judah? (v. 45, NIV) It probably refers to the people gathered at the conference, since "they" goes back to verse 40. The NASB translates it, "But they, righteous men..." referring to "they" (the delegates) in verse 44. But how could men from ungodly nations be called "righteous"? Ezekiel may have been using a bit of holy irony and saying, "These pagan Gentiles are more righteous than Judah who knows the true and living God but won't trust Him!" Of course, the prophets also passed judgment on Judah, and they were righteous men.

Chapter 8

1. In Amos 1:3–2:3, the prophet passed judgment on the Gentile nations on the basis of their inhumanity, their barbaric treatment of their enemies; but when Amos came to judging the Jewish people, it was on the basis of God's law and their covenant relationship to Him (Amos 2:4, 10; 3:1). See Romans 2:11-16.

2. See Isaiah 15–16; Jeremiah 48; and Amos 2:1-3. Note that "Seir" is another name for the land of Moab (Gen. 32:3; 36:20-21).

3. God had already told Isaac and Rebekah that both the blessing and the birthright were to be given to Jacob (Gen. 25:23), and He would have accomplished it apart from the scheming of Jacob and his mother. Both Jacob and Rebekah suffered for what they did, but God overruled their unbelief and fulfilled His plan (Rom. 9:10-16). When they finally met, Jacob's treatment of his brother was hardly honest and loving (Gen. 32–32). He tried to appease (bribe?) him with gifts, he refused to travel with him, and he lied when he said he would follow Esau. Instead, he went in a different direction! They met again at Isaac's funeral (35:28-29).

4. The word Palestine comes from Philistine.

5. Amos rebuked Tyre for selling slaves to other nations (Amos 1:9-10).

6. Isaiah 14:12-23 is a declaration of God's punishment of the king of Babylon, but there are certainly strong suggestions that the passage also involves Satan, the god of this age, who through his demonic forces is working in and through world leaders (Dan. 10).

7. For other prophetic denunciations on Sidon, see Isaiah 23; Jeremiah 25:22; 47:4. During our Lord's ministry, He visited the region of Sidon (Matt. 11:21-22; Mark 7:24-31), and people from Sidon came to see Him (3:8).

8. See Ezekiel 11:17; 20:34, 41-42; 29:13; 34:13; 36:24; 37:21; 38:8; 39:27.

Chapter 9

1. Many ancient peoples had myths concerning great sea monsters that fought one another to gain control of creation, and this imagery occasionally shows up in Scripture (Job 9:13; Ps. 74:13-14; Isa. 27:1). One of Egypt's names in Scripture is "Rahab" and Egypt is portrayed as a water monster (Pss. 87:4; 89:10; Isa. 51:9-10). Of course, the ancient mythology is not approved by the biblical writers but only used in an illustrative way.

2. When you look at a map of ancient Egypt, keep in mind that "lower Egypt" is at the top of the map (north) in the delta region, and "upper Egypt" is at the bottom of the map (south).

3. The alternate spelling of his name (Nebuchadrezzar) may be more correct than the spelling we're most accustomed to in Scripture. Both identify the same person.

Chapter 10

1. The Jews might have been thinking of Isaiah 51:2. Actually, Abraham didn't inherit the land during his lifetime (Acts 7:5). All he owned was a tomb where he had buried his wife (Gen. 23) and where he himself was buried (25:7-10).

2. Instead of following Abraham's example of faith, the Jews sometimes used their connection with Abraham as an excuse for disobeying the Lord. Because they were "children of Abraham," the religious leaders refused to submit to John's baptism, and they also argued with Jesus

using the same excuse (John 8:33ff).

Chapter 11

1. "Defiled" means "ceremonially defiled" from coming in contact with someone or something unclean. See Leviticus 11–15.

2. The parallel between the present spiritual experience of the believer and the future spiritual experience of the Jewish nation shouldn't lead us to conclude that these Old Testament promises to the Jews should really be applied to the church. Whether in an Old Testament Jew, a New Testament Christian, or a future Jewish citizen in the Messianic Kingdom, regeneration is regeneration. It's the work of the Spirit in response to saving faith, and it's a miracle of God.

3. There is an interesting parallel between Ezekiel 37 and Ephesians 2, for both chapters deal with resurrection and reconciliation. Paul deals with the dead sinner raised to life (Eph. 2:1-10) and saved Jews and Gentiles reconciled in the one body, the church (vv. 11-22). It's clear, however, that Ezekiel's focus is on God's dealings with the nation of Israel and not the salvation of individual believers.

4. To interpret this vision as announcing the return of the remnant from Babylon or even the emergence of a nation of Israel in the world community is to misinterpret the message. Political Israel today is like the standing army without life, and there has been no great return of the Jews to their Holy Land. The fulfillment of the vision is yet to come.

5. *The Metropolitan Tabernacle Pulpit*, vol. 10, 426.

6. The Hebrew word *shakan* means "to dwell" and gives us the phrase "the Shekinah glory," the glory of God dwelling in His sanctuary.

Chapter 12

1. Ezekiel describes a six-nation coalition invading from the north (Ezek. 38:6, 15; 39:2), while the Battle of Armageddon involves all nations from the four quarters of the earth (Rev. 20:8). Before Gog and his hordes can do anything, God will attack them with pestilence, hailstones, and brimstone and the armies will fight each other (39:17-23), while the army at Armageddon will be destroyed by our Lord at His coming (Rev. 19:11-21). It will take seven months to bury the corpses from Gog's invasion (Ezek. 39:12), but the Armageddon army will be

annihilated (Rev. 20:9). Gog will head the armies that invade Israel for wealth (Ezek. 38:7, 12), but the Beast will lead the armies at Armageddon (Rev. 19:19). Gog's army won't have a chance to do any damage, but the Armageddon army will do damage before the Lord descends to conquer them (Zech. 14:1-9).

2. For an exposition of the prophecies of Daniel, see my book *Be Resolute* (Chariot Victor).

3. These names are not symbolic but belong to actual people who founded nations bearing their names. See Genesis 10:1-7; 1 Chronicles 1:5-7; Ezekiel 27:13-24; 32:26.

4. Though it's frequently called "The Mosque of Omar," the building is technically not a mosque but a monument.

5. Even if archeologists discover that the Jewish temple stood on another site, it's likely that the Islamic nations would prefer that the temple not be rebuilt in Jerusalem.

6. Which of the prophets besides Ezekiel foretold the invasion of the land by these nations? (v. 17) Perhaps this isn't a reference to specific prophecies but to the fact that God has always promised to punish those nations that attacked Israel. This assurance from the Abrahamic Covenant (Gen. 12:1-3) is demonstrated frequently in Scripture.

7. Ezekiel described the invasion using language that the people in the ancient world would understand. If he had used modern military language, it would have conveyed nothing.

8. What this wealth is, the text doesn't say; but the mineral wealth in the Dead Sea area is immense. However, see Joel 2:1-8. At the same time, the claim of the Prince of Magog that he wants Israel's wealth may be a lie. What he may really want is control of the land for his Muslim allies, or perhaps he simply wants to keep the European leader from taking over.

9. Some writers suggest that world disarmament would make it necessary for Gog and his army to use ancient weapons and ride on horses. But ancient weapons and cavalries don't lend themselves to surprise attacks in a world equipped with satellites, the Internet, radar, and television reporters!

10. The KJV phrase "stop the noses of the travelers" gives the impression that it's the odor of the decaying bodies that creates problems, but

it's the burial ground and the burial operation that get in the way of the travelers. The name of the cemetery will be "The Horde of Gog."

Chapter 13

1. For an excellent presentation of this view, see Patrick Fairbairn's *Commentary on Ezekiel* (Kregel, 1989), 439–58.

2. Of course, the Gentiles will be welcomed to the temple worship (Isa. 2:1-5).

3. The long cubit was twenty-one inches long. If the rod was six cubits long, that equals ten feet six inches. Some make the long cubit twenty-four inches, making the rod twelve feet long. As I follow Ezekiel and his guide touring the temple precincts, I will not convert each measurement into feet and inches, unless the number is important to the meaning of the text.

4. In Herod's temple, the inscription on this wall of separation reads: "No foreigner may enter within the barricade which surrounds the sanctuary and enclosure. Anyone who is caught so doing will have himself to blame for his ensuing death." This explains why the Jews wanted to kill Paul when they saw him in the temple, because they thought he had brought unclean Gentiles into the sacred courts (Acts 21:26ff).

5. The prohibition against approaching the altar by steps (Ex. 20:24-26) applied to altars of stones or earth erected elsewhere than the tabernacle or temple.

6. See Leviticus 1–7. For an exposition of these chapters, see my book *Be Holy* (Chariot Victor, 1994).

7. When, at the Transfiguration, Peter offered to build some booths for Jesus, Moses, and Elijah, his motive was right but his timing was wrong (Matt. 16:27-17:8). When Jesus comes in glory, the people will celebrate Tabernacles and live in booths.

8. We wonder if disciplining the descendants because of their ancestors' sins isn't a reversal of what Ezekiel taught in chapters 18 and 33:12-20, that the children are not punished for the sins of the fathers. But Ezekiel is speaking of the corporate apostasy of the Levites and not their individual sins.

9. The population of the millennial kingdom will include some peo-

ple who will already have glorified bodies: the Old Testament saints who were resurrected (Dan. 12:2, 13), New Testament Christians (1 Thes. 4:13-18; 1 John 3:1-3), and Tribulation martyrs (Rev. 20:4). But believers who have survived the Tribulation, both Jews and Gentiles, will be in mortal bodies and subject to death. People will live long lives, but deaths will occur (Isa. 65:20). Children will be born and will be sinners needing salvation One would think that the miraculously ideal conditions in the kingdom would motivate everyone to trust in the Lord, but at the end of the millennium, Satan will be able to raise a large army to oppose the Lord (Rev. 20:7-10). During the thousand years, many people will feign obedience to the Lord and yet not trust Him. But can we be sure even today that everyone who belongs to a church is necessarily born again? (Matt. 7:21:29)

10. The KJV of 45:1 and 47:22 reads "divide by lot," but a better translation would be "to assign, to allot." It's clear from the text that the Lord partitioned the land and assigned it according to His own will. The places are already identified that mark the borders, although we aren't sure where some of these cities are located.

11. This eastern gate must not be equated with the one in present-day Jerusalem. The eastern gate in the millennial temple will be closed to the public because the glory of God entered through it (43:1-5).

12. In the promises to the "overcomers" in our Lord's letters to the seven churches (Rev. 2–3), you see a similar progression through the Old Testament periods, beginning with the tree of life in the Garden (Rev. 2:7) and concluding with reigning with Christ on His throne (3:21).